BUSINESS DEVELOPMENT

STRATEGY

FOR THE

UPSTREAM

OIL AND GAS INDUSTRY

BUSINESS DEVELOPMENT
STRATEGY
FOR THE
UPSTREAM
OIL AND GAS INDUSTRY

scarsdale
press

ROBIN WINKLE

For information about this title or to order other books
and/or electronic media, contact the publisher:

Scarsdale Press
https://scarsdalepress.com
inquiries@scarsdalepress.com

Library of Congress Control Number: 2022908755

ISBNs:
979-8-9861706-0-2 (hardcover cloth with dust jacket)
979-8-9861706-1-9 (eBook)

Printed in the United States of America

Cover and Interior design: 1106 Design

To Sophia, Alexander and Jonathan.

PREFACE

THE BOOK STARTED AS AN ARTICLE that was prompted by an experience earlier in the author's career. A senior executive was meeting with a group of bankers to discuss acquisition options and was struggling to explain what kind of asset he wanted to acquire. After conceding that both oil and gas were interesting, he finally concluded that what he wanted to buy was cash flow. While this is undoubtedly and almost universally true, it isn't useful. The bankers had no guidance on what to show him, and he had no basis to evaluate what was put in front of him. If you don't know what you are looking for, how will you know when you find it? In this case, the search went nowhere, which isn't necessarily a bad outcome but may have been a missed opportunity.

The upstream oil and gas industry, despite diminishing importance in stock markets around the world, remains the world's largest acquisition and divestment market, with $256 billion of deals concluded in 2018. It is a complex industry, with many participants: the upstream oil and gas companies who buy, sell, and operate assets, the private equity firms and banks who finance them, and the geologists, engineers, bankers, consultants, attorneys, and accountants who advise on the transactions. The transactions involve very large sums of money, span years from inception to closure, and are fascinating in their complexity and infinite variety. This book does not attempt to address that process, but rather the much-shorter and less-involved process that buyers and sellers should engage in up front—understanding the health of the portfolio, what they are good at, and what kind of asset mix they should aim for.

The book is intended to provide some guidance for those who work in the industry on how to think through their asset-acquisition strategy, as well as serve as an introduction for those who are interested in learning more about the subject.

The first chapter of this book introduces the concept of business development and the acquisition and divestment of assets in the upstream oil and gas industry; it also provides some context on the size of the industry and explains what makes it distinct. The first chapter also introduces two industry examples—the Apache acquisition of the Forties field and the BHP acquisition of a portfolio of shale assets—that are referred to throughout subsequent chapters to illustrate how the concepts presented can be applied in practice.

The second chapter presents some key industry concepts that readers who are new to the industry or have previously worked in a different area may be unfamiliar with. This chapter serves as a reference section; some of the concepts that are touched on in the second chapter are discussed in more detail in later chapters. The next three chapters focus on describing a methodology for defining and articulating a business-development strategy, through examination of the question from three perspectives—portfolio health, organizational capability, and asset mix.

The third chapter links business development to business strategy by analyzing the current portfolio of assets in the context of businesses' financial framework, using thematic scenarios to test for strengths and weaknesses. This technique is best illustrated by example: unfortunately, there is a lack of publicly available information on financial performance broken out at asset level, and so, we use Indie Oil, a fictitious independent international oil company, for illustrative purposes. Indie Oil is introduced in Chapter 3 and revisited again in subsequent chapters.

The fourth chapter presents a discussion on organizational capability, how this can be assessed, and how this impacts the business-development strategy. The purpose here is to help you understand what you are good at and what skills need to be learned, so that these forms of competitive advantage can be incorporated into your business-development strategy.

The fifth chapter addresses asset mix by breaking down assets into their constituent characteristics. This approach allows for the identification and analysis of assets according to their commonalities and differences, facilitating the design of notional portfolios.

The sixth chapter discusses how to bring together portfolio health, organizational capability, and asset mix into a business-development strategy, with Indie Oil, first introduced in Chapter 3, serving as an example. Finally, Chapter 7 concludes the book.

TABLE OF CONTENTS

TABLES

FIGURES

Chapter 1

INTRODUCTION

THIS CHAPTER INTRODUCES THE OIL AND GAS INDUSTRY and explains the role of "upstream" within that industry. It then goes on to examine the distinctive aspects of the industry that make a coherent business-development strategy so important. It addresses the industry's business-development track record before introducing two transactions—Apache's acquisition of the Forties field and BHP's assembly of an onshore shale-oil position—that will be used for illustrative purposes throughout the rest of the book. The chapter closes with an explanation of the structure of the rest of the book.

1.1 THE OIL AND GAS INDUSTRY

The oil and gas industry finds and develops crude oil and natural gas, converts them into usable products, and sells them to customers. The industry produces transport fuels and provides feedstock for power generation and the base chemicals used in the manufacture of plastics as well as other associated products such as bitumen and lubricants. The industry can be roughly broken down by function into upstream, midstream, and downstream. Figure 1, below, provides an illustration of each of the segments and how they are connected.

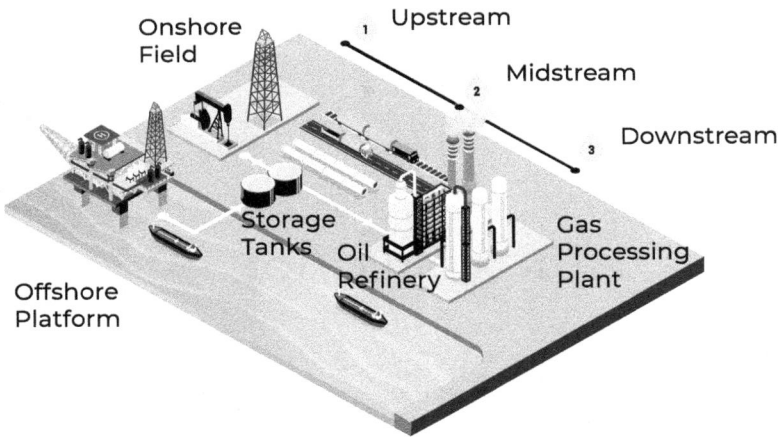

FIGURE 1: Oil and Gas Industry Value Chain

The upstream oil and gas industry, the focus of this book, finds and develops crude oil and natural gas. This segment of the business is commonly referred to as Exploration and Production (E&P) as well as "upstream."

The midstream segment of the business is responsible for gathering and transportation of oil and gas as well as gas processing. Crude oil can be transported by pipeline, truck, railcar, or tanker. Natural gas can be transported by pipeline or compressed or liquified for transportation by truck or tanker. Gas processing is undertaken in order to bring a gas stream to sales specification. This objective is achieved by blending with other gas streams, adding industrial gases, and removing liquids. With a few exceptions, this is normally undertaken as a midstream activity.

The downstream segment of the business consists of refining, petrochemicals, and marketing. Refining uses crude oil as an input and breaks it down into usable products such as gasoline, kerosene, which is used as jet fuel, and diesel, which is used as a transport fuel or for home heating. The refining process also creates a number of other fractions, such as refinery gases, naptha, and lubricating oils that are used in a range of products such as candles and wax paper and form the building blocks for plastics. The petrochemicals business uses refined products to create industrial chemicals such as aromatics, used in the creation of polymers and ethylene, which are used to make polyester, soaps, detergents, cosmetics, and paints. Marketing consists of selling the end products to the customer.

Standard Oil, the early industry leader, was initially focused on the midstream and downstream segments, leaving the upstream segment to individual wildcatters. Having achieved dominance in refining and distribution, Standard Oil became a fully integrated company in the late 1880s through acquisition of fields straddling the Ohio/Indiana border. By 1891 Standard Oil was responsible for 25% of United States oil production[1].

This vertically integrated approach—combining upstream, midstream, and downstream—became the norm for the industry, and most familiar names still use the vertically integrated model. Many National Oil Companies (NOCs), companies that governments have created and in which they maintain control, have also adopted this model.

Over time, some alternatives have emerged. Utilities and chemical companies, such as DONG (now Ørsted) and Dow diversified into upstream oil and gas assets as a way of hedging commodity-price risk for their key inputs. Many smaller companies purely focused on the upstream business have emerged over the years; these are the companies that dominated the United States shale revolution, but they have been around in one form or another since the birth of the industry. The last decade saw a trend—for integrated companies such as ConocoPhillips and Marathon—toward breaking with the integrated business model by establishing separate upstream and downstream businesses.

Historically, midstream infrastructure was built by integrated oil and gas companies to transport their own product, and this is still the case outside of North America. In the United States and Canadian markets today, midstream businesses such as Enterprise, Enbridge, and Cheniere, huge companies in their own right, dominate midstream. It is these midstream companies, rather than the International Oil Companies (IOCs), that have pioneered the development of the United States as a Liquefied Natural Gas (LNG) exporter. At the same time, some IOCs in the United States have chosen to maintain ownership of their midstream assets, because either they generate attractive returns or control of access is considered strategic.

1.2 THE ROLE OF BUSINESS DEVELOPMENT

Business development in the context of the upstream oil and gas industry is the acquisition or divestment of all or part of an interest in a lease, a granting instrument, or a contractual right to production from a wellbore. The upstream oil and gas industry is an extractive industry, which means that it must continuously find and develop new oil and gas fields as existing fields decline.

To provide a sense for the scale of this activity, in 2019, the world produced more than 100 million barrels per day of oil under the broadest definition—crude oil, condensate, biofuels, and natural gas liquids[2]. Once an oil field has achieved peak production, it will enter a natural decline. Decline rates vary by field size and setting. Super-giant fields decline more slowly than large fields. Deepwater fields decline more quickly than onshore fields, as greater capital intensity and higher operating cost require higher early production to satisfy economic hurdles, even at the cost of ultimate recovery. The most recent shale-oil wells in the Permian can see decline rates of 65% to 85% in their first year of production[3].

The aggregate natural decline of the world's oil production as a whole has been estimated at around 5%[4]. That means that 5 million barrels of new production must be brought on-stream each year, just to stand still—and, historically, the world has had to do more than just stand still. Oil-demand growth averaged more than 1.2 million barrels per day over the period 2009 to 2019[5]. While the relationship between economic growth and oil demand has weakened, it has not been eliminated. If the world economy keeps growing, the oil and gas industry will need to find and develop more than 6 million barrels per day of new production, year after year.

The world produced 386 billion cubic feet of gas per day in 2019[6]. Gas developments differ from oil, in that, as gas, LNG aside, is not fungible; the gas producer and customer are typically contracted to receive an agreed level of production over many years. Consequently, while gas fields do experience natural declines, the rates are less pronounced than for oil. The author is not aware of work on the natural decline of global gas supply, although it would be reasonable to assume it is lower than the 5% for oil. Global gas demand, on the other hand, is rising faster than oil, averaging demand growth of 2.5% between 2009 and 2019. It is fair to say that the world needs to add somewhere between 10 and 20 billion cubic feet per day of gas-production capacity to satisfy demand.

In order to address this additional oil- and gas-production capacity, oil and gas companies are continuously finding and developing new sources of supply. This involves identifying and entering new basins or securing new positions in existing basins, drilling exploration and appraisal wells, and, if successful, moving forward with the construction of facilities and development drilling. This process takes many years and requires billions of dollars of capital and a highly trained and experienced workforce. The process can be thought of as a funnel, with lots of potential fields being added in the front end, and a lot falling out over time as they are screened out or sold for one reason or another.

In addition to organic growth, oil and gas companies continuously adjust their portfolios to match their investment opportunities with the capital they have available and their view of the external environment. To give a sense of the size of this activity, the global market for mergers and acquisitions was $3.78 trillion in 2018[7], of which $256 billion, or 7%, were oil- and gas-industry transactions. Of this, $129 billion, or 50%, involved upstream oil and gas assets. Of those transactions, $72 billion, or 56%, were asset rather than corporate transactions.

Things were more subdued in 2019, with asset-deal value falling to $48 billion and collapsing to $16 billion in 2020 as the COVID-19 pandemic and its impact on the oil and gas industry effectively froze the business-development market. The most active regions of this period by deal value have been the United States and, in 2020, Latin America, as illustrated in Figure 2:

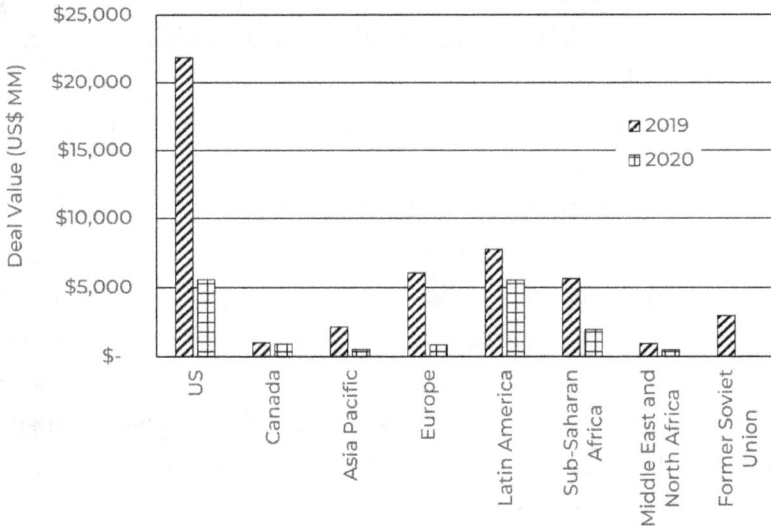

FIGURE 2: Business-Development Deal Value by Region

The role of business development in the oil and gas industry is to build and maintain a healthy portfolio of assets, a portfolio that provides upside but is resilient. This portfolio is built both organically, through the access to new acreage, and through the acquisition and divestment of more mature assets. The creation and maintenance of a healthy portfolio involves more than the addition of assets. Healthy companies are constantly reviewing their portfolios and making adjustments where necessary through divestment.

There are a number of situations where divesting assets is a sound course of action. For the largest IOCs, who typically have more options in their portfolio than they have resources to execute, this point comes not when the asset is exhausted but rather when an asset can longer compete for capital within the portfolio. This trend has been repeated over and over again, on the United States Gulf of Mexico shelf, in the UK North Sea, and in Norway. The fact that an asset can't compete for capital does not mean that there are no longer profitable development opportunities to exploit. As we will discuss later in this book, the relationship between the size of a project and the organizational resources required to execute it is not linear. There is a point where incremental investment opportunities in mature assets are simply not material, and, thus, another asset owner with fewer options is more likely to realize the incremental value. The IOC can realize part of this incremental value through a sale, creating the kind of differential value that produces a willing buyer and a willing seller.

The largest IOCs also enjoy differentiation in terms of technology, business processes, and balance sheets. They are often referred to as "premium operators" because they provide a premium capability, but also because that capability comes at a premium cost. Simply put, it costs money to build and maintain this capability, and, while business processes *do* improve overall value, they also increase cost. Where an incremental investment in an existing asset is of low complexity, technically, commercially, or politically, a smaller, simpler company can often generate better returns from the investment. This is the second reason to divest an asset; even if it competes for capital, it may be more profitable for a large company to divest the asset, secure part of the upside in the sale price, and allow a smaller company to develop it profitably.

A third reason for divestment is to complete a country or region exit. Maintaining a broad geographical spread of assets is usually considered a good practice, as it provides a hedge against political risk in any single geography. However, the cost of maintaining each geographical or regional presence is high. It requires a physical presence with staff and offices to run the asset, as well as the cost of complying with local laws, filing, paying taxes, and so forth. If the anchor asset falls below a certain materiality threshold, this additional overhead cost can impair the profitability of the geography. At some point, it is better to exit completely or, alternatively, to farm-down and allow someone else to operate, than to retain a diminished in-country presence.

A fourth reason to divest involves farming-down rather than exiting completely. A farm-down can be used to reduce an asset risk profile, especially common in the exploration phase, raise additional capital for ongoing development, as a means of introducing expertise or financial capability, or in an asset trade to access other opportunities. In each of these cases, there is some overriding reason to undertake a transaction that creates a willing seller.

The fifth reason to divest is to maintain a robust portfolio of options. Over time, some assets will outperform others, knowledge of the potential of individual plays or technologies will improve, and the portfolio will gradually drift off center as values are adjusted. Under these circumstances, full or partial divestment of assets provides a means of bringing the portfolio back to true.

The final reason for selling an asset—because you need to raise cash—is the worst reason of all. The oil and gas industry is cyclical, with profitability driven by commodity prices. If you are in a situation where you need to sell to raise cash, it is likely caused by depressed commodity prices. Depressed commodity prices mean depressed valuations and, as everyone else is in the same situation, a very small group of willing buyers. There have been circumstances where companies have been forced to sell assets for cash outside of a downturn—the case of BP following the Macondo disaster, for example—where there is really no choice. However, in general, asset sales in a downturn is an example of when *not* to sell and is indicative of poor portfolio management.

1.3 BUSINESS-DEVELOPMENT STRATEGY

What is strategy, and why do you need one? There are a lot of definitions of "strategy," but for the purposes of this discussion, we will define strategy as "how you compete and where you compete." This is clearly important in all areas of business but is particularly critical in the upstream oil and gas industry for two reasons:

- ⮑ The industry produces a commodity
- ⮑ Industry cycle times are unusually long, in effect locking up capital

These reasons are discussed in more detail in the sections below.

1.3.1 The Product

The end products of the upstream oil and gas industry, be it crude oil, condensate, natural gas liquids (NGLs) or natural gas, are commodities. There is differentiation in oil quality and gas richness between fields, and thus a degree of differential pricing, but there is nothing much that you can do to influence it.

To explore the implications of this, we can take a counterpoint from the technology industry. Apple and Xiaomi compete in the smartphone market, with Apple competing at the premium end and Xiaomi competing in the mass market. Apple sold 217 million iPhones[8] in 2018 at an average price of $793[9]. Xiaomi sold 118 million phones in 2018, at an average price of $143[10]. Apple and Xiaomi produce a product that does essentially the same thing, but Apple is able to sell that product at more than five times the price of Xiaomi. People will pay a premium for an iPhone to associate themselves with the brand, because they admire the sleek design and because it provides them with access to Apple's ecosystem.

You can't do this in upstream oil and gas. People do not gather around the water cooler to discuss where they filled up the gasoline tank of their vehicle that morning. Exxon can't decide that it wants to try to sell its crude at a premium because it has a valuable brand and excellent marketing. Its product is priced at a discount or premium to a marker crude based on its composition and delivery date. That is the end of the story.

The only way to differentiate yourself from your competitors is to find, develop, and produce the commodity more efficiently than they do. An asset transaction requires a willing buyer and a willing seller. The only way to create value in a transaction is for the buyer to generate more value from the asset than the seller; the asset brings something that the buyer needs or allows the buyer to leverage a capability that they have.

The only way to do this consistently is to acquire assets where you enjoy a competitive advantage. To do this, you need to understand your own capability and where they can be leveraged to your advantage.

1.3.2 The Commitment

The upstream oil and gas industry is extremely capital intensive and works on very long timelines. A good basic assumption for a typical offshore hub-class project would be ten years for exploration and development and twenty years for production. Many fields wait decades for development after discovery, for technological, political, or economic reasons, like Lunskoye in the Russian Federation. Some have much longer field lives—the Troll A platform in Norway is designed for 70 years, for example. In either case, an asset acquisition is a long-term commitment that ties up a large amount of capital. Asset sales, even in a seller's market, can take years to complete, and, while that capital is tied up in the wrong place, your competitors are exploiting better opportunities.

1.3.3 The Cost of Being Opportunistic

Deciding to be opportunistic is sometime seen as a strategy in itself. It is also the default in the absence of a defined strategy. One purported benefit of this approach is that you won't miss an opportunity—but on closer examination, this isn't true. As discussed later in this book, most assets are available on the right terms, but most of them are not in a formal sale process. It isn't practical to approach every operator about every asset, and, even if it were, you wouldn't make a lot of headway—people don't like dedicating their time and resources or granting access to confidential data if they suspect a fishing expedition.

The challenge with this approach is that you spend a lot of time looking at whatever is in a sale process, without any structured way to screen out the majority of assets where there is no fit. It means that you waste a lot of time because you look at anything with a price tag that falls within your acquisition budget and with projected cash flows that meet or can be made to meet your firm's economic hurdles.

As well as being labor intensive, opportunism introduces additional risk to the evaluation process by avoiding the discipline required to define a strategy in the first place. Put simply, if you don't know what you are looking for, how will you know when you find it? The process of defining an acquisition strategy, presenting, defending, and obtaining an endorsement for it, defining the parameters of coveted assets, and drawing up target-asset lists based on those parameters serves to provide a degree of protection from the inherent biases that we are all susceptible to in decision-making. Opportunism exposes the acquiring party to a number of identified biases that are common in decision-making[11]:

⮑ The Anchoring Trap, which describes the mind's tendency to give disproportionate weight to the first evidence that it receives.

⮑ The Confirming Evidence Trap, which describes our tendency to seek out information that supports our point of view and ignore evidence that contradicts it.

Research has shown that highly intelligent people are capable of constructing rational arguments to defend almost any position,[12] and all of the people involved in these types of transactions *are* highly intelligent. Once someone decides the acquisition is a good idea, they tend to interpret the data to support that view. Is their argument compelling and supported with data? Yes, it probably will be. Is it fully aligned with the company's optimum underlying acquisition strategy? Probably not. Can this end in an acquisition? Yes, sometimes it does.

Consciously defining a strategy up front and testing it with the organization is one of the best ways to negate this kind of bias.

1.4 BUSINESS-DEVELOPMENT TRACK RECORD

How successful is business development in the upstream oil and gas industry in creating value? The upstream oil and gas industry acquires access to acreage, searches for oil and gas, and, if successful, develops, produces, and then abandons the field. Asset acquisition in the broadest sense, which includes the acquisition of exploration acreage, is essential for the industry to survive. Thus, the debate on whether organic growth or the value of mergers and acquisitions (M&A) is the best way to grow a business is not applicable. Acquiring upstream oil and gas assets is not a choice for firms in the sector; if they cease to acquire, eventually, they will cease to exist.

If the upstream oil and gas industry creates value and acquisition is an essential part of that business model, then it is fair to conclude that process acquisition is value adding—otherwise, the industry would have disappeared by now.

The answer as to whether the upstream oil and gas industry creates value seems to depend on the data set that you pick. If you had taken a straw poll in 2020 of those who had invested in the industry of the previous five years, the answer would likely be "not very much." Look back a little further, however, and a different picture emerges. One study[13] that looked at the period from 2006 to 2013 concluded that the upstream industry average return on capital employed (ROCE) was 21%, with the average of the top quartile delivering an ROCE of 38%. Even the bottom quartile managed to deliver an ROCE of 9%. In contrast, the ROCE of the global technology industry between 2007 and 2020 was between 8.8% and 11.7%[14]. The industry as a whole is clearly profitable, and the variance indicates that participants are able to differentiate themselves. Bearing in mind that the study period straddled the worst recession since the Great Depression, the old maxim that the next best thing to a well-run oil company is a poorly run oil company seems apt.

This performance, however, did coincide with a period of sustained high oil prices. If we look at the more recent ROCE performance of Shell, traditionally a strong performer and one that delivered an average upstream ROCE of 42% over the period 2006 to 2013, then a different picture emerges. Shell's average upstream ROCE from 2016 to 2018[15], a period of weaker oil prices, was 5%, below most industrial companies' cost of capital.

As Figure 3 illustrates, Shell exhibited a higher average ROCE over a period of sustained higher oil prices. From this, we can infer that the upstream oil and gas industry creates value but also that it may require an oil-price environment at a certain level to do so. As asset acquisition is an essential component of the upstream oil and gas industry, we can conclude that asset acquisition, in the broadest sense, is a value-adding activity but may require a prevailing oil price above a certain floor.

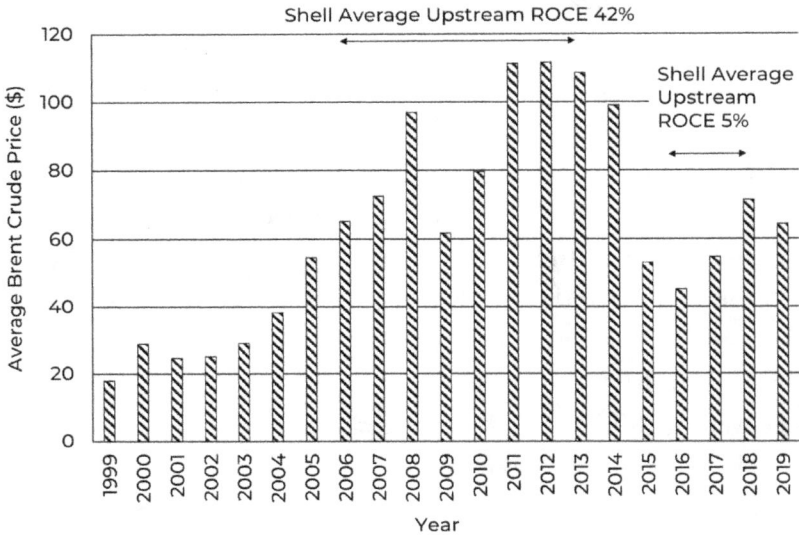

FIGURE 3: **Average Annual Brent Crude Prices (1999 to 2019)**

While the acquisition of assets is not a choice for the upstream oil and gas industry, which assets to acquire and how to acquire them is. The author has been unable to identify any published analysis of whether any one strategy is more or less successful than any other. One reason for this may be that publicly listed companies do not disclose financial performance at the asset level.

There are, however, examples of assets that were acquired and, as a result of their geographic location or distinct field type, were reported separately at least for a period. One example is the Forties field in the UK sector of the North Sea, which was acquired by Apache in 2003. The other is a collection of shale assets, assembled by

BHP in 2011. This book will use each of these examples to illustrate the points made in each chapter of this book. Both acquisitions are introduced in the sections below.

1.5 APACHE'S ACQUISITION OF THE FORTIES FIELD

The Forties field, discovered by BP in 1970, is located 110 miles east of Aberdeen in the United Kingdom's (UK) sector of the North Sea, started production in 1975. It remains the largest discovery in the UK, with STOIIP* estimates in excess of 4.2 billion barrels and at peak produced more than 500,000 barrels per day of oil. By the time BP sold the field to Apache, it had already produced more than two billion barrels of oil.

Apache acquired the field in 2003 for $680 million. The acquisition was aligned with Apache's stated strategy at that time, which is summarized in the excerpt from their 10-K Filing for the fiscal year ending in 2003[16].

> "Over the years our strategy for achieving profitable growth has evolved. Over the most recent decade Apache has been an active acquirer of properties, following up with proactive exploitation operations, including workovers, re-completions, and drilling, to increase production, and efforts to reduce costs per unit produced and enhance profitability. Also over the past decade, we added an international component to our strategy, which exposed our shareholders to larger reserve targets and a greater ability to grow production and reserves through drilling."

The press coverage at the time highlighted the relative position that Forties occupied in the respective portfolios of BP, where the asset

---

* STOIIP—Stock Tank Oil Initially In Place—is the volume of oil initially in place in the reservoir, calculated at surface pressure and temperature, rather than reservoir conditions.

ranked 30th in their global portfolio, and Apache, where it ranked 2nd[17]. BP's announcement at the time highlighted the underlying rationale of the deal[18]:

> The Forties asset "may be worth more to others than to us," adding, "We believe this is an excellent deal for BP and Apache. Among other things, it brings to the UKCS a powerful US independent for which Forties will be a highly material asset and therefore more likely to attract necessary future investment."

This prediction proved prescient. Forties was Apache's only North Sea asset from 2003 until its acquisition of a number of Mobil assets in 2011. Apache's annual 10-K filing includes a North Sea geographic segment, which between 2003 and 2010 consisted only of the Forties asset. Apache made significant investments in the field over that period, a total of $3.8 billion, including the original acquisition price[19]. This investment is shown in Figure 4, below.

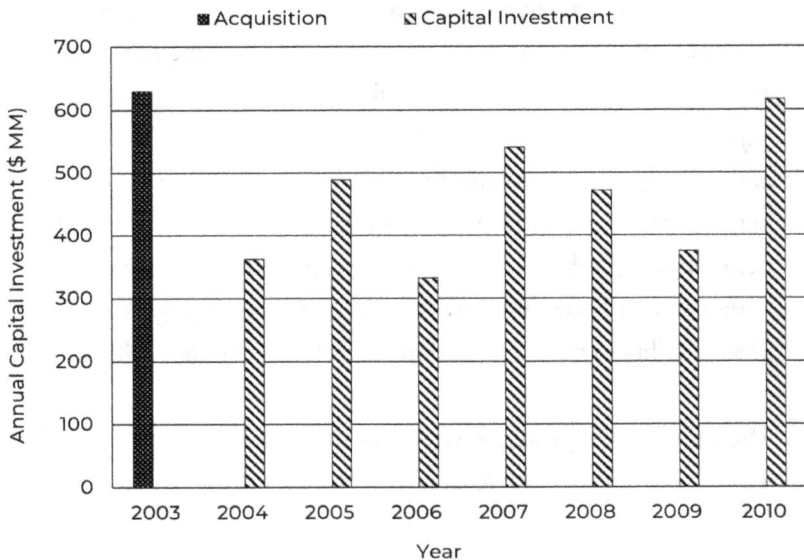

FIGURE 4: Apache Investment in the Forties Field (2003 to 2010)

This investment consisted of a combination of new seismic to identify additional reserves, facility upgrades, and additional wells and recompletions. As Figure 5 shows, this investment resulted in an initial increase in both reserves and production.

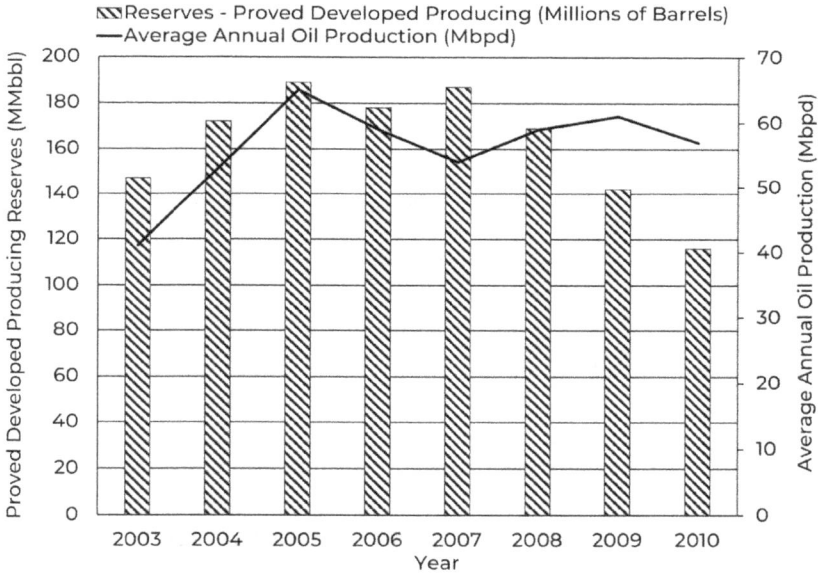

FIGURE 5: Forties Oil Reserves and Production Data (2003 to 2010)

Apache's investment in the Forties field achieved cumulative cash-flow breakeven in 2008, as illustrated in Figure 6.

The Internal Rate of Return (IRR) over the period from 2003 to 2010 was 7%, which would likely have fallen short of Apache's threshold return for the investment. The results for Forties cannot be broken out from publicly available data after 2010, but the field was still producing 55,000 barrels per day in 2010, and the period through 2014 saw sustained higher oil prices. The field is still producing today, in 2022 and has a projected further field life of 15 years. While we don't have access to the data to calculate the IRR across the investment cycle, it is reasonable to conclude that it was well in excess of the 7% through 2010 and that the acquisition was economically accretive to Apache.

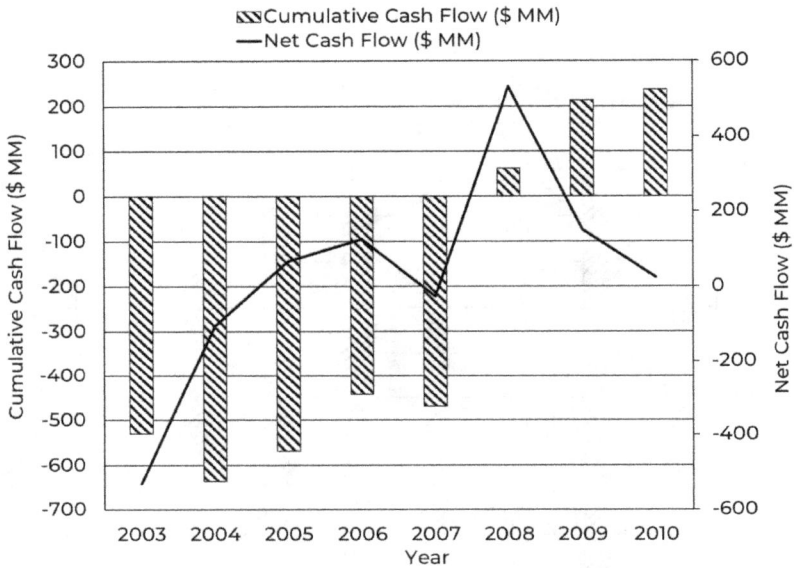

FIGURE 6: Forties Net and Cumulative Cash Flow (2003 to 2010)

1.6 BHP'S SHALE POSITION

BHP Billiton is an international energy and mining conglomerate with a petroleum division, headquartered in Houston, Texas. In 2011, BHP made two large investments in the United States onshore. The first was the acquisition of Chesapeake's Fayetteville shale assets for $4.75 billion in February of that year. The acquisition consisted of 487,000 acres of leasehold and producing natural gas properties in Arkansas. Chesapeake was one of the original shale pioneers and at that time was pursuing a strategy of transitioning from dry gas fields toward liquid-rich fields[20]. At the time of the transaction, BHP made the following statement:

"The acquisition is consistent with BHP Billiton's strategy of investing in large, long-life, low-cost assets with significant volume growth from future development. It also supports our goal of diversification by geography, customer, and product."

This deal was followed up later that year with BHP's acquisition of Petrohawk. Petrohawk was founded in Houston, Texas, in 2003 and grew rapidly through a series of mergers and acquisitions. It was acquired by BHP for $12 billion in cash and the assumption of $3.8 billion of outstanding debt. At the time of the acquisition, Petrohawk had established a position in three prominent shale basins—The Eagle Ford, the Haynesville, and the Permian. The company was producing approximately 950 MMscf/day of gas and 158 Mbpd of oil[21]. Speaking at the time, the BHP Billiton CEO, Marius Kloppers, said:

"The proposed acquisition of Petrohawk is consistent with our well-defined, upstream, Tier 1 strategy and provides us with even greater exposure to the world's largest energy market, while also broadening our geographic and customer spread. Importantly, our offer and the associated substantial premium represent a unique opportunity for Petrohawk shareholders and recognize the growth opportunities embedded in its portfolio immediately."

The Fayettesville, Haynesville, Eagle Ford, and Permian Assets were consolidated in a single BHP subsidiary for operational and reporting purposes.

The acquisition fared poorly from the beginning, with BHP taking a $2.835 billion gross/$1.839 billon net impairment on the Fayettesville assets in 2012. Asset impairments were recorded in subsequent years as summarized in Table 1, below[22].

YEAR	ASSET	IMPAIRMENT (GROSS)	IMPAIRMENT (NET)
2012	Fayettesville	$MM 2,835	$MM 1,839
2013	Permian	$MM 266	$MM 167
2014	-	-	-
2015	Onshore Assets	$MM 2,787	$MM 1,958
2016	Onshore Assets	$MM 7,184	$MM 4,884
2017	-	-	
2018	Onshore Assets	$MM 2,859	$MM 2,750

TABLE I: Summary BHP Onshore United
States Impairments (2012 to 2018)

In 2018 BHP announced the sale of its Haynesville, Eagle Ford, and Permian assets to BP for $10.8 billion. It also announced the sale of its Fayetteville assets to a subsidiary of Merit Energy Company for $300 million. This constituted BHP's exit from onshore shale after seven years. BHP made the following statement at the time of the sale[23]:

> "The move is a part of the company's plan to focus on its most profitable core long-life operations—iron ore, copper, petroleum, coal, and potash."

BHP had continued to invest in the assets throughout the period that it held them, and, while they were producing assets and were generating some cash flow, they did not generate enough to cover that investment. Figure 7, below, shows a reconstruction of cash flow for the onshore asset based on BHP's annual reports.

As Figure 7 shows, capital investment in the onshore fields greatly exceeded EBITDA in all years except 2017. The cash-flow profile of the asset, including acquisition and sales prices, is shown in Figure 8.

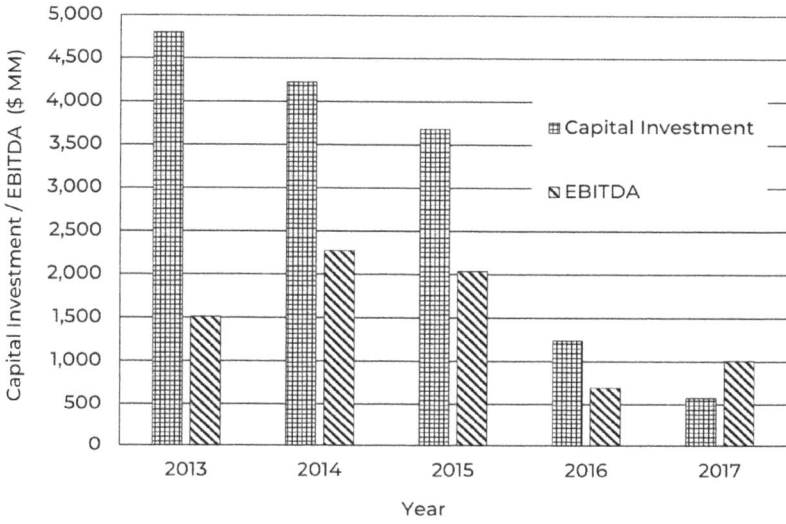

FIGURE 7: BHP Onshore Capital Investment and
EBITDA (2013 to 2017)

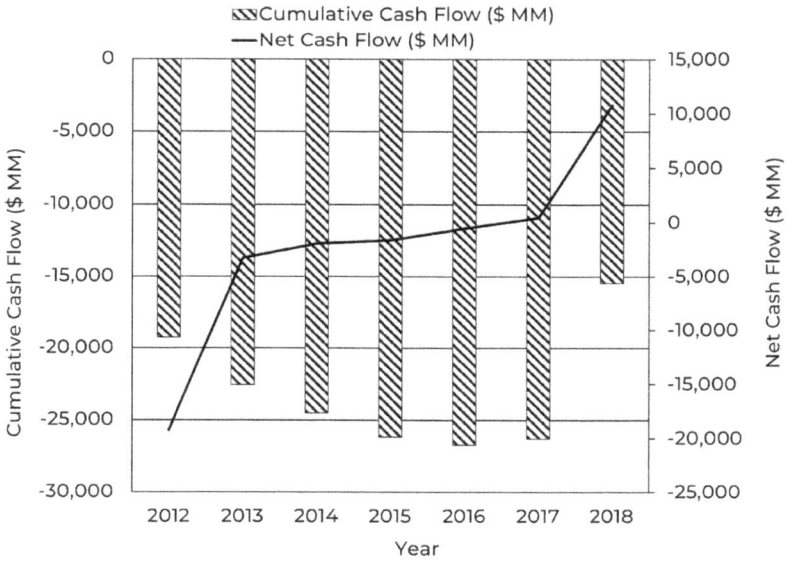

FIGURE 8: BHP Onshore Net and Cumulative Cash Flows

This shows that the asset takes a $15 billion cumulative loss over the period in question. The BHP acquisition of these onshore fields is clearly an example of an asset acquisition that destroyed financial value.

1.7 CREATING A BUSINESS-DEVELOPMENT STRATEGY

Having established what we mean by business-development strategy and why it is of particular importance to the upstream oil and gas industry, the rest of this book will focus on how to develop one. Both Apache and BHP espoused business-development strategies in the press releases that accompanied the announcement of the transactions. These press releases provide a clear contrast in the granularity of the strategies that they were presenting. Apache was clear about how it wanted to grow and what it would—or would *not*—do to achieve that end. BHP was far more equivocal; everyone wants access to large, long-life, low-cost assets with the potential for volume growth. This book approaches strategy development through three lenses. The first is an understanding of the health of the current portfolio, the second is an assessment of corporate capability and resources, and the third is consideration of asset mix, using constituent characteristics.

The intent of approaching strategy from the perspective of portfolio health is to ensure that the strategy that is selected is consistent with the business's overall financial framework and robust against prospective fluctuations in the price of commodities. It informs divestment decisions and builds guardrails around the materiality and maturity of the desired portfolio. The approach is discussed in detail in Chapter 3 of this book, using the fictional oil company Indie Oil to illustrate how this works in practice.

Understanding the capabilities and resources of your organization and how far these can realistically be extended through acquisition is a prerequisite for success in upstream business development.

Given the technical complexity and capital intensity inherent in the business, acquiring assets that are poorly understood or where value cannot be realized will damage the business over the long term. This is discussed in detail in the fourth chapter of this book.

Defining asset mix using constituent characteristics, discussed in Chapter 5, is the precursor to constructing a coveted asset list. Asset characteristics define the type of asset that you are looking for or the type of asset that you need to divest. The approach of defining asset characteristics rather than immediately identifying target fields allows the buyer to look across the full sweep of what is—or what could be—available. As a seller, this approach creates optionality in divestment targets, reducing exposure to an overall set of asset characteristics, rather than an individual asset itself, providing flexibility in the marketing process.

The approach advocated here is circular, rather than linear, with the strategy refined as it is viewed from each of these perspectives. The use of multiple scenarios to construct and evaluate multiple notional-aspired portfolios is described in Chapter 6. Indie Oil is again used as an example to show in detail how these scenarios can be put together.

Chapter 2

KEY CONCEPTS

THIS CHAPTER INTRODUCES some key upstream oil and gas industry concepts in order to provide a common vocabulary and some context to discussions in subsequent chapters. The content covers technical, commercial, and economic areas that are likely to be a feature of most transactions and is organized as follows.

The first group of topics is technical in focus and provide an introduction to some of the ideas that form the core of finding and developing oil and gas fields. The author is neither a geologist nor a petroleum engineer but has found that a degree of familiarity with these processes is useful in helping the developer communicate and understand risks and opportunities as they arise.

- ⮑ Geology
- ⮑ Fluid Type
- ⮑ Recovery Mechanism

The second group of topics is commercial in focus:

➲ Fiscal Regime
➲ Reserves Classification
➲ Risk Classification

The final section focuses on the methodology employed in the maturation of oil and gas fields, and their economic evaluation:

➲ Asset Maturity
➲ Economic Evaluation

The purpose of this chapter is to provide the reader with a general background on the industry. The intent is to provide familiarity with industry terms and methods of classification, rather than to act as a textbook for evaluation.

2.1 GEOLOGY

Geology is central to the upstream oil and gas industry. It is neither the subject of this book nor an area of expertise that the author has any claim to. But it is worth spending some time to introduce some of the most basic concepts that are likely to come up in the course of a discussion of oil and gas fields.

Conventional oil and gas fields require five prerequisites to form a working hydrocarbon system—source rock, reservoir rock, migration path, trap, and seal. These are topics that will typically come up in any discussion about the risk profile of a basin or exploration prospect. There is a temporal element as well, as the trap and seal have to be in place at the point at which the hydrocarbons are generated by the source rock. If they form afterwards, then the oil will have migrated to surface.

Unconventional reservoirs—shale oil and gas—work differently. In the case of shales, the oil is produced directly from the source rock using a process called hydraulic fracturing to stimulate flow. This negates the need for a reservoir rock, migration path, trap, and seal, which greatly reduces the exploration risk with this type of field. This in one of the main reasons for the recent interest in shale oil and gas reservoirs.

The following provides a description of the geological prerequisites for both conventional and unconventional fields.

2.1.1 Source Rock

Hydrocarbons are generally agreed to have their origin in organic matter, consisting mainly of marine phytoplankton and, more recently, plants. Marine phytoplankton first emerged about 700 million years ago, in the Precambrian, and from that point onward, the seas were rich with these invertebrates, which would sink to the seabed and form rich layers of organic matter within marine sediment. This source was augmented by the emergence of land plants around 450 million years ago.

In circumstances where the sediment has sufficient bacteria, a process known as diagenesis would occur, which converted the organic matter into an organic chemical compound called kerogen. As the sediment is buried, pressure and temperature increase, which leads to the conversion of kerogen first into oil and then into gas. Oil is produced through a process called catagenesis, which occurs at temperatures of 125 to 300 degrees Fahrenheit, found at depths of 3,000 to 15,000 feet. Catagenesis is the breakdown of chemical bonds within kerogen, resulting in the release of liquid hydrocarbons. At the higher end of this temperature range, secondary cracking of the oil molecules generates gas molecules.

If burial continues, from 15,000 to 20,000 feet, the temperature continues to increase, from 300 to 500 degrees Fahrenheit, and a process called metagenesis occurs, in which the oil molecules are further broken down into gas molecules. Beyond this depth and temperature, the hydrocarbons are broken down completely.

Layers of sediment that have been buried in this way form the source rock that generates oil and gas. These source rocks can be classified as being within either the oil window or the gas window, depending on an understanding of their burial depth and temperature history. They are a source rock rather than a reservoir rock, because sediments that have undergone these processes do not have the porosity and permeability characteristics required for an economically viable conventional hydrocarbon reservoir. Instead, these sediments act as a source rock, and, in addition to the correct burial history, they must also be close to a suitable reservoir rock, one with a seal to prevent migration to surface and a trap to prevent the hydrocarbons moving around the seal. There must also be some path for the hydrocarbons to travel between the source rock and the reservoir rock.

Source rocks can, however, be exploited, using hydraulic fracturing to stimulate flow. Shale oil is produced from source rock in this way.

2.1.2 Reservoir Rocks

The most important characteristics of reservoir rocks, from the perspective of oil- and gas-field development, is that they have porosity—spaces between the rocks to store hydrocarbons—and permeability—so that the pores are connected to allow the hydrocarbons to flow. Beyond porosity and permeability, size and, in particular, the thickness of the reservoir section support oil and gas economics. An ideal reservoir would also have the same properties throughout (it would be homogeneous) and in every direction (it would be isotropic). It would be perfectly connected (continuous), as these characteristics greatly simplify and, therefore, reduce the cost of field development. Unfortunately, no such reservoir exists, but the closer to that ideal, the better.

The two main kinds of reservoir rocks are clastics, like sandstone, and carbonates, like limestone. Under certain circumstances, other rock types can form reservoirs—shale, in particular, over the last decade. The formation and characteristics of these rock types are discussed below.

Clastics

Clastic reservoirs are formed by the weathering and deposition of other types of rock[24]. Depositional environments can be desert or marine environments such as rivers, deltas, or deep-sea fans. The performance of a sandstone reservoir will be impacted by its depositional environment—the grain size and distribution of the sands, the presence of other minerals, the angle of deposition, and the thickness of the sheets. These differences impact the porosity and permeability of the reservoir and productivity of a production well. Across the field as a whole, these different depositional mechanisms result in fields with different levels of heterogeneity and anisotropy, which complicates reservoir description and field development. About 60% of oil and gas reserves are found in clastic reservoirs[25].

Carbonates

Carbonate reservoirs are formed from the deposition of calcium-carbonate material from plant and animal matter. They tend to form in warm seas. The method of deposition means that carbonate reservoirs are often very thick and cover a large area, both positive factors in an oil or gas reservoir. However, the depositional environment means that the grains are typically not well sorted, meaning that carbonate reservoirs are normally more heterogeneous than sandstone reservoirs.

Carbonate reservoirs also undergo a variety of diagenetic processes that alter their geometry after initial deposition. These processes can result in local increases or decreases in porosity and can open or close connections between the pores.

The result of this combination of depositional and diagenetic processes is that carbonate reservoirs generally exhibit greater heterogeneity and isotropy than sandstone reservoirs and are thus more complex to develop. In some cases, the benefits of large pore spaces can outweigh these difficulties. About a third of oil and gas fields are carbonate reservoirs[26], including some of the world's largest and most productive fields, such as Ghawar in Saudi Arabia.

Shale

The formation process for shale, which is a source rock, is described in 2.1.1. As noted there, source rocks have poor productivity and require hydraulic fracturing to produce hydrocarbons. The industry has less experience in the production of hydrocarbons from shale than from conventional reservoirs, so it is harder to say what characteristics support a strong economic performance. Current thinking is that the total organic content of shale is the key to determining both its oil content and productivity[27].

One of the key benefits of shale is that only source rock is required for a working hydrocarbon system. This eliminates much of the exploration risk. This challenge instead becomes whether the source rock can be produced at economic rates.

2.1.3 Migration

Migration describes the movement of oil and gas from the source rock to the reservoir rock. This occurs in two phases. Primary migration occurs when the oil and gas move from the source rock to a carrier rock. Secondary migration occurs when the oil and gas move through a carrier rock until it accumulates in a reservoir rock.

Not much is understood about how this primary migration occurs. Hydrocarbons are lighter than water, and, as porous subsurface rocks are saturated with water, they will tend to rise in rock that is sufficiently permeable, until they reach an impermeable barrier.

2.1.4 Traps and Seals

The trap is the end point of this secondary migration process. A trap consists of a permeable reservoir rock covered by some impermeable cap rock that prevents continued migration. This impermeable cap rock is referred to as the *seal*. Traps are divided into structural and stratigraphic traps.

Structural traps are the result of some structural deformation. Structural traps can be further subdivided into anticline traps, fault traps, and salt domes. Anticlines are formed by the folding of a sandstone layer beneath a shale layer. The sandstone layer acts as the reservoir, the shale layer acts as the seal, and the fold forms the trap that the hydrocarbons migrate into. A fault trap occurs when reservoir rock is split across a fault line, resulting in a permeable layer abutting an impermeable layer and creating the trap. There must be sufficient pressure across the fault to prevent the hydrocarbons from migrating along it. The third type of trap is a salt dome, where hydrocarbons are trapped in reservoir rock beneath the overhang of an impermeable salt dome. In this case, it is the salt dome that provides the seal.

Stratigraphic traps occur through sedimentation, where there are alternating deposits of permeable and impermeable rocks.

2.1.5 Conclusion

The purpose of this section was to provide some background on the geological prerequisites of a working hydrocarbon system and touched on some of the physical characteristics that are desirable in the economic development of an oil field. In the next section, we will look at the different fluid-type definitions that the industry uses to describe oil and gas fields and how they can impact field-development economics.

2.2 FLUID TYPE

Section 2.1 described the components of a working hydrocarbon system. This section discusses the different fluid types that fall

under the umbrella of hydrocarbons and some of the considerations given to each. All oil and gas fields contain hydrocarbons,
combinations of hydrogen and carbon, and other components.
This section discusses conventional field types and then introduces
shale oil and oil shale.

Oil and gas fields exist across a spectrum, and differentiating
between them is not a precise science. Although not precise, an
attempt at differentiation is useful, as each field type has different
technical- and commercial-development approaches and different
ranges of recovery. Thus, a broad classification supports a quick first
pass at a likely development scheme and recovery range.

There is general agreement that conventional oil and gas fields
can be classified by their fluid properties into six different types and
the basis on which this division should occur. These classifications
serve more as guidelines rather than hard and fast rules.

Classification can be based on molecular weight, formation
volume factor (FVF), and gas/oil ratio or condensate/gas ratio in solution. The formation volume factor describes the ratio of the volume
of oil at stock-tank conditions, at surface pressure and temperature,
to the volume of oil at reservoir conditions. Attempts to classify field
types by American Petroleum Institute (API) gravity, as an index
for the density of oil and refined products, is more difficult, given
the extent of the overlap between different field types, especially for
volatile and black oils, and volatile oils and condensates.

The properties of these six different field types are summarized
in Table 2, below[28,29].

The second column of Table 2 shows the formation volume
factor. This is designated as Bg for gas and Bo for oil, and in both
cases defines the ratio of volume at reservoir conditions with volume
at standard conditions.

Table 2 shows a gas/oil ratio for dry and wet gas, and gas-
condensate fields. In most cases engineers will use a condensate/gas

ratio when talking about liquid yields from gas fields. This convention was not applied in Table 2, as the objective was to illustrate the relative gas content of each of the fluids, and maintaining gas/oil ratio throughout facilitates this.

FLUID TYPE	INITIAL FVF	INITIAL GOR (SCF/STB)	C7+ FRACTION (MOL %)	OIL API (º)
DRY GAS	>20 ft³/scf	>100,000	<0.5	N/A
WET GAS	>20 ft³/scf	15,000–100,000	0–1	60
GAS CONDENSATE	3.0–20.0 ft³/scf	2,000–30,000	1–6	45–70
VOLATILE OIL	1.5–3.0 rb/stb	900–6,000	10–35	40–55
BLACK OIL	1.1–1.5 rb/stb	50–900	35–50	15–45
HEAVY OIL	1.0–1.1 rb/stb	Negligible–50	>50	10–20
BITUMEN	1.0 rb/stb	Negligible		4–10

TABLE 2: Fluid Type

There are overlaps in API between the different fluid types, and nomenclature can vary by region—what may be classed as a heavy oil in one region may be classed as a black oil in another.

On top of the six conventional field types, there is also shale oil and oil shale, which are discussed separately, due to a combination of rock or fluid properties, as these have different reservoir characteristics and require different approaches.

2.2.1 Dry Gas Fields

Dry gas fields occur where hydrocarbons are in the gas phase at initial reservoir conditions, at abandonment reservoir conditions, and at separator conditions. Dry gas has a high methane content, typically 95% or more, with few higher fractions[30]. Dry gas is also referred to as lean gas and has a lower calorific content than wet gas (also referred to as a "rich gas"). Dry gas can contain gases other than methane, such as nitrogen or carbon dioxide (CO_2), that need to be processed before the gas can be used. The high proportion of methane has two major benefits. The first is that flow assurance is greatly simplified, as dry gas should remain in the gas phase, with no liquid drop-out, during transportation. The second is that dry gas is cheaper to process than rich gas. On the second point, while processing is cheaper, lean gas does not yield valuable Natural Gas Liquids (NGLs), and, therefore, that revenue stream is lost. Dry gas is also suitable for conversion to LNG, without prior processing, given its low liquid content.

The Groningen field in the Netherlands, Europe's largest onshore gas field, is an example of a dry gas field. The gas is 82% methane and 3% heavier fractions, 14% nitrogen, and 1% CO_2[31]. Groningen was discovered in 1959, and gas from the field has been used for residential and commercial cooking and heating, industrial applications, and power generation.

Dry gas fields have typical recovery factors of between 40% and 95%, depending on permeability, abandonment pressure, well spacing, and pressure support.

2.2.2 Wet Gas Fields

Wet gas fields occur where hydrocarbons are in the gas phase at initial reservoir conditions and at abandonment reservoir conditions, but the gas has a higher proportion of NGLs. Wet gas fields differ from retrograde-condensate fields, as liquid drop-out will not occur in the reservoir, and, so, there is no benefit to gas cycling. Wet gas has a higher proportion of longer-chain hydrocarbon and hence has a higher calorific value than dry gas. Wet gas streams can be susceptible to liquid drop-out during separation and transportation, and require additional processing to remove NGLs. Wet gas streams typically require more processing than dry gas streams to achieve sales specifications, but the NGLs that are recovered are a valuable source of revenue, and, consequently, wet gas normally has superior economics to dry gas.

The Marcellus gas field in the United States is the largest gas field in North America and contains both wet-gas and dry-gas regions. In the northeast of Pennsylvania, the gas is mainly dry, whereas in the southwest, it is wet. Two example compositions, one from a wet-gas well and one from a dry-gas well in the Marcellus, are shown in Table 3, below[32].

COMPONENT	DRY GAS WELL (%)	WET GAS WELL (%)
METHANE (C1)	95.5	79.4
ETHANE (C2)	3.0	16.1
PROPANE (C3)	1.0	4.0
NITROGEN (N2)	0.3	0.1
CARBON DIOXIDE (CO2)	0.2	0.4

TABLE 3: Marcellus Gas Composition

Wet-gas fields have recovery factors of 40% to 95%, similar to dry-gas fields.

2.2.3 Retrograde Condensate Fields
Condensate is a term used to describe light oil fractions, primarily pentane and hexane, that are liquid at ambient conditions. The key difference between a retrograde-condensate field and a wet-gas field is that liquid hydrocarbons will condense in the reservoir as

pressure drops, as well as in the separator and further downstream. This characteristic has an important impact on development planning and valuation of the reservoir. To maximize recovery of the high-value liquids, some form of pressure maintenance will be required to maintain the reservoir pressure above bubble point. This often leads to a development plan premised on gas cycling, which requires liquids to stripped from the gas stream at surface, before the gas in reinjected into the reservoir for pressure maintenance.

Gas-condensate fields have typical recovery factors of 60% to 85% gas, and 20% to 75% of the oil under a depletion-recovery mechanism. The presence of a strong aquifer or aggressive production will typically increase the proportion of liquids recovered and lower the proportion of gas recovered[33].

Gas cycling has implications for the cost and complexity of surface facilities, wells, and the phasing of production, as a retrograde-condensate field development in this manner will produce liquids for several years, followed by a wet- or dry-gas stream near the end of field life. Gas cycling will typically result in incremental recovery of about 50% of the hydrocarbons that would otherwise have been lost[34].

If the initial reservoir pressure is below the bubble point, then retrograde-condensate fields may have an oil rim beneath the main retrograde-condensate reservoir. The presence of an oil rim can add value to a retrograde-condensate field and lend a field additional development opportunity.

The South Pars/North Field, which straddles the border between Iran and Qatar, is an example of a gas-condensate field. The field holds an estimated 1,800 trillion cubic feet of gas and 50 billion barrels of condensate, making it the world's largest conventional hydrocarbon accumulation[35]. A typical gas composition is shown in Table 4, below[36]. As the table shows, the composition is clearly different from the dry-gas well shown in Table 3 but is quite similar to the wet-gas well shown in that table. The principal difference from the production perspective is that the North field will see liquid drop-out in the reservoir, whereas the Marcellus will not.

COMPONENT	NORTH FIELD (% MOL)
METHANE (C1)	83.2
ETHANE (C2)	5.2
PROPANE (C3)	1.9
C4+	4.0
NITROGEN (N2)	3.4
CARBON DIOXIDE (CO2)	1.8
HYDROGEN SULPHIDE (H2S)	0.5

TABLE 4: Typical Gas Composition North Field

Given the higher proportion of liquid hydrocarbons, retrograde-condensate fields are typically more valuable than either dry-gas or wet-gas fields. Gas cycling also provides some flexibility in the scale and timing of gas demand, as gas can be re-injected until a gas market has been developed.

2.2.4 Volatile Oil Fields

Volatile oil fields are similar to retrograde-condensate fields, with the only distinction being that they contain a higher proportion of heavier hydrocarbons. The API gravity of retrograde-condensate liquids is mid-50s to 70, whereas the API gravity of volatile oil liquids ranges from the low 30s to the low 50s[37]. Here, the terminology is also different. Whereas a retrograde-condensate field gas may have an oil rim, a volatile oil field can have a gas cap, if initial reservoir pressure is at the bubble-point pressure.

If a gas cap is present, a gas-cap-drive recovery mechanism would typically yield recovery factors of 30% to 40%[38]. In the absence of a gas cap, primary recovery from a volatile oil field is usually on the order of 17% to 25%[39]. This can be boosted through secondary recovery. If the reservoir has adequate vertical permeability, then segregation will occur, which will boost the recovery to between 40% and 80%, given sufficient time[40]. Volatile oil fields will produce a lot of associated gas, between 500 and 6000 scf/barrel[41].

The Mbede field in Nigeria is an example of a volatile oil field with good vertical permeability. The field consists of four main reservoirs and is particularly interesting because it has reservoirs with and without natural water drive. A detailed study of the field, undertaken in 1992[42], after 20 years of production, estimated ultimate recovery from reservoir 3I/4A at 65% and 4D at 50%. The high recovery factors in both reservoirs were ascribed to the high vertical permeability of around 500 mD. Counterintuitively, reservoir 4D was the one with natural water drive. The study found that the presence of water drive inhibited the gravity-segregation-drive mechanism that produces high recovery factors in volatile oil fields with adequate vertical permeability. This conclusion has implications for the design of appraisal programs for volatile oil fields as well as for the selection of recovery mechanism for these fields. A typical composition for the Mbede field is shown in Table 5, below.

Volatile oil fields contain a high proportion of gas and valuable NGLs, coupled with the potential for very high primary recovery factors, given a benign combination of rock and fluid properties. Volatile oil fields contain large quantities of gas—more than 50% methane in the case of Mbede, for example.

COMPONENT	MBEDE (% MOL)
METHANE (C1)	54.2
ETHANE (C2)	6.8
PROPANE (C3)	6.8
ISOBUTANE (iC4)	1.7
BUTANE (C4)	2.8
ISOPENTANE (iC5)	1.5
PENTANE (C5)	1.4
HEXANE (C6)	2.3
C7+	21.8
NITROGEN (N2)	0.3
CARBON DIOXIDE (CO2)	0.4

TABLE 5: Mbede Fluid Composition

2.2.5 Black Oil Fields

Black oil fields have a higher proportion of heavier hydrocarbons than volatile oil fields, with an API of between 20 and 30 degrees.

Black oil fields with the initial pressure at bubble point are described as "saturated" and exhibit a gas cap. Saturated black oil fields have similar recovery factors to volatile oil fields. Recovery mechanisms and recovery factors for saturated black oil fields are similar to those for volatile oil fields, although productivity will typically be lower, given the reduced mobility of the heavier oil.

Black oil fields with an initial reservoir pressure above the bubble point are described as "undersaturated." Undersaturated black oil fields will typically yield recovery factors of 5% to 30%[43].

Undersaturated black oil fields with high formation compressibility and high-pressure drawdowns can yield higher recovery factors. The presence of strong aquifer support or the application of water injection can increase undersaturated black oil recovery factors up to 70%, with an average of 35% to 40%[44].

Black oil fields will typically produce between 50 and 900 scf/barrel of associated gas. Black oil fields are some of the most straightforward to develop from a technical perspective; the low gas/oil ratio minimized gas-handling requirements and, therefore, facilities costs. A typical fluid composition from an undersaturated black oil field[45] is shown in Table 6, below.

COMPONENT	UNDERSATURATED BLACK OIL FIELD (% MOL)
METHANE (C1)	41.4
ETHANE (C2)	5.9
PROPANE (C3)	5.5
ISOBUTANE (iC4)	0.9
BUTANE (C4)	2.3
ISOPENTANE (iC5)	0.8
PENTANE (C5)	1.2
HEXANE (C6)	1.7
C7+	39.8
NITROGEN (N2)	0.5
CARBON DIOXIDE (CO2)	0.0

TABLE 6: Fluid Composition from Undersaturated Black Oil Field

Note that the fluid still contains a high proportion of methane, but the C7+ component is nearly 40%, almost twice the level of Mbede.

2.2.6 Heavy Oil

Heavy oil fields are those with an API of between 10 and 20 degrees and are also characterized by higher viscosity. Heavy oil fields will exhibit low recovery factors using primary recovery, on the order of 5% to 10%, and secondary and tertiary recovery mechanisms are often applied, as discussed in section 2.3. These methods are expensive and energy-intensive, and, as a result, heavy oil fields tend to have higher breakeven costs than other fields.

Heavy oil field development is quite a specialist undertaking, and a greater degree of technical due diligence should be applied to ensure that the field is well understood before consideration is given to an acquisition. One of the benefits of heavy oil fields is that there are large heavy oil deposits available in Organization for Economic Co-operation and Development (OECD) countries on reasonable terms; hence heavy oil could constitute part of a portfolio if the field is well understood, and the acquiring party has the wherewithal to see it through.

2.2.7 Bitumen

Bitumen fields are those with an API of between 4 and 10. Bitumen is extracted through either mining of shallow deposits or steam injection of deeper deposits. The bitumen is then pressed through an upgrader, which breaks down the long hydrocarbon chains to create a synthetic crude oil, which can be transported and refined.

Bitumen production is relatively high-cost and has a bigger environmental impact than other field types, as it requires a lot of energy to extract and uses a lot of fresh water to process. Alberta, in Canada, is home to some vast deposits of bitumen. The combination of huge resources in an OECD country advantageously located for the United States market was enough to make bitumen projects popular in the '90s and 2000s, as this was seen as a resource-access solution by the major oil companies. Several bitumen projects are in production today, although a view on peak oil and long-term oil prices has evolved, and the industry has become more environmentally conscious; there are likely to be fewer of these developments in the future.

2.2.8 Shale Oil and Light Tight Oil

Shale oil and Light Tight Oil (LTO) are both produced from low-permeability formations, often shale or sandstone. The difference between them is that true shale oil is produced from the source rock in which it was generated, whereas LTO is produced from a low-permeability sandstone. Shale/LTO is the play at the source of the last decade's shale revolution and the basis for the United States establishing itself as the world's largest oil producer. The reservoir fluid itself is very light at 45 to 50 degrees API, almost a condensate. Shale/LTO wells also produce large volumes of associated gas, which require processing facilities and export infrastructure. Shale/LTO oil has three key characteristics that distinguish it from conventional oil and gas.

The first difference is the properties of the rock formations in which it is found. The rock is tight; it exhibits low permeability—to the extent that the oil would not flow into the wellbore from a conventional completion. Porosity would typically be less than 10% and permeability less than 0.1 mD. The solution is to artificially fracture the rock, by injecting water at high pressure, followed by sand, to fill the fractures and keep them open. Oil will then flow from the fractured surfaces, through the permeable sand, and into the wellbore. As a result, shale/LTO wells require large volumes of water and sand to effectively complete—not to mention the associated environmental considerations of sourcing and disposal, as well as concerns about groundwater contamination and earthquakes caused by the fracturing activity. The other consequence is that shale/LTO wells experience aggressive production declines—on the order of 70% in their first year.[46] It is, therefore, necessary to continuously drill and complete new shale/LTO wells in order to maintain production levels.

The second characteristic of shale/LTO is that these fields are abundant, even in mature oil provinces. While there are areas that are better—*sweet spots*—there is no exploration risk in the geological sense. This does not mean that there is *no* exploration risk; the commercial risk is still there, as some areas are more productive than others, and some are more gas than liquid prone.

The third characteristic is cycle time. Shale/LTO development is simple and repetitive, and can, lease-maintenance requirements notwithstanding, be ramped up and down by adding or removing drilling rigs and frac spreads. The cycle time from investment to return on greenfield exploration is a decade or more, whereas, in shale oil, it is a year or more.

These three characteristics make shale/LTO distinct as a resource type from conventional oil and gas fields—and any resource type with different characteristics can be useful in the construction of a portfolio.

2.2.9 Oil Shale

Oil shale is distinct from shale oil and is noted here as a footnote; there is no longer much interest in the commercial development of this resource. Oil shale is a shale that contains kerogen, which is a mixture of organic compounds that will produce hydrocarbons when heated. Oil shale and kerogen form the source rock from which oil and gas are naturally produced, given the right history of temperature and pressure. Oil shale is source rock that has not been exposed to the right temperature and pressure and, therefore, has not expelled its hydrocarbons.

Oil-shale development can be undertaken either above ground, through mining, or underground, through the application of heat to the formation. When oil shale is mined, it is either burned to generate electricity directly or heated to release oil and gas. Underground—*in situ*—development involves heating the shale underground to create oil and gas.

Oil shale is more energy intensive than conventional oil and gas developments, as it requires the application of energy to create the oil and gas prior to extraction. The technology has been in use for decades, but the resource type has yet to be demonstrated as being commercially competitive with conventional oil and gas, despite studies showing that breakeven prices could be as low as $25/barrel[47].

2.2.10 Conclusion

Having read this section, it should be clear to the reader that there is no such thing as a standard oil and gas field. Behavior is influenced by not only geology but also by the properties of the reservoir fluids. In the next section, we will introduce different recovery mechanisms, which are a choice rather than nature's endowment, but the next section will illustrate how the interaction of recovery mechanism with geology and fluid type introduces another layer of complexity to field development.

2.3 RECOVERY MECHANISMS

While section 2.1 described the geology of a functioning hydro-carbon system and section 2.2 described different fluid types in a reservoir, this section focuses on recovery mechanisms, or how the hydrocarbon will be recovered from the reservoir. While geology and fluid types are nature's endowment, recovery mechanism is something that the developer controls.

Recovery mechanism is not a plan for the development of the field; rather it is the underlying philosophy that will deployed in development. The reason that it is addressed here is that recovery mechanism is one of the earliest and most important decisions that can be taken in the course of a field development, and it is closely tied to the capability of the executing organization, something which is discussed in Chapter 5. Organizational capability in the execution of advanced recovery mechanisms can serve as a differentiating factor for a company—Occidental, for example, has established a track record in tertiary recovery. It is, therefore, worthwhile to develop an awareness of the different recovery mechanisms and the considerations associated with each of them.

In the first instance, recovery mechanisms are divided into primary, secondary, and tertiary. In theory, a field will be developed using primary, then secondary, and then tertiary recovery mechanisms, with each successive mechanism employed to improve recovery over the prior mechanism. This is also a useful way to think about increasing levels or technical complexity, cost, and risk, together with increasing levels of recovery.

In practice, many fields are initially developed with secondary or tertiary recovery only. A phased field development can consist of a primary, secondary, and tertiary recovery phase. A phased field development can also consist of a sequence of phases that are all primary or secondary recovery—infill drilling campaigns, for example. Each of these definitions and the sub-mechanisms within each are described below.

This section also provides a short definition and discussion on Enhanced Oil Recovery (EOR) and Improved Oil Recovery (IOR), to provide the reader some familiarity with these terms.

2.3.1 Primary Recovery

Primary recovery involves producing hydrocarbons without adding any energy to the reservoir, which, in a practical sense, consists of drilling production wells but no injection wells. There are six different drive mechanisms used to produce hydrocarbons under primary recovery:

- ⊃ Solution Gas Drive
- ⊃ Natural Water Drive or Aquifer Drive
- ⊃ Gas Cap Drive
- ⊃ Segregation Gas Drive
- ⊃ Gravity Drainage
- ⊃ Compaction Drive

These mechanisms can work independently or in combination.

In solution-gas drive, the initial reservoir pressure will be at or above the bubble point, and, so, there will be no gas cap. Production is driven by the expansion of solution gas as reservoir pressure falls. Solution-gas drive is the principal drive mechanism for approximately one third of the world's oil reservoirs and provides an average recovery factor of 15% to 17% (varying between 5% and 30%)[48].

In natural-water drive, the initial reservoir pressure will again be at or above the bubble point. In this scenario, there is an oil-water contact, and the underlying aquifer encroaches into the reservoir as oil is produced, serving to maintain reservoir pressure. Natural-water drive occurs in about one third of the world's oil reservoirs and provides an average recovery factor of 35% to 40% (varying between 10% and 70%)[49].

In gas-cap drive, the initial reservoir pressure will be at the bubble point, and a gas cap will have developed. Gas-cap drive differs from segregation-gas drive, discussed below, in that the vertical permeability of the reservoir is limited (less than 50 mD). The gas cap expands as reservoir pressure falls, with this expansion displacing the underlying oil. Gas-cap drive provides an average recovery factor of 30% to 40%.[50,51]

Segregation-gas drive occurs in reservoirs with higher vertical permeability (more than 50 mD), where gas migrates to the top of the reservoir, and oil migrates to the bottom. Segregation-gas drive provides a recovery factor of 40% to 80%[52].

Gravity drainage is seen in reservoirs where the structure dips and there is sufficient lateral permeability. Under gravity drainage, the oil migrates downdip, while the gas migrates updip, resulting in high oil saturations downdip, even as reservoir pressure falls. The mechanism is analogous to segregation-gas drive but takes place on a lateral rather than vertical plane, and it provides similar recovery factors of 40% to 80%. Gravity drainage is often used in combination with secondary-recovery methods such as gas injection or tertiary-recovery methods such as steam injection in more viscous oils.

Compaction drive refers to the compression of rock as fluid is drawn from a reservoir. Compaction drive has a greater impact on shallow, unconsolidated sands, as these have greater potential for compaction. Chalk reservoirs in the North Sea also have significant compaction potential. The Valhall field, in the Norwegian sector of the North Sea, experienced up to 10 meters of compaction, over a reservoir thickness of 70 meters, in the first twenty years of production[53]. This was an important recovery mechanism for Valhall, with BP attributing up to 50% of the reservoir drive energy to this mechanism. It also resulted in substantial seafloor subsidence of up to 6 meters in some areas, which clearly constitutes a risk to offshore production.

2.3.2 Secondary Recovery

Secondary oil recovery entails the injection of water or an immiscible gas, normally hydrocarbon gas, to increase the recovery factor in a field. An immiscible gas is one that will not be absorbed by the oil. Miscible gas floods, where the gas is absorbed by the oil, are classified as tertiary recovery and will be covered in section 2.3.3. Secondary recovery works in two ways: in the first instance, injecting water or gas works to mitigate the decline in reservoir pressure that occurs in the course of production. Secondary recovery also works by displacing *in-situ* hydrocarbons. In a water flood, where the water would be injected below the main oil sections in the reservoir, the oil would be displaced upwards, as oil is lighter than water. In an immiscible gas flood, the gas would be injected in the crest, above the oil zone, displacing the oil downwards.

Secondary recovery can be undertaken following an initial development premised on primary recovery, or it can form the basis for an initial development plan. In many parts of the world—the Russian Federation, for example—secondary recovery is the default development scheme. Some regions have more experience in using these techniques than others. The North Sea and West Africa use some form of secondary recovery in most cases, whereas it is seldom used in the United States Gulf of Mexico.

A description of the physical mechanisms by which the injection of water and gas impact the performance of a reservoir lies beyond the scope of this book and the capability of this author. The key point to retain is that secondary recovery is intended to improve overall recovery, by maintaining pressure and displacing oil, with its ability to do so impacted by the field type and design of the recovery mechanism itself. As discussed in section 2.2.4, the application of inappropriate secondary recovery can reduce the overall recovery from certain types of fields. The other consideration with secondary recovery is cost. The requirement to separate and inject either water or gas increases facility and wells costs substantially. Additional facilities are required to lift, treat, and pump water, or separate and compress gas to injection pressure, which requires additional power and, in an offshore setting, space and weight provisions. Additional injection lines and wells are required to inject the hydrocarbons or water. In many cases, the additional costs, together with uncertainty around actual reservoir performance, undermines the business case for secondary recovery, at least for initial development.

2.3.3 Tertiary Recovery

Tertiary recovery involves injecting materials other than regular water or immiscible gas; it works by changing the physical properties of the reservoir rock or the reservoir fluid, usually to improve mobility. There are a number of different types of tertiary recovery:

- Chemical floods, which work to reduce to improve the mobility of the oil by reducing the forces holding it in place.
- Miscible gas floods, where the gas is absorbed in the oil to reduce its viscosity and thus improve its mobility.
- Alternative flood fronts, where treated water or other chemicals are injected to provide a more effective flood front than secondary recovery.
- Thermal techniques, such as steam injection or fire floods, which increase reservoir temperature and, thus, mobility of the oil.

Tertiary-recovery techniques are commonly used in certain niche applications. Gas cycling in a retrograde-condensate reservoir, for example, is a form of miscible gas flood. Steam injection is common in older heavy oil fields in California. Occidental has developed a distinct expertise in CO_2 injection in shale-oil fields. Beyond these niches, tertiary-recovery mechanisms tend to start out as pilot projects in specific, usually large fields, as a result of the high cost of application and uncertainty of outcome.

2.3.4 Enhanced Oil Recovery (EOR) and Improved Oil Recovery (IOR)

Enhanced Oil Recovery (EOR) and Improved Oil Recovery (IOR) are commonly used industry terms that overlap with the primary, secondary, and tertiary framework. EOR typically refers to the techniques employed in tertiary recovery. IOR refers to methods to improve recovery that are based on primary- or secondary-recovery techniques, drilling additional production or injection wells (infill drilling), hydraulic fracturing, or acid treatment of a well to improve performance, for example. The water- or gas-injection techniques discussed in section 2.3.2 would also fall under the umbrella of IOR rather than EOR, and, so, the expansion of an existing water or immiscible gas flood would be considered IOR. Hydraulic fracturing, which can be undertaken on shale, tight sandstones, or conventional reservoirs to improve flow, is also commonly considered to be an IOR technique.

2.3.5 Conclusion

This section was intended to provide an overview of the different types of recovery mechanisms that can be used in the production of hydrocarbons. If nothing else, these sections should serve to demonstrate that there is no such thing as a standard oil and gas field and no such thing as a standard way to go about developing it.

2.4 FISCAL REGIME

Fiscal regimes define the financial relationship between the oil and gas company and the host-country government. While rock and fluid properties have the greatest impact on the potential value of a field, you must take them as you find them. However, it is the fiscal regime that determines an investor's ultimate return and, just as importantly, the risk profile of that return. While nothing will make a poor field profitable, a competitive fiscal regime can make an average field attractive for investment.

This relationship is distinct from the regulatory relationship, with the branch or branches of government that control operation of the industry, or local political relationships. The fiscal regime is a good place to start when considering an opportunity, because it is easily quantified and, with adequate preventative measures, should be relatively stable.

Before looking at different types of fiscal regime, it is worth spending a few words on ownership of mineral rights. With the exception of the United States and Canada, mineral rights are owned by the government, rather than by the landowner. Thus, outside of the United States and Canada, the relationship will always be with the host-country government in some form. In the United States and Canada, the relationship can be with an individual landowner or the state or federal government, depending on who owns the land. Offshore mineral rights in the United States of America are split between the state and federal governments, depending on their proximity to shore.

The fiscal regime is defined as the lease or granting instrument, a written agreement that sets forth the terms and conditions of the lease or grant. While each fiscal regime is unique and subject to change with each new licensing round, extension, or renegotiation, there are some general comments that can be provided about the different types of granting instruments that form the substructure upon which the fiscal regime is built. The oil and gas industry works with three different types of granting instruments:

- Tax, Royalty Regimes—Concessions, Licenses, and Leases
- Production Sharing Agreements
- Service Contracts

As a general rule, tax/royalty regimes introduce a higher level of technical and economic risk and potential economic reward, as they are mainly OECD-based, so the remaining fields are more challenging but provide greater exposure to oil prices. Production Sharing Agreements (PSAs), also sometimes referred to as Production Sharing Contracts (PSCs), tend to allocate a greater share of the economic reward to the host-country governments, while providing additional legal stability and downside protection for the oil and gas company. Service contracts pay the oil and gas company a fee based on some defined performance metric. It is important to emphasize that the stability of a fiscal regime is, in many ways, more important than its relative attractiveness at any point in time. If we assume that it will take ten years to progress a hub-class field from discovery to production and a further twenty to thirty years of production from there, then it is clear that a high level of certainty will be required on future royalty and tax payments to support the decision to invest.

The three types of granting instrument are discussed in more detail, below.

2.4.1 Tax/Royalty Regimes

Tax/Royalty regimes are the original and most straightforward granting instrument. Concessions, Licenses, and Leases are the three different forms of tax/royalty regime. In some respects, Concessions, Licenses, and Leases all work in the same way. They grant the holder a right to access certain minerals over a defined area for a predetermined period of time. The holder usually pays some form of ground rental, a royalty on production, and tax on profits for the corporate entity at the national level. A royalty is a percentage of revenue, either in production or in cash. There is sometimes a bonus payment at the time of award, especially if award is part of a competitive-bid process. In some cases, there is also an additional tax levied on profits from oil and gas production.

While Concessions, Licenses, and Leases work in the same sort of way, there are some important differences[54]. A Concession is closer to a contract than a License regime. This means that each individual Concession is negotiable and, in theory, should be easier to adjust if required. Licenses are administrative/regulatory acts granted by the state, which means there is less scope for negotiation and less flexibility but also that the terms are publicly available. License regimes can also be subject to unilateral change. Leases exist in the United States of America and Canada in both private and public forms, differing depending on land ownership. A private lease is more contractual and comes with those benefits—it is negotiable, flexible, and private. A public lease is more like a license, as there is a contractual component but also a reliance on law and regulation.

As noted above, the United States and Canada are unusual in that the landowner owns not just the land but also underlying minerals. Here the oil and gas company can buy the land and the mineral rights or lease them from the property owner. If access is leased, the operator pays a royalty to the mineral-rights owner. The last few years has seen the emergence of a market in mineral rights, with companies that have been established to buy, sell, and lease out mineral rights, rather than produce oil and gas.

The taxation of profit at the corporate level introduces a valuation difference between existing taxpayers and newcomers. Existing taxpayers are able to offset a proportion of their capital cost against their income tax for the year, introducing a valuation gap over newcomers. Companies that are carrying forward a prior-year tax loss can also realize a value gap, as the acquisition of existing production allows them to accelerate their tax-loss write-off. Premier's attempted acquisition of BP's assets in the North Sea in 2020 was designed to take full advantage of this facility.

Traditional Concession agreements are less and less common these days, as they have developed a reputation for being unfairly weighted against the interests of the host-country government. Instead, License regimes have become increasingly common in OECD countries, Leases are used in the United States of America and Canada, with Leases on public lands functioning in a similar way to Licenses in other countries, and PSAs are common in emerging markets. Table 7, below, compares License/Public Lease terms from the UK, Australia, Norway, and the United States[55]. While tax/royalty regimes are simple, their terms can vary significantly.

COUNTRY	ROYALTY	BONUS	TAX
UK	0%	0%	Corporate Income Tax—30% Supplementary Charge—10%
AUSTRALIA	10%-12.5%	0%	Corporate Income Tax 22% Resource Rent Tax 56%
NORWAY	0%	0%	Corporate Income Tax 22% Resource Rent Tax 56%
USA	Onshore 12.5%-30% Offshore 12.5%-18.75%	Negotiation or bid	21%

TABLE 7: Comparison of Selected Concession Terms

As shown in Table 7, the United States imposes a higher royalty but a lower corporate tax rate, resulting in a more profitable industry at high oil prices. The UK appears to take a middle-of-the-road position, but its taxation of the industry has varied over the years through additional taxes as production levels and commodity prices have fluctuated[56]. These fluctuations can be significant, and a high-level summary of the history of the UK Concession terms is provided in the following paragraph by way of illustration.

The UK first introduced a tax/royalty regime in 1964, with a royalty of 12.5% and a number of special deductions for the industry that lowered its effective tax rate below the prevailing rate of 40%. The UK introduced an additional Petroleum Revenue Tax at 40% in 1975, rising to 60% in 1979, 70% in 1980, and 75% in 1983. Corporation tax rose to 52% in 1972. In 1981, the UK introduced an additional Supplementary Petroleum duty of 20% of gross revenue. This was replaced by an Advance Petroleum Revenue Tax in 1982, which was phased out in 1983. In 1983, Royalties were abolished for Northern North Sea fields that received development consent after 1983, and a number of additional tax allowances were introduced. Between 1984 and 1992, Corporation Tax fell gradually from 52% to 33%. The Production Revenue Tax was reduced to 50% in 1993 and eliminated for fields that received development consent after 1993. Corporation Tax fell progressively to 30% in 1999, and remaining royalty obligations were abolished in 2003, when an additional Supplementary Charge of 10% on "ring fenced profits" was introduced. The Supplementary Charge was then raised to 20% in 2006 and 32% in 2011; then it was reduced to 20% in 2015 and 10% in 2016. The Petroleum Revenue Tax was reduced to 35% in 2016 and was essentially abolished in the March 2016 budget.

This summary does not include changes to the various allowances, exclusions, and ring fences that changed over the period. The purpose is to illustrate that License regimes in OECD countries are not necessarily stable and should not be assumed to be so.

2.4.2 Production Sharing Agreements

PSAs, also known as PSCs, first emerged in Indonesia in the 1960s, in response to criticism that the Concession system transferred ownership of minerals to foreign companies[57]. PSAs addressed this by maintaining national ownership of the minerals, while incentivizing investment by granting the contractor a share of production.

PSAs grant the holder a share in production from the field as opposed to ownership of the mineral rights themselves. They are intended to provide a separate, self-contained fiscal regime for each license and, in doing so, provide stability for the investor and the potential for a greater share of revenue for the host-country government. PSAs feature some or all of the recovery mechanisms described in Table 8, below:

MECHANISM	DESCRIPTION
BONUS	These are lump sums paid at key milestones such as contract award, extension, start of production, or renewal.
RENTAL	This is an annual rental paid for the contract area.
FEES	Assorted fees, in addition to Bonus and Rental payments. These can include state and local taxes, a Value Added Tax, and customs duties.
DOMESTIC MARKET DISCOUNT	This refers to a requirement to supply the domestic market with a proportion of the oil and gas production from the contract area at a discount to prevailing market prices.
STATE PARTICIPATION	This is state participation in the contract as a partner. The state is normally carried; the contractor must cover their proportion of cost during the exploration and appraisal phases. Once commerciality has been declared, the state may have a carried interest in the development, an option to take a funded interest in the development, or a combination of the two.
ROYALTY	Royalty is a proportion of revenue, paid either in production or in cash. This can be a flat rate, but PSCs often contain a sliding-scale royalty that adjusts with either hydrocarbon price, cumulative production, production rates, or a combination thereof.
SOCIAL RESPONSIBILITY	Many PSCs contain some form of hypothecated tax, applied to gross revenue, usually linked to some form of social fund.
REVENUE SHARING	Revenue sharing is the proportion of overall revenue set aside directly for the host-country government. Again, this can be a flat rate, but it is more common to have a sliding scale that adjusts with price, cumulative production, production rates, or a combination thereof.
COST RECOVERY	Cost Recovery is the portion of exploration, appraisal, or capital costs that is paid to the oil company from their proportion of revenues, before the profit split is calculated. This usually has a cost stop and a depreciation schedule—i.e., cost recovery is capped at 75% of cost, depreciated over five years.

MECHANISM	DESCRIPTION
PROFIT SHARE	This is the split in profit between the contractor and the state, which is calculated from the contractor's share of the revenue once they have been reimbursed from cost recovery. The profit share can be a straight percentage or use a sliding scale, as for royalty or revenue share. A common recent method is to link the profit-share percentage with the R factor, the ratio of contract profit to contract cost. The idea is that the state takes a progressively higher share of the profits as the project becomes more profitable.
CORPORATE INCOME TAX	This is corporate income tax payable on the profits from the contractor's corporate entity in-country, minus their allowable deductions.

TABLE 8: PSA Mechanisms

As the table shows, the flexibility in PSA terms allows host-country governments to craft contracts that grant progressively larger shares of revenue from contract areas as production levels, cumulative production, price, and overall profitability increase. When host countries undertake tenders, they can make some or all of these parameters biddable and use a formula that determines the highest score. This results in an almost-infinite array of different contractual terms.

A key feature of these agreements is that the state maintains ownership of the minerals, which is of political importance in many countries. The investor, or contractor, is reimbursed in oil and can usually book this production as reserves. There are some variations on these contracts in which the contractor is paid in revenue from the sale of the hydrocarbons, rather than in the hydrocarbons themselves, and, in these cases, reserve bookings may not be possible. As reserves replacement is a key external metric for most upstream oil and gas companies, it is important to secure early advice on reserves booking.

PSAs are common outside the OECD. In general, PSAs provide a lower level of risk and reward. The risk is lower as development costs are at least partially recoverable, but the reward is lower as government share increases with high production outcomes or oil prices. Government take is an estimate of the financial benefit of the development of an oil or gas field that accrues to the government. An illustration of the range of government take is included in the figure below[58].

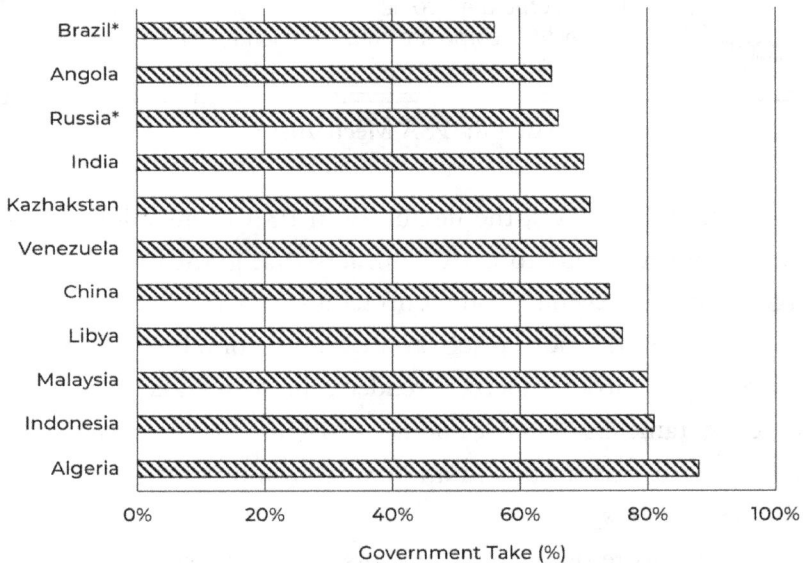

Denotes a fiscal regime that has a combination of Concession and PSA granting instruments.

FIGURE 9: Government Take Selected Fiscal Regimes (2009 to 2014)

2.4.3 Service Contract

The third model is the service contract, where the contractor recovers cost and is then paid a fee for production or is allowed to produce but with a capped rate of return. Service contracts are not common in the industry. The most recent, high-profile example was Iraq, where the rationale for IOCs participating on that basis was just that the fields were so exceptional. It should be noted that several IOCs have since withdrawn.

Some of the large service companies have participated in service contracts in the past. Schlumberger formed a unit called Schlumberger Production Management in 2011, in the hope that the business could achieve higher margins than the sale of equipment and services but decided to wind down the unit in 2019, after struggling with profitability[59].

Migration from service contracts was one component of Mexico's Energy Reforms Law, which was passed in 2014. This initiative consisted of "migrating" twenty-two work-financed contracts (COPFs) and integrated exploration and production contracts (CIEPs), two forms of service contract, to PSAs. The intent was to attract investment in the fields, which had languished, as the existing service contracts capped returns at a level below that at which it would compete for capital within a conventional oil company. Four contract migrations were completed before PEMEX canceled the remaining seven migrations in June 2019[60]. Investors would be wise to be cautious about promises of future transfers.

There is something to be said for avoiding the revenue volatility that comes with a service contract, but that can be achieved through hedging, which provides more flexibility and potential upside. Care should be taken to ensure that cost-recovery limits are clear, that the oil and gas company can abide by these exclusions, and that the host-country government has a track record of abiding by them. The oil and gas company should also be realistic about the terms; a service contractor does not enjoy a strong negotiation position.

2.4.4 Conclusion

This section was intended to provide an overview of fiscal regimes and impress a number of points on the reader. The first is that, after geology and fluid properties, the fiscal regime is the consideration that will have the biggest impact on investment performance. The second point is that there is no "best" fiscal regime, as they will also behave differently, depending on external circumstances such as commodity price and the risk profile of activity being undertaken. The third point to note is that it is not the *terms* of the regime but the *stability* of the regime that is important from an investment point of view. Fiscal regimes can change over time, and, so, it is important to gauge what may happen, what the impact would be on a given investment, and how either the change or the impact can be mitigated.

2.5 RESERVES CLASSIFICATION

Conversations about oil and gas companies and assets quickly move to a discussion on reserves, resources, reserves-replacement ratios, how much was paid for a certain volume of reserves on a $/bbl basis, and so on. The purpose of this section is to provide the reader with an appreciation of what reserves are and what they are not.

Reserves classification is the language used to discuss the maturity of an asset with the investment community, host-country governments, and host-country government agencies. Discussions of oil and gas fields within oil and gas companies revolve around estimated ultimate recovery (EUR), which is the volume of hydrocarbons that will be ultimately recovered. Each EUR estimate is dependent on the data available, level of maturity, development assumptions, and a large number of external factors, such as assumed commodity price.

Reserves classifications are different—they are primarily a legal rather than a technical or commercial description of the asset. They have been codified to standardize the set of assumptions inherent in the estimation of EUR. Unfortunately, there is not one standard, but many. The situation is complicated because a lot of the standards use the same terms but have different meanings or different technical levels of proof to qualify. The differences can appear small but have a far-reaching impact. The Security and Exchanges Commission (SEC), for example, requires the use of year-end prices and costs for its economic test, while the Society of Petroleum Engineers (SPE) guidelines will allow the use of average annual prices and costs if these can be justified.

Industry practitioners in general are very loose in their use of reserves-classification language; reserves are often used as a proxy for EUR or confused with resources. Within reserves, there are different levels of maturity—PDP and PUDS—Proved Developed Producing and Proved Undeveloped are both reserves but require very different levels of capital investment to bring to market and have very different levels of certainty around final production levels.

The SPE have attempted to map the different regimes to allow a practitioner to translate between different systems[61]. There are some common themes that each of the systems address.

- ⊃ Classification by discovery criteria
- ⊃ Classification by commercial criteria
- ⊃ Classification by uncertainty

2.5.1 Classification by Discovery Criteria

This splits the world's hydrocarbons into those that have been discovered and those that have yet to be discovered. For an accumulation to be classified as "discovered," then it has to have been penetrated by a well that finds a reservoir containing hydrocarbons and some indication that it can move to surface. Hydrocarbons that are undiscovered are described as Prospective Resources.

2.5.2 Classification by Commercial Criteria

The next consideration is whether the field can be commercially developed. There can be a myriad of reasons why even a large, productive field cannot be developed economically—fiscal regime, market, and technology, for example. Discovered fields that cannot be commercially developed are described as contingent resources by the SPE; other jurisdictions use terms like "sub-commercial" or "marginally economic."

For a field to be classed as "commercial," it needs to be economically viable, and there needs to be demonstrated intent to develop it. Both of these criteria are subjective; what constitutes an economic investment case to one company may not present an economic investment case to another. The question of "demonstrated intent" is also open to interpretation. In some fiscal regimes, the Declaration of Commerciality, or an approved Field Development Plan may constitute a commitment to develop. There is a link here to the hydrocarbon-maturation funnel outlined in section 2.7, as the further along the funnel a project is, the greater the intent to develop.

Fields that satisfy both the economic and intent tests can be classified as Reserves rather than Resources.

2.5.3 Classification by Uncertainty

Reserves are also classified by likelihood of recovery, to reflect uncertainty in ultimate recovery. These are sometimes described using words—"Proved," "Probable," and "Possible"—to denote low, mid, and high cases. These can be approximated to probabilistic methods if those are applied. "Proved" is more than 90% certain, "Probable" is more than 50% certain, and "Possible" is less than 10% certain. Most agencies have additional requirements to classify reserves as "Proved," and, so, in practice, "Proved" reserves will have a greater than 90% probability of recovery.

2.5.4 Reserves Restatements

All reserves estimates are undertaken assuming a prevailing commodity price, which naturally moves from year to year. Sharp declines in commodity prices can result in write-downs of Proved Developed

Producing reserves, as the economic life of the well—the point where its operating costs exceed the value of its production—will be shortened, and, consequently, fewer reserves will be produced. These can be very substantial. In 2017, Exxon Mobil Corp. revised down its proved crude reserves by 3.3 billion barrels as a result of low oil prices in the prior year[62].

2.5.5 Application of Reserves Classification in Transactions

Reserves classifications are used in this book when discussing the Apache and BHP acquisitions, because that assessment is based on publicly available data, which means reliance on the proved reserve disclosures required by the SEC in their annual reports.

Data rooms may not include disclosures of reserves from individual fields, and this is not necessarily problematic. As outlined above, there are many different approaches to the calculation of reserves and a lot of scope for interpretation. Reserves do not link directly to underlying economics—50 MMBoe recovered over a 5-year period is far more valuable than 50 MMBoe recovered over 10 years. The reserves disclosure makes no account of this. The focus should be on understanding that a field's EUR from first principles is more productive than trying to back-calculate it from a reserves disclosure.

The exception to this—once more—is shale oil, which is typically priced off a discount to Proved Developed Producing Reserves, with some allowance given for Proved Undeveloped. This subgroup may have emerged because of the uniformity of the resource, together with a lack of physical basis for production estimates, or the common fiscal regime, makes discounted reserves estimates a useful valuation shorthand.

2.5.6 Conclusion

The intent of this section was to provide an overview of reserves classification and where reserves should and shouldn't be used. One analogy could be made with financial statements, with reserves acting as the income statement, whereas EUR acts as the statement of cash flows. Individual investment decisions should be made based on EUR, but reserves should be considered when looking at the long-term health of the company, as a robust reserves base should be the result of a series of good EUR-based investment decisions.

2.6 RISK CLASSIFICATION

The process of maturing hydrocarbons could be described as an exercise in identifying and mitigating risk. In both maturation *and* acquisition and divestment, it is important to have a clear view of what the risks with a given field are, which of those risks will be taken, and which will be mitigated to a greater or lesser degree.

Throughout this book, we will use a TECOP system to classify risk. TECOP is the system that Shell uses to classify risk, and the author has always found it a useful system, as it forces participants to think of risk beyond their own personal contribution to the endeavor. In an industry which is very heavy with geoscientists and engineers, it is beneficial to force people to think beyond technical when scanning the horizon for danger. TECOP is an acronym and is used to subdivide risks as follows:

    T: Technical
    E: Economic
    C: Commercial
    O: Organizational
    P: Political

This framework is useful, as it forces the individual to think outside their normal frame of experience; it provides a trigger for someone from a technical background to consider political risk, for example. It should be noted that there can be an overlap between these categories, for example, an environmental incident is classified as a technical risk but will also have a negative-reputation impact, which is a political risk.

Each category is discussed in more detail, below.

2.6.1 Technical

Technical risks associated with upstream oil and gas are normally things like volumetric and recovery-factor estimates, well or project capital cost, operating cost, and schedule estimates. This category also includes deployment of new technology—that is, technology that is new to you as well as to the industry in general—and Health, Safety, Security, and Environmental (HSSE) risks.

Of these, the risk with the largest economic impact is typically STOIIP, followed by recovery factor, followed by either Capital Expenditure (CapEx) or schedule. Asset types that exhibit high technical risks are typically early stage and in frontier regions like the Arctic. The United States Gulf of Mexico is a high-technical-risk region, despite the industry's long track record there, as it is where new play concepts and technology are often tried out first. Nigeria, on the other hand, is an established oil province, with much lower technical risk, but with other, political, hurdles to moving projects forward.

2.6.2 Economic

Economic risks are those associated with commodity prices and fiscal regime. There is an overlap between technical and economic risks; a lower recovery factor is a technical risk with a clear economic impact, for example. Under Concession agreements and most License agreements, project economics will be most sensitive to commodity-price risk.

Some fiscal regimes provide more protection against oil-price fluctuations than others. The economic performance of a project is more sensitive to commodity-price fluctuations in a low-tax environment than a high-tax environment. The United States Gulf of Mexico is an example of a region with high economic risks—projects are very profitable at high oil prices but perform very poorly at low prices.

Fiscal-regime stability is another important consideration when it comes to economic risk. This is the risk that the government will make changes to the fiscal regime over time, often in response to changes in commodity prices or to plug shortfalls in revenue. This is not just a consideration for non-OECD countries. The UK has made numerous wide-ranging changes to its fiscal regime over the last fifty years, introducing, adjusting, and withdrawing various taxes and royalties as the political climate changed and commodity prices rose and fell. A brief history is provided in section 2.4.1 to illustrate how wide these swings can be. Outside of the OECD, PSAs, which codify a fiscal regime contractually, have become the norm.

A portfolio approach is the best defense against commodity-price fluctuations; failing that, smaller producers can focus on maintaining a low breakeven cost and hedging to protect against these fluctuations. Unfortunately, there is not much that can be done to provide fiscal stability in a tax/royalty regime, other than rely on the host-country's requirement to attract capital on an ongoing basis. Most PSAs include stabilization clauses, which are designed to prevent a host-country government from retroactively adjusting a fiscal regime; the industry has decades of experience with these, and there are some examples available that are considered gold standards.

2.6.3 Commercial

Commercial risks cover contracting with third parties and compliance with host-country and third-party regulations. This is a short summary for a large topic, as it includes things like contractor and counterparty capability and solvency, as well as international sanctions, anti-bribery and -corruption legislation, and legal liability.

Commercial risks exist throughout the maturation life cycle, with contract capability and solvency, and anti-bribery and -corruption being most prominent during the early phases and the potential for legal liability being most prominent during the operating phase.

The best mitigation for commercial risk is good legal advice. It is particularly important to engage legal counsel who have expertise in that jurisdiction.

2.6.4 Organizational

The main organizational risks are associated with organizational structure, capabilities, and culture. Organizational risks can be harder to identify and mitigate than other types of risk but are particularly important when looking at acquisition and post-acquisition integration. Chapter 4 of this book discusses the assessment of organizational capability in detail.

2.6.5 Political

Political risks include things like the impact of oil and gas development on local communities, and the company's reputation and relationships with regulators and institutions in both the home and the host country.

Oil and gas investment does not represent an unalloyed good for local communities. During the development phases, there will be disruption, health and safety impacts on the local community, and a demand shock to the local economy that will create both winners and losers. The impact of the Sakhalin II project on Yuzhno-Sakhalinsk was transformative for the local economy, but those with public-sector jobs, like schoolteachers, did not realize any benefits in terms of higher salaries but did experience the negative impacts of food- and house-price inflation.

The focus during the operations phase is on HSSE impact to the local community. Upstream oil and gas facilities employ a lot of capital but not a lot of people, and, so, it is important to ensure that the host community enjoys some benefit and does not suffer negative consequences for hosting this activity.

Failure to accommodate host communities can create some of the most intractable problems in the industry. Corrib could be summarized as a project which benefited Ireland at the expense of the small local community at Bellanaboy. The protest by local people delayed the project for more than a decade; the consequence for the owners is a project that will never recover its initial capital investment. Nigeria is another example, where the Rivers State hosts most onshore production and associated disruption and pollution; the revenue from production flows to the central government, which then parcels the revenue out to the country as a whole. The result is a cycle of violence in the Rivers State that has forced most IOCs to withdraw.

The best way to gauge political risk is by establishing a local presence—the only real way to understand the unique nuances of a place. While this is possible on a development timeline, it isn't practical for acquisition of a new country entry, placing the buyer at an information disadvantage. The best available solution for an acquisition timeline is to retain the services of one of the many political-risk consultants, who should be able to provide a view on the political risk of a given activity in a given region. This can be used during the strategy-formulation stage, to establish which host-country nations fit with the risk profile of the acquiring company, or, in more detail, during the due-diligence phase.

2.6.6 Conclusion

Risk is a component of the business-development process, both in acquisition and divestment, and so it is important to identify and classify the risks in a systematic way, to build a complete picture of the attractiveness of an investment. In the author's experience, technical risks are the most abundant but can generally be solved with the application of time and money. Political risks, on the other hand, while less numerous, can prove more intractable.

2.7 HYDROCARBON MATURATION

In order to understand a business-development strategy, it is necessary to consider what the upstream oil and gas industry does, how it goes about it, and how it thinks about assets. At its core, the industry finds, develops, produces, and sells hydrocarbons. Each company has its own internal definition of how they think about these stages, but, in all, there are seven steps to the hydrocarbon-maturation life cycle, as outlined in Figure 10, below.

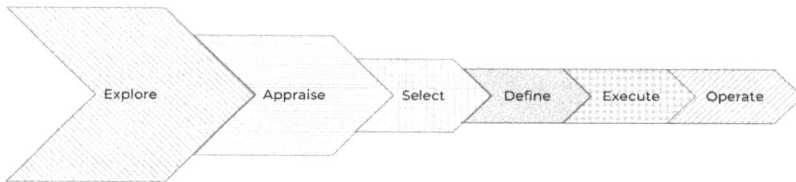

FIGURE 10: Hydrocarbon Maturation Life Cycle

This process applies to conventional oil and gas fields, but not to shale oil, which has a truncated life cycle, described in section 2.2.8. The phases for a conventional oil and gas field are described in this section. The life cycle can be thought of as a funnel, with a large number of potential opportunities entering the exploration phase, which are then gradually whittled down through exploration, appraisal, and selection, to the few that will move forward to become projects and eventually producing assets. The industry has organized itself in this way, as the costs of maturing a field rise exponentially the further down it moves. In order to maintain a healthy queue of projects and options, the industry has organized itself in such a way as to address key concerns early, at low cost, and to eliminate projects that will ultimately fail to move forward.

2.7.1 Explore

The exploration phase is where new oil and gas fields are discovered. The exploration phase begins when the oil and gas company secures acreage. The acreage can be secured through a new award of a lease or granting instrument or through a farm-in into existing acreage.

The process by which leases are auctioned varies from country to country. The more established basins will typically hold regular auctions—the United States Gulf of Mexico or the UK North Sea (UKNS)—while countries that do not yet have an established industry may have a system of open application—Greenland, for example. Some regimes require a signature bonus, while some may also require a work-program commitment.

Exploration acreage can be further classified into four categories, based on the maturity of the play[63]:

Activity during the exploration phase will consist of obtaining and analyzing seismic data, and planning and drilling exploration wells. The oil and gas company may be required to commit to a work program as a condition of securing the acreage and risks forfeit if it fails to execute this program. The exploration phase for a prospect is complete when a well is drilled and technical success or failure is established. In some cases, it is possible to establish technical success but commercial failure from an exploration well, but typically demonstration of commercial success requires additional appraisal activity. Technical success occurs when the exploration well encounters hydrocarbons, but in insufficient volume, or with insufficient rock or fluid properties for commercial development. A commercial success occurs when both technical and commercial criteria are satisfied. Exploration acreage can contain multiple exploration prospects, and, so, it is possible to complete the exploration phase on one prospect while pursuing exploration activity on other prospects.

The relatively low likelihood of success—a company has to drill nine independent wells in a frontier basin to have a 50% probability of making one or more commercial discoveries[64], even in maturing basins—determines the way in which exploration should be conducted. To give a feel for the magnitude of this, an exploration well in a deepwater frontier basin could easily cost $200 million, which would mean a $1.8 billion investment for a 50% chance of one or more commercial discoveries. This reality drives the structure of exploration within the industry, as discussed below.

EXPLORATION PLAY TYPE	DESCRIPTION
FRONTIER	Frontier plays are those in which there is no prior exploration activity or very recent exploration activity. Frontier plays are characterized by low technical and commercial success rates—32% and 7%, respectively—based on recent research.
EMERGING	Emerging plays are those in which a commercial discovery has already been made but before the discovery rate in the play starts to decline. Emerging plays are characterized by high technical and commercial success rates—64% and 34%, respectively.
MATURING	Maturing plays are those in which the discovery rate has started to decline but before the extended tail of small incremental discoveries. Maturing plays are characterized by declining technical-success rates but high commercial-success rates—59% and 34%, respectively. Average discoveries in maturing plays are also smaller.
MATURE	Plays are characterized by a large number of small discoveries. In many cases, exploration is infrastructure led; the focus is on developing small incremental volumes from discoveries near existing infrastructure. Mature plays have lower technical- but similar commercial-success rates—53% and 34%, respectively—and still smaller average-discovery sizes.

TABLE 9: Description of Exploration Play Types

Given the odds, exploration should be conducted only as a campaign, with each well designed to test the underlying hypothesis, rather than find hydrocarbons. The aim is to fail quickly and cheaply, an approach which is difficult to explain to investors and hard to stomach for a company of any size as the expenses rise. Therefore, companies should employ a mix of high-impact/low Probability of Success (POS) and low-impact/high-POS campaigns in their exploration programs. It is also why exploration acreage is usually farmed down to bring in new participation—the risk is shared, and it provides more "shots on goal" for a limited exploration budget.

One of the distinctions of shale oil is that there is no uncertainty as to the presence of hydrocarbons, and, so, there is no technical exploration risk. This is clearly an attractive characteristic of shale, especially for firms that lack exploration expertise. There is, however, still a risk that the field cannot produce at commercial rates, or that the oil and gas company cannot achieve the scale to produce commercially.

Given all this, what is the incentive for the industry to keep exploring? Access to discovered oil and gas resources is expensive, whereas access to exploration acreage is not. Successful exploration can also be transformational for a small company and is the lowest-cost approach to reserve replacement for large companies.

2.7.2 Appraise

The appraisal phase applies to fields that have been discovered but not yet declared commercial. The appraisal-phase work program consists of additional appraisal drilling, rock and fluid sampling, and sometimes well testing or the deployment of an early-production system to provide sufficient data to support a conclusion that the field is technically and economically feasible to develop.

The objective during the appraisal phase is to reduce the range of subsurface uncertainty to the point where there is at least one feasible development scenario. Uncertainty about the size and distribution of in-place resources is tested through additional drilling and subsequent analysis of well results and seismic. Uncertainty in rock and fluid properties is addressed through additional coring or fluid sampling. Productivity and connectivity risk can be addressed through well testing or early-production systems.

The end of the appraisal phase is usually marked by some form of regulatory milestone—a declaration of commerciality, for example, which can commit the operator to proceed with development. There may also be a transition in the operating agreement, a requirement to form an Integrated Project Team (IPT), where all participants nominate staff to work on the next phase of the development.

2.73 Select

Concept Selection is the phase where a field has been declared commercial, but work is ongoing to determine the best way to develop it. The end of the selection phase is marked by submission and approval of the Field Development Plan (how the field should be developed) and the Concept Selection Report (why the field should be developed this way). The definition of "best" in this case is open to debate as the operator, joint-venture partners, and host-country regulator will often have different priorities.

The duration of the selection phase varies from field to field and operator to operator. The larger and more complex the development, the larger and more complex the joint venture. A rule of thumb for a deepwater, hub-class development in an established deepwater basin would be 18 to 24 months. A deepwater tie-back, or shelf or onshore development could be shorter; a larger or more-complex development could be longer.

Many people, inside and outside of the industry, can find these timelines frustratingly long. The work that has been done on project performance, however, indicates that spending time in these early phases leads to better outcomes, especially for larger or more-complex projects[65]. The concept-selection phase is the last point at which the stakeholders are able to effectively alter the shape of the project. If the project is later found to be cost prohibitive, or cannot proceed for some other reason, then it will often recycle to this phase.

2.7.4 Define

During this phase, the operator will be completing Front End Engineering (FEED) and obtaining bids from contractors to finalize the cost-and-schedule estimate for Final Investment Decision (FID). The Define phase is normally split into two sub-phases—the creation of a Project Specification, sometimes referred to as Pre-FEED, and the FEED itself. The Project Specification is a definition of the project sufficient for execution of FEED. Pre-FEED is sometimes undertaken by the operator, but, these days, both the Pre-FEED and the FEED are often outsourced to contractors.

This phase will typically run for around six months on a small project and twelve to eighteen months on major projects.

2.7.5 Execute

Project execution involves the completion of detailed design, fabrication, transportation, and installation of facilities, drilling and completion of production and injection wells, followed by commissioning and start-up. The duration of this phase is dependent on the complexity of the project but is hard to complete in less than two years and can last for more than a decade.

2.7.6 Operate

The operation phase of a project involves the production of hydrocarbons and can run for decades. Fields are frequently redeveloped during the operation phase—adding additional fields through near-field exploration, drilling additional wells, or adding facilities. Typical field lives are 20 years, but some facilities can be designed for longer. There are likely to be additional projects during this phase;

these can be small in scale, involving additional wells or facilities, or can be much larger in scope, involving full-scale redevelopment.

2.7.7 Abandon

Abandonment occurs when the field is exhausted and involves the removal of facilities, the plugging and abandonment of wells, and remediation of the site. Abandonment liabilities can be significant and in some cases need to be funded through the production life of the field. Abandonment typically occurs when revenue from the field can no longer cover operating costs.

2.7.8 Shale Oil

As noted earlier, the life cycle of shale oil differs from conventional fields in that there is no exploration phase. Instead, shale-oil fields are developed through a continuous process of drilling, production, and then testing new techniques to either reduce well cost or improve well productivity. This approach has three key advantages.

The first is the elimination of technical exploration risk. The second is short cycle time—the fields generate cash quickly, which can then be plowed back into additional wells or used to pay off debt. This is a valuable characteristic for a number of reasons:

- ⮑ It enhances the economic performance of the field, as cash is returned more quickly.
- ⮑ Short cycle times allow the operator to take advantage of periods of high oil price.
- ⮑ Short cycle times reduce the risk of assets being stranded due to projected future declines in oil demand.

The third advantage enjoyed by shale oil is the ability to adjust the capital program from year to year as the external price environment dictates.

2.7.9 Conclusion

This section was intended to provide an overview of the hydrocarbon-maturation life cycle. Maturity is an important concept in the context of this book, as an asset's maturity will have an impact on portfolio performance, the capabilities required to mature it, and the overall asset mix of the business. This impact is discussed in greater detail in Chapter 3 and Chapter 5.

2.8 UPSTREAM OIL AND GAS VALUATION METRICS

Valuation is an exercise that is undertaken during the acquisition, divestment, and maturation of oil and gas assets. It will determine which basins to enter, which wells to drill, and which concepts to select. In the context of acquisition and divestment, valuation of assets is clearly important, not only in pricing the asset but also in analysis of the portfolio.

This section introduces some of the valuation metrics that are commonly used in the upstream oil and gas industry. These metrics are used in the decision-making process when screening or ranking projects as well as in transaction evaluation. Most upstream oil and gas companies will define screening criteria and ranking criteria. Screening criteria are hurdles that a project must clear to be considered for investment. Ranking criteria are used to decide which projects to invest in when a company is capital constrained and has limitations on the number of projects it can invest in.

These metrics will be referenced at various points throughout this book. The upstream oil and gas industry uses many of the same metrics as other industries, but, in some cases, there are nuances to their use. A good general guide to finance is referenced in the endnotes.[66]

2.8.1 Net Present Value

Net Present Value (NPV) is one of the primary metrics used to screen and rank projects in the upstream oil and gas industry. It is calculated by adding the sum of all of a project's discounted cash flows. The discount reflects the fact that the forecast of future cash flows is just that, a forecast, and, so, is inherently risky. This risk is accounted for by discounting cash flows, with the discount rate selected to reflect the level of risk. If a project has an NPV above zero, then it's profitable at that discount rate; if it has an NPV below zero, then it is not profitable at that discount rate.

There are a number of advantages to using NPV. It is based on cash flows rather than some other financial or non-cash metric; it uses all cash flows in the calculation and discounts those cash flows correctly. One other useful characteristic of NPV is that multiple NPVs can be added together to show the value of a portfolio as a whole. One disadvantage is that it is harder to compare the relative profitability of projects using NPV than is the case with some other metrics, because absolute NPV values are a function of the materiality as well as the profitability of a project.

The most significant drawback with the technique in the oil and gas industry is in the selection of discount rate. In theory, each individual project should be discounted at a rate that reflects its overall level of risk. As a practical matter, this is hard to objectively assess, as each project tends to be unique, and there is no large, accessible database to evaluate analogs. In practice, most companies who employ NPV as a valuation metric apply either their Weighted Average Cost of Capital (WACC) or 10%. Both approaches imply that each project is equally risky, presumably based in the assertion that the risk has been normalized through application of a standardized set of processes.

The argument that all projects are equally risky—that the 25th small, infrastructure-led development in the Netherlands carries the same risk as a frontier megaproject in the Arctic—is, by inspection, incorrect. In practice, most companies struggle to apply different discount rates, and, consequently, these projects are often discounted at the same rate.

2.8.2 Internal Rate of Return

The Internal Rate of Return (IRR) is the rate of return provided by the project. The internal rate of return can be thought of as a back-calculation of NPV, as it represents the discount rate at which NPV is zero. Thus, if the IRR exceeds whatever discount rate the company in question would have employed in its NPV calculation, then an investment will be profitable. IRR is a commonly used metric for evaluating projects in the upstream oil and gas industry, with many companies imposing an IRR threshold as the basis for making an investment.

IRR can be thought of as the profitability of the project and has the benefit of presenting all the economic information of the project as a single number. It is easy to compare different projects using IRR, but IRRs cannot be combined to reflect the *overall* profitability of a number of projects. Notwithstanding these benefits, there are some practical and theoretical constraints to the use of IRR of which the reader should be aware.

Some projects will exhibit a negative cash flow, a positive cash flow, and then a negative cash flow again. This is quite common in oil and gas, where there is an initial development, some production, and then redevelopment or abandonment. In cases where cash flows flip from positive to negative in this way, the calculation will yield multiple IRRs. If a project has X changes in cash flow from positive to negative, it will have X different IRRs. This is an artifact of the calculation method; the project cannot really have multiple IRRs, but this shortcoming does render IRR meaningless for projects with this type of cash-flow profile.

The second technical issue with IRR is materiality, and this is a particular shortcoming in the upstream oil and gas industry. IRR does not account for the size or materiality of a project—only its profitability. Upstream oil and gas projects can be subdivided into new hubs and infill opportunities. New hubs are true greenfield developments; infill opportunities take advantage of existing hubs to access additional oil and gas. Hubs are more capital intensive and take longer to execute but are more material than infill opportunities. As a consequence of these characteristics, infill opportunities typically yield higher IRRs than hubs. The organizational bandwidth required to execute an infill opportunity is smaller than that for a hub, but not by a great deal. The risk is that if you optimize your portfolio on IRR, then you will tie up your organization developing things that are highly profitable, but, because they lack materiality, they do not actually generate a lot of cash. If you fail to establish new hubs, you will also eventually run out of infill opportunities.

The final consideration with IRR is more theoretical. The Capital Asset Pricing Model (CAPM) states that the expected return on an asset can be calculated as the risk-free rate plus the risk premium associated with the asset. If we consider two projects, Project A has an IRR of 10%, and Project B has an IRR of 20%. We can say that Project B is more profitable than Project A, but the CAPM tells us that Project B is also riskier than Project A, as it attracts a higher risk premium. According to the CAPM, building a portfolio of high-IRR projects is actually building a portfolio of high-risk projects. Efficient markets are a prerequisite for the CAPM to apply, which requires that the value of every asset fully reflects all available information.

Is this the case for upstream oil and gas? The market for assets is illiquid, and there is substantial information asymmetry between the operator of the asset and the rest of the market. The infill opportunities discussed in the previous paragraph are themselves open only to owners of current hubs, so they represent a monopoly rather than the market model. While the CAPM does not apply to upstream oil and gas assets in the same way as it applies to publicly listed stocks, there is an element of truth to it. Lower-risk areas tend to attract more capital, and, therefore, over time, returns in those locations moderate. High-risk areas remain high margin because it is the only way they can continue to attract capital.

IRR is a useful metric when it can be reliably computed, but its shortcomings should be recognized when it is used.

2.8.3 Profitability Index

The profitability index is the ratio of discounted cash flow after the initial investment divided by either the discounted or the undiscounted initial investment. It is less commonly used than NPV or IRR. It works in the same way as NPV for investment decisions but can also be used as a measure of profitability in the same way as IRR.

The profitability index does lack some of the benefits of IRR. For example, whereas IRR provides a feel for profitability relative to other everyday financial measures—interest rates, bond prices, stock-market returns—the profitability index does not.

2.8.4 Break-Even Prices

The break-even price is the commodity price at which a well, a field, a project, a region, a company, or a country satisfies some defined economic hurdle, commonly cash-flow neutrality or an IRR of 10%. This metric has become more common in recent years, as it has become the most common method of expressing the relative profitability of shale-oil wells and has moved into focus for conventional fields as the energy transition raises the possibility of oil demand peaking. In the latter case, the theory is that the entity with the lowest break-even prices will be the last one to be forced from the market.

The metric itself is a useful one because it provides a sense for how resilient a given entity is to variations in price. If you are operating a field that breaks even at $20/barrel, then there is not much need to worry about hedging. If the break-even is $65/barrel, then that is a different story. The two drawbacks to the metric are a lack of definition of what is included as a cost and the difficulties of comparing fields at different levels of maturity.

The first point can be illustrated by the break-even convention employed in shale oil in the United States. This convention is to compare per-well break-evens, which is literally the oil price required for an individual well to generate a return of 10%. This does not include the cost of leasing the land, facilities, transportation of the product, corporate overhead, or debt service. This is why many companies that advertise break-even prices in the $30 to $40 per-barrel range are unable to generate positive cash flow at $60 per barrel, much to the frustration of the investment community. This also makes it difficult to compare different assets, as they may advertise the same per-well break-even prices but have drastically different break-even prices when looked at holistically.

The second issue concerns life-cycle economics versus go-forward economics. Projects should be assessed on a life-cycle basis, but decisions are invariably taken on a go-forward basis. Less-mature projects will usually have higher break-even prices than more-mature projects on a go-forward basis simply because they have more spend ahead of them. The best way for a company or country to lower its break-even price is to stop investing in new production, but, eventually, a company or country that does this will cease to produce. Again, this makes it hard to compare corporate or national health based on claims of break-even price alone.

2.8.5 Exposure

Upstream oil and gas projects require the upfront investment of a large amount of capital and a return that is realized over many years. This leads to a cumulative cash-flow deficit in early years, which is gradually reversed, resulting in a surplus toward the end (hopefully). If we use the analogy of digging a hole and then filling it in, exposure represents the maximum depth of the hole.

Exposure is more of a secondary metric than NPV and IRR, as it is hard to determine a basis for setting an absolute threshold that a project should not breach. If you are considering an investment that has high risk, then understanding maximum exposure is important and could be a basis for restructuring an investment. This can be achieved by farming down working interest or re-organizing the project so that it is executed as a series of small projects, a practice known as *phasing*. *Farming down* serves to share the risk with other participants, while *phasing* focuses on matching ongoing capital expenditure to cash flow. A phased project will usually not be as profitable as a project that is executed in one go, but phasing can reduce risk by limiting exposure.

When faced with a choice between two investment opportunities that have a similar economic profile, exposure can be used as a way to distinguish the relative attractiveness of the two. One of the reasons that shale oil has been so popular is that the financial exposure is theoretically very low. Wells are drilled and brought onstream in a matter of months, and, so, cash is continuously being returned to the business.

2.8.6 Payback

The payback period is the amount of time it takes for a project to return the cash that was initially invested. Payback can be calculated using either discounted or undiscounted cash flows. It is similar to exposure in that it acts more as a secondary measure that gives a feel for the riskiness of a project but is hard to define payback levels that could be considered good, bad, or threshold.

Payback acts as a proxy for risk in much the same way as exposure does. A project that returns the investment in two years (Project A) rather than five years (Project B) sounds like it should be lower risk, because more can go wrong in five years than in two years. But if Project A involves greenfield development in a new play in a host country that has no track record with the industry, and Project B is an infill-drilling opportunity in an established play in a country with an established petroleum industry, Project B is actually lower risk.

The use of payback has become more prominent in recent years as concerns about climate change have mounted. The concern is that long-life assets, those with long payback periods, will never be fully exploited as the world will transition to alternative energies. Assets with short payback periods provide some mitigation to this risk— another reason why shale oil has become popular in recent years.

Payback is useful to consider in the same way as exposure if there is a choice to make between two similar projects.

2.8.7 Finding and Development Cost

Finding and development cost is the ratio of the cost of finding and developing a resource divided by the volume of the resource to be developed, expressed in $/barrel. Finding and development costs can be useful when comparing different plays within the same fiscal regime but are not useful for comparing individual fields or plays between fiscal regimes. They should not be used for field comparisons because they incorporate a finding component—the cost of the exploration campaign, which has to be spread across the entire play. They should not be used as a basis for comparison between plays in different fiscal regimes, because the different fiscal regime will impact the profitability of the development.

Finding and development cost is more of a leading indicator than a real economic metric. It is useful for comparative purposes, but not to support decision-making across multiple fiscal regimes.

2.8.8 Unit Development Cost

Unit-development cost is the ratio of the cost of developing a resource divided by the volume of the resource to be developed and is expressed in $/barrel. Unit-development costs can be useful when comparing different fields within the same fiscal regime but are not useful for comparing individual fields between fiscal regimes. They should not be used for comparing plays within a fiscal regime, because they exclude the exploration-cost component. They should not be used as a basis for comparison between plays in different fiscal regimes, because, as with finding and development cost, the different fiscal regime will impact the profitability of the development.

As with finding and development cost, unit-development cost is more of a leading indicator than a real economic metric. It is useful for comparative purposes but not to support decision-making across multiple fiscal regimes.

2.8.9 Unit Operating Cost

Unit-operating cost is the ratio of the cost of operating a field to the production from the field and is expressed in $/barrel. Projected or forecast unit-operating costs can be used to inform an investment decision on an asset when compared with other assets currently in operation. They are most useful for benchmarking the operational performance of different assets and can be used to estimate the potential for operational improvements during an acquisition evaluation. Caution should be used when selecting analogs for this kind of activity, though, as different field types and maturities will have different profiles. Older fields tend to have higher unit-operating costs for a given nameplate capacity than newer fields because of higher maintenance costs and lower production. Fields that rely on enhanced recovery methods such as gas injection will have higher costs because of the requirement to purchase gas.

As with the other unit-cost metrics, these are not really economic measures but can be useful for comparative purposes.

2.8.10 Transaction Metrics

Transactions in the upstream oil and gas industry are often benchmarked by analysts using metrics like $/flowing barrel, $/barrel reserves or $/acre for onshore fields. $/flowing barrel is the ratio of the value of the transaction to the average production from the field over a specified period. $/barrel reserves is the ratio of the value of the transaction to the proved or proved and probable reserves of the field. $/acre is just the ratio of the price of the lease to the areas that are being leased. The use of these kinds of multiples is common for transactions in other industries—small businesses will typically sell for 3–5 x EBITDA, for example. However, it isn't appropriate for the upstream oil and gas industry for a number of reasons.

Let's consider $/flowing barrel. In other industries, there is an expectation that revenues will continue to grow in line with economic growth. This is not the case for extractive industries such as oil and gas. If each of the assets shown in Figure 11 were purchased in year two for $100,000, each would have been purchased for $5/flowing barrel. However, each of the three assets obviously has very different economic value based on the five-year production profile shown.

The second reason is that even if the production profiles of two assets are the same, their capital and operating costs will not be. The third is a difference in fiscal regime and even the difference between license terms in the same fiscal regime. There are so many reasons why asset valuations in the upstream oil and gas industry differ that employing $/flowing barrel as a basis for valuation has no real value.

$/barrel reserves and $/acre have a little more rationale but suffer from many of the same drawbacks as $/flowing barrel. The exception is shale oil in the United States, where application of these metrics can be useful because the fields are so similar. Decline curves, reserves/well costs, and fiscal terms are generally very similar, and, thus, in these settings, these metrics can be meaningful.

2.8.11 Price Premises

The variable that has the biggest impact on upstream oil and gas economics is oil price. The industry has high fixed costs and low

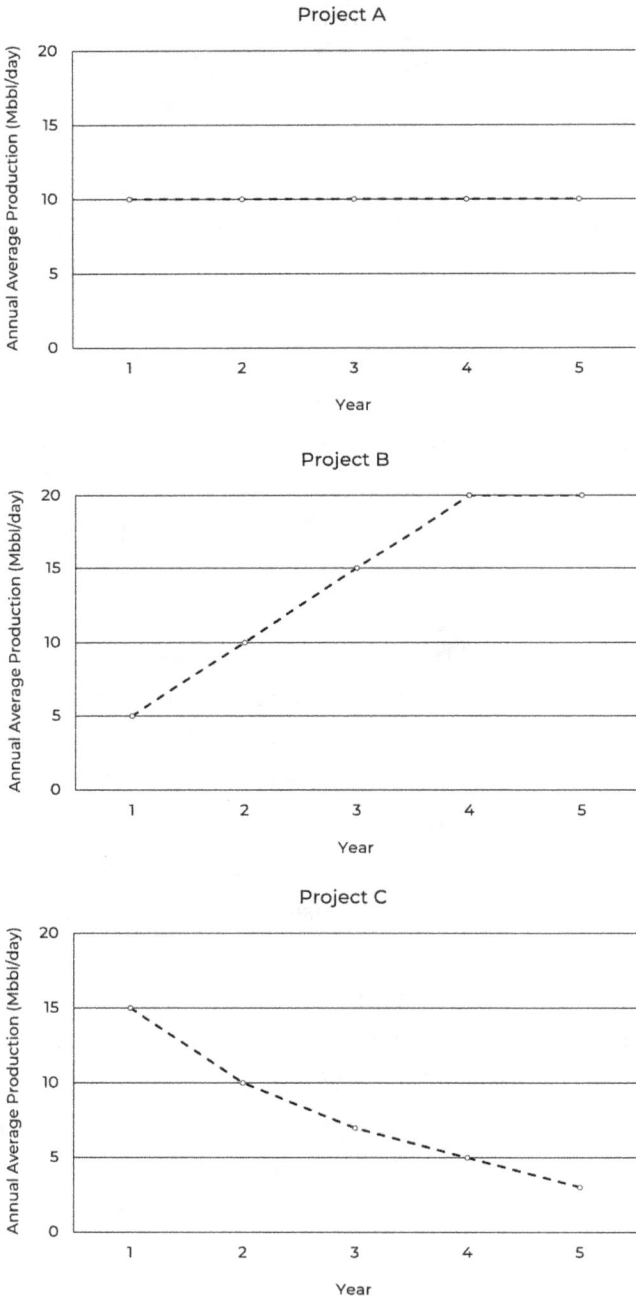

FIGURE 11: Asset Production Profiles

variable costs, which means that changes in price fall straight to the bottom line. Oil prices can vary substantially over the short term, and oil- and gas-investment decisions are made based on years of investment and decades of production. The industry has addressed this disconnect by adopting long-term price forecasts, commonly referred to as "price premises." The idea is that, over the long term, these forecasts reflect the average price and iron out the short-term noise.

Most companies will carry multiple premises for different applications. They will have an expectation or reference case, which is the basis for investment-decision economics. They will typically carry a low case to test how a given investment will perform if the oil price follows a more pessimistic path. They may also have an upside case, which tests how assets perform if the price turns out to be higher. Some companies have additional price premises—they may use one set of prices to screen assets and a second set to rank them, for example. The ranking premise could be higher or lower than the screening premise, depending on whether the company wanted to adopt a more-defensive or more-aggressive price position.

As these price premises are intended to support multi-decade decisions and are based on long-term forecasts of oil price, it would be reasonable to expect that they are constant. Unfortunately, this is not the case, for a couple of reasons. The first is that price premises are the single biggest determinant of whether an asset meets economic hurdles, and people are bad at forecasting it. If your premise is too conservative, you won't be able to compete for assets with your peers, and your business will suffer. If your premise is too aggressive, then you will go out of business. It requires a lot of faith to sanction an asset that meets investment hurdles at $80/barrel, when it is $40/barrel outside and has been for a year. The result is that price premises are regularly adjusted as the external environment changes, undermining the original intent.

The second reason is that while oil and gas assets produce over decades, which insulates their economics from short-term fluctuations in price, the companies that own those assets do not enjoy that same luxury. Low oil prices starve companies of the cash flow that they need to invest consistently, and one common method of tightening investment criteria is to adopt a lower price premise; it serves to quickly eliminate from consideration a swath of potential assets. The drawback is that some of those assets may have been more attractive at a higher reference-case price, resulting in missed opportunities.

2.8.12 Conclusion

There is no single "correct" metric to use in the economic evaluation of oil and gas fields. Fortunately, it doesn't take a lot of effort to calculate all of them, and, once this step has been taken, any single metric, or combination, can be used for either screening or ranking purposes. The process of applying these metrics to analyze a portfolio of assets is outlined in Chapters 3 and 6.

2.9 CONCLUSION

This section was intended to provide an overview of some of the key concepts underlying the oil and gas industry and was broken off into a separate chapter to avoid long digressions later in the book. The author has tried to refer both forwards and backwards to provide the reader with more background than can be accommodated in context-specific sections of the book.

The next three chapters cover the building blocks of an upstream oil and gas business-development strategy, with the next chapter, Chapter 3, focused on assessing the health of the portfolio.

Chapter 3

PORTFOLIO HEALTH

This chapter looks at how to define a business-development strategy that is consistent with the needs of the business. This ensures that the strategy aligns with the business's financial framework and is robust against prospective commodity-price fluctuations. Focusing on the health of the portfolio provides the insights necessary to determine where more and less exposure are required.

Section 3.1 describes the role of business development within the hydrocarbon-maturation process and illustrates how underlying field declines force upstream oil and gas companies to continually acquire new properties. Section 3.2 discusses corporate strategy and the corporate financial framework. Section 3.3 introduces Indie Oil, their business strategy, and financial framework. Section 3.4 then goes on to discuss how to define the current portfolio and the evaluation metrics that are appropriate for assessment of a portfolio as opposed to evaluation of an individual asset. In section 3.5, we screen and rank the individual assets within the portfolio, and, in section 3.6, we evaluate the unconstrained portfolio and apply the financial framework to create a portfolio that conforms with those restrictions. Section 3.7 introduces scenarios and shows how these can be used to analyze the portfolio's strengths and weaknesses, highlighting the value of options. We then look at some real-life examples with Apache and BHP at the time of the Forties and the Petrohawk acquisitions.

3.1 BUSINESS DEVELOPMENT IN UPSTREAM OIL AND GAS

What is the purpose of business development for an upstream oil and gas company? To answer that question, we need think about what an oil and gas company does. At its core, it finds, produces, and sells hydrocarbons. It is an extractive industry, and, so, its assets experience a natural decline in production. The main reason for acquisition is to replace declining production. The main reason for divestment is to free up capital, to pay down debt, return equity, or fund exploration, development, or acquisition. Both acquisition and divestment contribute to a healthy portfolio. Then comes the question of how to position the portfolio for the future.

3.1.1 The Current Portfolio

In order to maintain a given level of production, an oil and gas company must continuously replace the hydrocarbons that have been extracted. Publicly listed oil and gas companies in the United States are required to publish annual reserves statements and report a reserves-replacement ratio. This ratio is calculated by dividing proved-reserves additions over the prior reporting period by production over the prior reporting period. As discussed in Chapter 2, reserves must satisfy technical, economic, and maturity tests to be classified as proved.

Finding and developing hydrocarbons takes time, meaning an oil and gas company must maintain a steady stream of prospective new fields. This can be thought of as a funnel, a widely used industry concept, illustrated in section 2.7 of this book. The core competence of an upstream oil and gas company is the maturation of resources through this funnel.

Estimates are that production from existing, conventional oil fields declines at an underlying rate of around 5% per annum.[67] Shale wells exhibit much faster declines, with rates as high as 75%[68] in the first year of production, and terminal declines, where the rate of decline has stabilized, of 15%[69].

To put these numbers into perspective, assuming a 5% annual decline, a company that produces 100,000 barrels a day of conventional oil needs to bring 5,000 barrels per day of new production on stream every year just to stand still. If we assume a 20% commercial-exploration-success rate, this company needs to target more than 9 million barrels of additional recoverable resource every year in order to maintain its level of production. Assuming a recovery factor of 15%, that means that the company needs to target more than 61 million barrels of STOIIP every year, just to stand still.

If the funnel is well stocked, there is no need for acquisition. If the operator is competent to fully develop the field and has no capital constraints, there is no need to divest. The obvious example here is Saudi Aramco. They have exclusive access to the best oil resources in the world for many years to come at the world's lowest break-even price. Although they do maintain an active exploration program over acreage that they currently hold, they have no acquisition requirements. They are capable of fully developing all of the fields they have access to and have essentially unlimited capital; they have no divestment requirements.

Most upstream oil and gas companies are not in this enviable position. They have gaps in their funnel, need to reload with exploration acreage, or are working under a mandate to increase production. Unfortunately, not every field that enters the funnel through exploration makes it to the end; prospects and discovered fields will drop out of the funnel as they are matured. Acquisition strategy becomes the way in which you fill the gaps in your hydrocarbon funnel to achieve your business strategy. They may have assets that they do not have the capability to fully develop or that may not compete for capital within their portfolios. Divestment is a way to realize partial value from assets that you will not be able to develop.

3.1.2 Portfolio Growth

If the existing portfolio is healthy, the focus shifts to portfolio growth: how the portfolio will need to evolve in the coming years. The need to address portfolio growth typically stems from some underlying weakness in a company's portfolio, coupled with recognition that there are events on the horizon that could transform the deficiency from chronic to acute. It is hard to generalize, but concentration in a particular geography, play, or hydrocarbon type can be underlying portfolio weaknesses. Geographical concentration exposes the company to host-country risk and may prompt acquisition in other geographies in order to mitigate that risk. Deep expertise in a single play becomes less valuable as the play matures and the number and quality of discoveries begin to fall off. Exposure to some forms of hydrocarbon, such as Canadian oil sands, which are conventionally thought of as having low political risk, can move along the risk curve as societal concerns about energy intensity and water use intensify. Many of the large IOCs have made a conscious shift in their portfolios from oil to gas over the last twenty years; given concerns about climate change, gas has been seen as a bridge fuel, with more potential for demand growth than oil through the middle of the century.

There are examples of companies with very specialized business models that failed when the shortcomings of those business models became apparent. Cobalt is an example of a successful exploration company that discovered oil in places that it didn't have the technical or financial capability to develop. Venari is a recent example of a company that made a virtue out of being purely non-operated but was closed down when it became apparent that this meant it had no control over its development pipeline.

3.1.3 Conclusion

This section of the book was designed to explain the purpose of the business development in the upstream oil and gas industry and why it is of particular importance, given the nature of the industry. The section referred to the process of hydrocarbon maturation and natural field declines and introduced the idea of portfolio health, which includes not just the current portfolio but how that portfolio should evolve to meet the challenges of the future. In the next section, we will look at how hydrocarbon maturation must be reconciled with an enterprise's financial constraints.

3.2 BUSINESS NEEDS

This chapter deals with the process of reconciling the needs of the business with the business's asset portfolio. The purpose of this exercise is to understand where you are as compared to where your strategy says you should be with respect to your portfolio of assets. This is an iterative process that should be undertaken on a regular basis—in concert with the annual business-planning process, for example. The purpose of this section is to describe how those business needs should be defined. While the optimal workflow for this exercise is dependent on the organization and the situation, a generic workflow is outlined below.

3.2.1 Business Strategy

The first thing to understand is the strategy of the business and how this relates to the portfolio of assets. In order for this to be a meaningful exercise, the strategy should be defined with sufficient granularity to differentiate between asset types. This step can be the most difficult with the largest companies, as they are typically in everything, everywhere. For example, at one stage in the 2000s, Shell's stated strategy was "More Upstream and Profitable Downstream." There is nothing wrong with that, but it doesn't provide sufficient granularity to distinguish between different upstream assets. In contrast, BW Energy, part of BW Offshore until its recent spin-off, had a very specific strategy. It acquired and developed discovered fields using surplus FPSOs from BW Offshore's fleet. It took political rather than technical risk, operating in countries where BW Offshore had existing operations on shallow-water fields with well-understood geology. This is a level of detail that allows discrimination between asset types in the construction of a portfolio.

The other component of business strategy to consider is whether the business is intent on growth, maximizing profitability, or, increasingly these days, in transitioning to renewable energy sources. Companies in other industries will typically talk about revenue-growth projections—they see strong revenue growth in the early days, revenue growth flatlines as the market matures, and then it slowly declines. Upstream oil and gas companies have typically not talked in terms of revenue growth, because, as the price of the commodity they produce is so volatile, it isn't a meaningful measure. If the sale price of iPhones could double or halve from quarter to quarter, then Apple would not ask to be measured on revenue growth, either.

Until recently, oil and gas companies would articulate these goals through production targets—either annual production growth or quantitative, time-bound, production targets. When evaluating a portfolio, these growth targets are very useful. Unfortunately, this practice has fallen out of favor; the key criticism is that the approach tended to incentivize growth over profitability. For a time, some companies tried revenue at reference oil price, but this is, of course, just production multiplied by that price. This book is written between 2020 and 2021, when the notion of production growth is somewhat moot, as everyone is focused on survival, but the author anticipates that production growth will eventually come back into fashion as oil prices recover and the industry begins to attract capital once again.

For many of the largest IOCs, maximizing profitability and returning capital to investors has been the underlying strategy for some time. There appears to be some form of natural limit to the rate at which an IOC can grow; if the rate is somewhere around three and a half to four million barrels of oil equivalent per day, organic growth just seems to stall. The organizations become so large and complex—and require so much capital and human resources—that further growth just doesn't appear possible. Growth through M&A at that scale has never been tried, either, presumably because the overlaps between the businesses of the very largest oil companies are such that national regulators would impose so many asset sales that it would undermine the initial purpose. This limit applies to IOCs, but there are NOCs that have grown much, much larger. Saudi Aramco can produce something like 13 million barrels of oil per day, but it has a national monopoly on the world's best fields, and, so, it is not really an apples-to-apples comparison.

More recently, major IOCs have not just stopped growing—they have talked about shrinking their hydrocarbon business to redirect investment to renewables. In 2020, BP committed to reduce its oil and gas production by 40% by 2030. This represents the latest evolution of the industry, from maximizing production growth, to maximizing profit, to allowing production to fall and investing in new industries.

3.2.2 Corporate Financial Framework

The corporate financial framework provides the boundary conditions that the evaluation of the current and notional portfolios must observe. A discussion of the different financing methods employed by the oil and gas industry and the various considerations associated with each are beyond the scope of this book. However, it is important, in this context, to understand how much cash the underlying business generates as well as other sources of capital and the limitations on accessing them.

The focus for the purposes of this analysis is on cash flow: How much cash is and can be generated from current operations, how much cash for investment to deliver the portfolio, how much cash has been committed to pay out to shareholders in the form of dividends or share buy-backs, how much cash is required to service debt. Beyond that, what is the capacity for the company to raise additional capital by issuing new debt or new equity? How much financial flexibility does it have? The approach outlined here looks at the company from a cash-flow perspective, but the results can be used to build out a pro-forma income statement and balance sheet if required.

3.2.2 Conclusion

This section was intended to highlight the importance of a business strategy defined with sufficient granularity to be useful when considering the constituents of a portfolio. The business strategy provides the direction for business development; the financial framework provides the constraints. In the next section, we introduce Indie Oil, its strategy, and the financial framework that it operates under. Indie Oil is then used throughout the rest of the chapter as an example of how the portfolio should be evaluated in the context of the needs of the business.

3.3 INTRODUCING INDIE OIL

Indie Oil is a fictional upstream oil and gas company that has been invented to allow the concepts introduced in the rest of the chapter to be demonstrated in detail. This section defines Indie Oil's business strategy and the financial framework that it operates within.

3.3.1 Indie Oil's Business Strategy

Indie Oil is a fictional company—it is a composite built from a number of real companies, so the operational and financial metrics are grounded in reality.

Indie Oil is a listed, independent oil company, with annual production of about 80,000 barrels of oil per day, with some limited associated gas. It has operated and non-operated production in West Africa, development projects in East Africa, and exploration acreage in Africa and South America. Its stated strategy is the delivery of low-cost oil and gas production in Africa, while pursuing disciplined exploration and development. Its exploration portfolio included infrastructure-led opportunities, proven basins, and selected frontier opportunities. Indie Oil is focused on maintaining attractive returns while selectively growing production.

3.3.2 Indie Oil Financial Framework

Indie Oil's balance sheet at the end of 2019 is shown in Table 10, below:

ASSETS	$7,500
Current Assets	$1,500
Non-Current Assets	$6,000
LIABILITIES	**$4,250**
Current Liabilities	$1,000
Non-Current Liabilities	$3,250
EQUITY	**$3,250**

TABLE 10: Indie Oil Simplified Balance Sheet ('000s)

Indie Oil is coming off a sustained period of expansion and has accumulated a substantial debt load, with a debt/equity ratio of 1.3. The annual cost of debt financing is $200 million. Indie Oil has a Reserves Based Lending facility of $2,500 million, of which $1,500 million is drawn down. The balance of their non-current liabilities is in the form of three tranches of notes, with the following repayment schedule.

YEAR	2020	2021	2022	2023	2024	2025
6.25% SENIOR NOTES	$ -	$ 300	$ -	$ -	$ -	$ -
6.25% SENIOR NOTES	$ -	$ -	$ 650	$ -	$ -	$ -
7% SENIOR NOTES	$ -	$ -	$ -	$ -	$ -	$ 800
TOTAL	$ -	$ 300	$ 650	$ -	$ -	$ 800

TABLE 11: Indie Oil Debt Repayment Schedule ('000s)

Indie Oil would issue guidance on a target range of debt-to-equity ratios, but, for simplicity of calculation in this example, we will say that Indie has committed to maintain their liabilities to below $5,000 million through 2025. Indie Oil has established a dividend policy that requires an annual payout of $100 million, and it has committed to retain this.

Indie has annual SG&A costs of $100 million, and, for simplicity, it has been assumed that there are no additional taxes due at the corporate level. Post-tax cash generation for Indie Oil assets on production in 2020 has been calculated for three oil prices, and these values are shown in Table 12. These have been used, in conjunction with SG&A, debt service, and dividends to calculate cash flow available for capital investment or debt repayment, called Surplus Cash Flow here.

As Table 12 illustrates, Indie Oil is essentially cash-flow break-even at $40/barrel Brent but cannot fund investment or pay down debt. Indie Oil generates surplus cash flow at prices above $40/barrel Brent.

OIL PRICE (BRENT $/BBL)	$40	$60	$80
POST TAX CASH FLOW ($ MM)	$ 384	$ 663	$ 943
SG&A ($ MM)	$ (100)	$ (100)	$ (100)
DEBT SERVICE ($ MM)	$ (200)	$ (200)	$ (200)
DIVIDENDS ($ MM)	$ (100)	$ (100)	$ (100)
SURPLUS CASH FLOW ($ MM)	$ (16)	$ 263	$ 543

TABLE 12: Indie Oil 2020 Post Tax Cash Flow from Assets

3.3.3 Conclusion

This section introduced Indie Oil by describing both its underlying strategy and its financial framework. The next section discusses how to define an oil and gas company through its portfolio of assets and then returns to Indie Oil to illustrate how this can be done.

3.4 DEFINING THE CURRENT PORTFOLIO

In section 3.2, we looked at how to describe an upstream oil and gas company in terms of its corporate strategy and its financial framework, a top-down approach. In this section, we look at how to describe a company from the assets up and use Indie Oil as an example of how this can be done in practice.

3.4.1 Portfolio Description

How should a portfolio be described? What level of granularity and what parameters should be considered? In terms of the level of granularity, it is useful to think at the investment-opportunity level, rather than at the asset or the field level. For example, if the asset consists of the block with legacy production from four fields, one of which is a redevelopment candidate, then this could be broken into two investment opportunities. The first would be the legacy production from all four fields, and the second would be the incremental production from the redevelopment candidate. The objective of this approach is to link CapEx directly to production and Operating Expense (Opex), which will simplify things when it comes to shuffling assets around. In terms of the parameters, each of these investment opportunities should then be defined in terms of maturity, flexibility, and control.

Maturity distinguishes among exploration opportunities, discovered, undeveloped resources, and fields in production. Flexibility differentiates between firm investments and options. A firm investment is one where Final Investment Decision (FID) has already been taken, and, so, there is no longer flexibility in the commitment of capital. An option is a pre-FID project. There are circumstances in which a pre-FID project could be considered firm, if further investment were required to extend the license term on a core asset, for example, but, in general, pre- and post-FID is a good guideline.

The most obvious way to differentiate control is between operated and non-operated projects. One of the great benefits of operatorship is control. There are some situations in which the operator of a mature asset has a low level of control. This could be in a situation where the operator and host-country government are struggling to reach agreement on the plan of development, or where a license or contract is being renewed. Post-FID non-operated projects can be classified as firm, as, under normal circumstances, there is no way for any of the participants to reverse this decision. In a non-operated project, the non-operator can normally stop progress but cannot drive it. If the non-operator cannot stop progress, then the impact of this should be examined using a scenario, which is described in section 3.7.

Exploration opportunities should be grouped in the same tranche, regardless of whether they are operated or non-operated. This is because the uncertainty associated with their immaturity is greater than the uncertainty associated with control and because exploration opportunities need to be handled differently from the other tranches, as discussed later in this section.

Differentiating using these criteria leads to the following tranches of production.

TRANCHE	DESCRIPTION
ON PRODUCTION	This is existing production from operations.
FIRM	This is production from projects where there is a high confidence that the project will move forward, which usually means that the project is post-FID. Only non-operated projects that have been sanctioned should be included in the firm tranche.
OPTION	Options are projects that may or may not be sanctioned, either because they are still being matured, because they may not currently rank in the portfolio, or because they may be dependent on another outcome—the discovery of additional reserves nearby or the outcome of a dispute resolution, for example.
NON-OPERATED	Non-operated projects are classified separately because the non-operator does not control the pace or scope of their maturation. Granularity is important when considering non-operated assets in a portfolio context, as each jurisdiction and joint venture awards different degrees of control to non-operated partners. The United States Gulf of Mexico is a very operator-friendly environment, as it allows the operator to push through sanction under a lease-maintenance provision and strips the joint-venture partners of their working interest unless they elect to participate. Brazil, on the other hand, is more non-operator friendly, as it requires unanimity for the joint venture to move forward.
EXPLORATION	This tranche covers both operated and non-operated exploration activity.

TABLE 13: Production Tranches

3.4.2 Case Selection

It is likely that each investment opportunity will have multiple cases, based on different levels of subsurface performance or field-development approaches. This introduces the question of which case to select. It is generally recommended to use deterministic descriptions of each production tranche; the analysis is easier to perform, and it is easier to interpret which assets or attributes are driving a particular result. This should be whatever case is generally used as a reference for the asset—the base case, reference case, or a deterministic case that represents the expectation outcome, if a probabilistic analysis is available for the asset.

As noted above, it is recommended that exploration be treated separately, given the level of uncertainty inherent in that tranche of production. Exploration can be described per campaign or further subdivided into individual prospects. There are a number of different approaches to describe exploration within the portfolio, depending on the amount of data available and appetite for analysis. These are described below.

Deterministic

Using the deterministic approach assumes exploration success and subsequent development in all cases. This outcome is very unlikely, and this approach will tend to inflate production and CapEx forecasts. The benefit of this approach is that it shows what kind of capital and organizational capability would be required in an extreme case; this approach is more useful in a scenario than in the reference case.

Deterministic Scenarios

This is when various combinations of exploration success are selected. Depending on your portfolio, these may be linked to the success or failure of technical themes. As with the pure deterministic approach, this is better suited to building scenarios than examining a reference case.

Deterministic Risked

In this approach, each of the deterministic cases is risked at the commercial Probability of Success. This provides a more-grounded forecast of CapEx, Opex, and production than the other deterministic approaches but doesn't reflect where success is more or less likely. In the absence of data and time or support for more detailed analysis, this is probably the best approach for a reference case. This is the approach that we will use with Indie Oil in this book.

Probabilistic Recovery and Rate

This approach requires the construction of an exploration, appraisal, and development model for each exploration prospect or campaign. This model uses distributions of STOIIP, recovery, and rate per well to simulate tens or hundreds of thousands of different exploration and development scenarios, producing a distribution of economic outcomes. The most likely outcome can then be selected, and the discrete exploration and development program associated with that outcome can be used to represent that prospect or campaign within the portfolio. This approach produces a more representative reference case than the risked deterministic approach but requires a greater knowledge of the distribution of key parameters and more analysis time.

Probabilistic Parametric

This is the most sophisticated approach to describing an exploration prospect and extends to the previous analysis method by employing distributions of individual rock and fluid parameters, rather than volume and recovery measures. This approach requires a detailed understanding of the distribution of rock and fluid properties within a specific basin and extensive analysis. This approach is best suited to guiding an exploration and appraisal program, but the results can still be employed in the construction of a portfolio.

3.4.3 Indie Oil Example

Indie Oil has a mix of operated and non-operated producing assets in West Africa, no firm development projects, and three development options. It also has a diversified portfolio of exploration opportunities—one infrastructure-led opportunity in West Africa and several high-impact opportunities in South America. The maturity definitions used in the table are described in Chapter 2, section 2.7.

COUNTRY	ASSET	MATURITY	OPERATOR	WORKING INTEREST	GROSS RESERVES/ RESOURCES*
GHANA	Marlin	Operate	Indie Oil	25%	480 MMbbl
GHANA	Swordfish	Operate	Indie Oil	50%	160 MMbbl
GABON	Sailfish	Operate	Other	10%	600 MMbbl
EQUATORIAL GUINEA	Dorado	Operate	Other	20%	50 MMbbl
COTE D'IVOIRE	Tuna	Operate	Other	25%	40 MMbbl
GHANA	Marlin Expansion	Define	Indie Oil	25%	150 MMbbl
KENYA	Roosterfish	Select	Indie Oil	50%	360 MMbbl
UGANDA	Tarpon	Select	Indie Oil	25%	1200 MMbbl
GHANA	Swordfish Area	Explore	Indie Oil	50%	100 MMbbl
ARGENTINA	Wahoo	Explore	Indie Oil	50%	300 MMbbl
PERU	Bonefish	Explore	Indie Oil	100%	200 MMbbl
SURINAME	Giant Trevally	Explore	Indie Oil	80%	400 MMbbl

TABLE 14: Indie Oil Portfolio

Table 15, below, provides a summary of the fiscal-regime types for each asset. A description of the different fiscal-regime types and explanation of each of the parameters is provided in section 2.4 of Chapter 2.

ASSET	FISCAL REGIME	ROYALTY	CORPORATE INCOME TAX	OTHER PSC TERMS
MARLIN	PSC	3%	35%	10% State Participation Carried
SWORDFISH	PSC	15%	35%	75% Cost Stop, 5-Year Depreciation 10% State Participation Carried
SAILFISH	Tax/Royalty	12%	73%	N/A
DORADO	PSC	13%	35%	75% Cost Stop, 5-Year Depreciation 20% State Participation Carried
TUNA	PSC	12%	25%	Revenue Sharing Effective Rate 45%
MARLIN EXPANSION	PSC	3%	35%	10% State Participation Carried
ROOSTERFISH	Tax/Royalty	0%	37.5%	N/A
TARPON	PSC	2% to 15%	30%	Royalty Indexed to Oil Price 15% State Participation Carried; 60% Cost Stop, 5-Year Depreciation Profit Oil State Share 46%–70%
SWORDFISH AREA	PSC	15%	35%	75% Cost Stop, 5-Year Depreciation 10% State Participation Carried
WAHOO	Tax/Royalty	21% to 32%	30%	N/A—Royalty Indexed to Oil Price
BONEFISH	Tax/Royalty	15% to 35%	32%	N/A—Royalty Indexed to Cumulative Production
GIANT TREVALLY	PSC	6%	30%	100% Cost Stop, 5-year Depreciation; 5% to 50% Profit Share Based on R factor; 15% State Participation, State Funded

* Note for the purposes of this table, reserves are used to define the expectation production from a post-FID asset, while resources are used to define the expectation production from the pre-FID asset.

TABLE 15: Indie Oil Assets Fiscal Regime Overview

The following tables summarize some of the key metrics for each of the assets. Table 16 presents data for discovered assets, while Table 17 presents data for exploration assets. The category definitions in Table 17 are described in detail in section 2.7.1 in Chapter 2.

ASSET	EXECUTION CAPEX ($MM)	TIME TO FID (YEARS)	FID TO FIRST OIL (YEARS)	OPEX ($/BBL)
MARLIN	N/A	N/A	N/A	9
SWORDFISH	N/A	N/A	N/A	9
SAILFISH	N/A	N/A	N/A	22
DORADO	N/A	N/A	N/A	20
TUNA	N/A	N/A	N/A	19
MARLIN EXPANSION	2,600	0	1	9
ROOSTERFISH	5,400	3	4	12
TARPON	14,400	4	4	10

TABLE 16: Indie Oil Key Metrics Discovered Assets

ASSET	SWORDFISH AREA	WAHOO	BONEFISH	GIANT TREVALLY
CATEGORY	Mature	Emerging	Emerging	Frontier
E&A COST ($ MM)	200	1,200	240	1,200
E&A DURATION (YEARS)	2	2	1	3
START YEAR	2019	2020	2021	2022
CAMPAIGN COMMERCIAL POS (%)	34	72	49	41
EXECUTION CAPEX ($MM)	800	3,600	1,600	6,000
TIME TO FID (YEARS)	2	4	3	4
FID TO FIRST OIL (YEARS)	3	4	4	4
OPEX ($/BBL)	9	12	12	8

TABLE 17 Indie Oil Key Metrics Exploration Assets

Indie Oil's expectation portfolio production profile for the period 2020 to 2040 is shown in Figure 12, below.

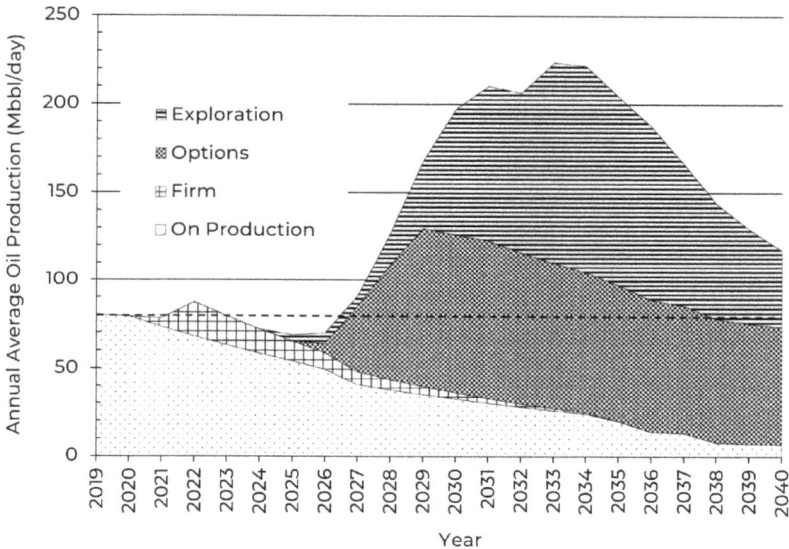

FIGURE 12: Indie Oil Production Forecast

The dashed line indicates Indie Oil's target production level. Referring to section 3.2.2, Indie Oil's corporate strategy was based on generating value rather than production growth. As Figure 12 shows, Indie Oil's portfolio will deliver broadly flat production through to the late 2020s, at which point production grows dramatically through options and risked exploration performance.

This is Indie Oil's unconstrained portfolio, which means that the constraints of Indie Oil's financial framework, as outlined in section 3.2.2, has not been overlaid. This exercise will be undertaken in the next section, but there are some conclusions that can be drawn from examination of the unconstrained portfolio, notably:

⊃ Indie Oil can meet its production target through Base Production plus Firm Investment over the next half decade, a good defensive position.

⊃ Indie Oil has a production gap that opens in the second half of the decade, before options and exploration barrels can be brought onstream.

⊃ Indie Oil can largely meet its production target through Firm Investment plus Options to the end of the next decade; it is not relying on exploration success to maintain production levels.

This last point is important and particularly comforting for investors as the exploration wedge will always have a far greater variance in potential outcome than the others—something which is hard to convey through tables and charts when shown with the other production wedges.

3.4.4 Conclusion

This section has described how to assemble the existing portfolio, in terms of granularity and the parameters that should be included, and used Indie Oil to illustrate this. The next section describes how to evaluate the portfolio and once more uses the Indie Oil portfolio example from this section.

3.5 SCREENING AND RANKING ASSETS

This section considers which evaluation metrics to apply and which evaluation techniques to use in evaluating individual assets within the portfolio. There is a detailed discussion of different economic-evaluation metrics and their benefits and drawbacks in section 2.8 of this book. In the previous section, we looked at the unconstrained portfolio—one in which all assets were included regardless of whether they satisfied investment criteria or conformed to the firm's financial framework. This approach is taken as it gives a sense for the health of the overall portfolio before any choices are made.

The first step, screening, is to evaluate the individual assets against investment criteria. There are three important tests at this stage:

- ⊃ The internal rate of return (IRR), calculated at the expectation asset-performance realization and the low-price premise, should be higher than the company's weighted average cost of capital (WACC).
- ⊃ The IRR, calculated at a more pessimistic asset-performance realization and reference-price premise, should be higher than the company's WACC.
- ⊃ The IRR, calculated at the expectation asset-performance realization and the reference-price premise, should be higher than the company's threshold investment rate.

If the IRR cannot be calculated reliably due to the nature of the asset's cash flows, then the project NPV, discounted at the company's cost of capital and threshold investment rate, can be used as a substitute, with a positive NPV required in each case.

The objective of this screening exercise is to select a subset of assets that will deliver target returns or better at your company's reference oil price and that will at least cover your cost of capital in the low-price premise or low asset-performance realization. Assets that do not meet these two criteria should be divested. A combination of low-price premise and low asset-performance realization will give a worst case but is likely too conservative to be applied as a screening criterion. If the company has no financial or human-resource constraints, then all of the remaining assets can be considered as suitable for investment. This is rarely the case, and, thus, there is a second step, focused on choosing the best assets for investment, given financial and other constraints.

Ranking involves assembling the economic and qualitative information required to differentiate between assets. The computational effort required to calculate and tabulate all of the economic indicators described in section 2.8 is minimal, so it is recommended that this be undertaken at the company's low-, reference-, and high-price premises.

3.5.1 Indie Oil Example—Screening

In this section, we take Indie Oil's portfolio through the screening process. Indie Oil, like many mid-size oil and gas companies, has a high cost of capital relative to its size, as its stock is essentially a leveraged bet on a volatile commodity. Indie Oil estimates its WACC at 14%, which places it at a competitive disadvantage to the large integrated majors and supermajors, which have WACCs in the single digits. As its capital is more expensive, Indie Oil focuses on higher-return projects, setting its threshold IRR at 20%. The large integrated majors and supermajors can maintain profitability with threshold IRRs in the low to mid-teens.

Indie Oils asset rates of return, at low- and reference-price premises, are shown in Table 18, below. Note that, for the producing assets, an NPV rather than IRR calculation was required, as the cash flow does not turn from negative to positive. The NPV calculations are shown on a total-gross basis for the asset.

We can see from Table 18 that all of Indie's producing assets satisfy their investment criteria, although Tuna is marginal. There is an argument for attempting to exit Tuna, to free up capital for more-profitable investments. It is not an operated position, making it less attractive to buyers who specialize in late-life operation, as they require operational control to realize performance improvement. Neither Dorado nor Tuna are really material, so it would be worthwhile adopting an open position in terms of offers, but not the effort and management attention of actively marketing.

ASSET	IRR ($40/BARREL)	IRR ($60/BARREL)	SATISFIES SCREENING CRITERIA
MARLIN	NPV 14: $4,159	NPV 20: $5,247	Yes
SWORDFISH	NPV 14: $1,286	NPV 20: $1,688	Yes
SAILFISH	NPV 14: $1,286	NPV 20: $2,168	Yes
DORADO	NPV 14: $226	NPV 20: $467	Yes
TUNA	NPV 14: (1)	NPV 20: $159	Marginal
MARLIN EXPANSION	79%	153%	Yes
ROOSTERFISH	10%	16%	No
TARPON	17%	22%	Yes
SWORDFISH AREA	11%	19%	No/Marginal
WAHOO	5%	9%	No
BONEFISH	14%	21%	Yes
GIANT TREVALLY	16%	20%	Yes

TABLE 18: Indie Oil Asset Rates of Return

The Marlin Expansion is extremely profitable, but, as shown in Figure 12, it isn't that material. The Marlin Expansion is a redevelopment or infill project, and these are typical characteristics of such projects. They are very profitable because they utilize existing infrastructure, but not very material, as the bulk of the volumes are usually recovered during the initial phase of production. This serves to illustrate the point made in section 2.8.2 of relying exclusively on IRR as a decision-making metric.

Of the two development options, Tarpon looks solid, but Roosterfish falls short of Indie Oil's screening requirements. Roosterfish is in the Select phase, with Indie holding 50% and operatorship, which means that Indie has made substantial investment in it but that there would still be scope for a new operator to come in and shape the project. Roosterfish is not a bad project, either: it has been de-risked, it is hub-class in terms of scale, and an IRR of 16% at $60 per barrel would satisfy a lot of larger companies with lower capital costs. Roosterfish calls for a two-pronged approach:

- ⊃ Engage with the host-country government seeking improved fiscal terms as a prerequisite for further investment.
- ⊃ Begin a discreet and selective marketing process to prepare an exit.

The perennial third option—telling the asset team to go back to the drawing board and make it more profitable—should be resisted. They will go back to the drawing board and may produce what appears to be a more-profitable project, but it won't turn out that way.

Swordfish Area is the nearfield or infrastructure-led exploration component of Swordfish field development. It doesn't meet Indie investment criteria, either, so it should be a prime candidate for divestment. Indie operates Swordfish and so would either have control or—at the very least—a great deal of influence over access and commercial terms to utilize the Swordfish infrastructure that will be required to develop the Swordfish Area discoveries. Swordfish and Swordfish Area also currently share the same joint-venture partners, something that is very valuable, as it eliminates metering and allocation complexity between the different wells, which would require additional infrastructure, and all partners are aligned commercially on operational priorities and allocation of cost. Ghana is Indie's most important operating region, and, so, it is critical to maintain cordial relations with the host-country government and regulator, which means continuing to make progress. Indie could attempt to initiate negotiations on an improved fiscal regime, but this would be ill advised, as it would inevitably lead to a counter that opened up terms at Swordfish, which is extremely profitable. In addition, Swordfish Area neatly fills a near-term gap in Indie's production. It is an exploration prospect, but as it's infrastructure-led, there is high confidence.

Swordfish Area is an example of a field being more valuable to the current owner than anyone else and where there are genuine strategic reasons for investment. It is also a good example of where strict application of investment criteria would be inappropriate.

Both Bonefish and Giant Trevally satisfy Indie's criteria and so can move through, although both are marginal. Indie holds a high working interest in both assets, and, given their maturity and marginal nature, it would make sense to start thinking about a farm-out, to spread risk and fund some additional options.

Wahoo, on the other hand, falls well short of Indie's investment criteria. The Wahoo work program was scheduled to start in 2020, and, consequently, there should not be a significant write-off in a simple exit. With luck, there may have been some prior discussions, and it may be possible to realize some value from a transaction, but the most likely outcome is that the asset will be relinquished.

Implementing these changes, exiting both Roosterfish and Wahoo, would leave Indie Oil's unconstrained production forecast as follows:

Production is substantially below the 80 Mbbl/day guidance through most of the decade, and exploration is required to maintain that production into the next decade, although there is still substantial scope of exploration-driven production increases in the future.

Here we looked at two of the three screening tests: rate of return at low- and expectation-price premises. In the interests of brevity, we will skip the last test; each individual asset should be screened at the pessimistic asset-performance realization and the expectation-price premise as outlined in section 3.5, but this should be completed in practice. Next, we will look at Indie Oil ranking.

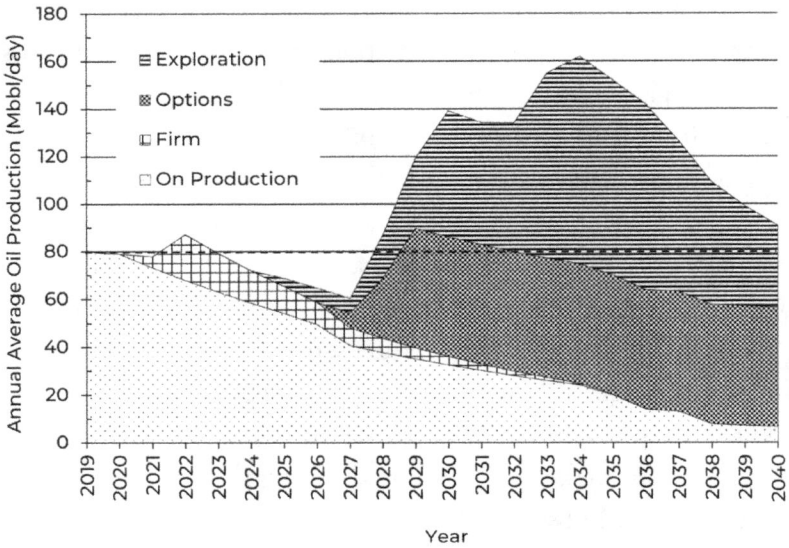

FIGURE 13: Indie Oil Production Forecast Post Screening

3.5.2 Indie Oil Example—Ranking

Table 19, below, shows the ranking metrics for each of the post-screening assets.

ASSET	IRR (%)	NPV1 $ MM	PAYBACK (YEARS)	EXPOSURE ($ MM)	PI	UDC $/BBL	UOC $/BBL	BREAK-EVEN PRICE3 ($)
MARLIN	N/A	5,247	N/A	N/A	N/A	N/A	9	9
SWORDFISH	N/A	1,688	N/A	N/A	N/A	N/A	9	9
SAILFISH	N/A	2,168	N/A	N/A	N/A	N/A	22	22
DORADO	N/A	467	N/A	N/A	N/A	N/A	20	20
TUNA	N/A	159	N/A	N/A	N/A	N/A	19	19
MARLIN EXPANSION	153	1,813	2	200	1.15	18	9	27
TARPON	22	2,692	10	3,576	0.60	10	10	28
SWORDFISH AREA	19	511	7	1,000	0.60	12	9	37
BONEFISH	22	1,138	10	1,740	0.96	11	12	33
GIANT TREVALLY	20	2,519	14	5,166	1.01	12	8	28

TABLE 19: Indie Oil Ranking Criteria

Notes:
1. NPV is discounted at 20%.
2. UDC for exploration prospects is Finding and Development Cost.
3. Break-even Price is in real terms, calculated at a discount rate of 10%, to facilitate external comparison.

On most metrics, Swordfish Area is the weakest option. Tarpon also falls behind the other exploration opportunities when it comes to Profitability Index (PI), a bang-for-the-buck measure, but is the most material discovered resource in the portfolio. The portfolio in general is very resilient to price, with break-evens in the sub-30s for the most material options and prospects and in the mid-30s for the others. The table is intended to illustrate that there is no correct metric to rank on; each field there will be trade-offs driven by the geology, the setting, and the fiscal regime, which should be evaluated holistically.

Looking back over the analysis conducted in this chapter has yielded the following insights:

➲ Neither Roosterfish nor Wahoo meets Indie Oils investment criteria.
➲ Indie has a production gap that opens up in the second half of this decade.
➲ Indie Oil has a heavy concentration of its most valuable assets in Ghana.

3.5.3 Conclusion
This section looked at how to rank assets or investment opportunities within a portfolio, and it quickly became clear that there is no one, correct metric for ranking. In general, you should see some assets come across as stronger and some as weaker, as shown in the Indie

Oil example. In the next section, we look at how to combine the business needs defined in section 3.2, with the screened and ranked portfolio that we developed through sections 3.4 and 3.5.

3.6 RECONCILING PORTFOLIO WITH FINANCIAL FRAMEWORK

In this section, we will look at how to reconcile the high-graded portfolio that we assembled in section 3.5 with the corporate financial framework. This is undertaken by looking at the financial performance of the portfolio under reference-case conditions, examining whether it satisfies the constraints of the corporate financial framework, and using the ranking work in the previous section to make adjustments where necessary.

The goal here is to understand how the sources and uses of cash required and generated by the portfolio fits within the company's financial framework, as described in section 3.2.2. The objective is to identify where the portfolio fits within that framework and where it falls outside that framework. It is testing consistency between the portfolio and the financial framework, rather than looking for absolute or relative economic value. The role of price is important here; long-term price is used as a decision basis for investing in assets, but short-term price impacts a company's cash flows. Consequently, the analysis should be performed for the full range of price premises. It is recommended that the expectation asset realization is used here; other, more optimistic or pessimistic asset-performance combinations, can be tested as a subsequent step, described under section 3.7.

In examining the results of this analysis, the following points are important to consider:

- ➲ Can the firm tranche of the portfolio be delivered at the low-price premise within the constraints of the financial framework? If the answer is yes, then all is well and good.

This tells you whether sanctioned projects can still be funded if prices fall in the short term. If the answer is no, then either the financial framework or the firm tranche will require adjustment.

⮑ Can the firm tranche and the options tranche of the portfolio be delivered at the reference-price premise within the constraints of the financial framework? If not, then this is a signal to prepare for farm-down or full divestment of some of the options tranche.

⮑ Can the exploration and appraisal components of the exploration program be funded under the reference-price premise within the constraints of the financial framework? If not, then this is a signal to prepare for farm-down or full divestment of some of the exploration tranche.

⮑ Is there surplus cash flow under the high-price premise? Excess cash flow is usually considered a good problem to have, but it also indicates a lack of options within the portfolio. There are other solutions to excess cash flow—increased dividends or stock buy-backs, for example—but they can also result in waste and corporate bloat. Surplus cash-flow projections should serve as a trigger for acquisition of additional investment options.

3.6.1 Indie Oil

We will look at how Indie Oil's portfolio fluctuates with commodity price. The cumulative cash flow and net debt of Indie's portfolio at $40/barrel is shown in Figure 15, below. As this shows, Indie would exceed its debt limit of $5 billion in attempting to execute its portfolio at that price.

If we repeat the analysis, but this time farm-out fifty percent of the available working interest in Bonefish and Giant Trevally, then they can remain within the $ MM 5,000 debt ceiling and maintain a dividend payment of $MM 100 per annum. This is shown in Figure 15.

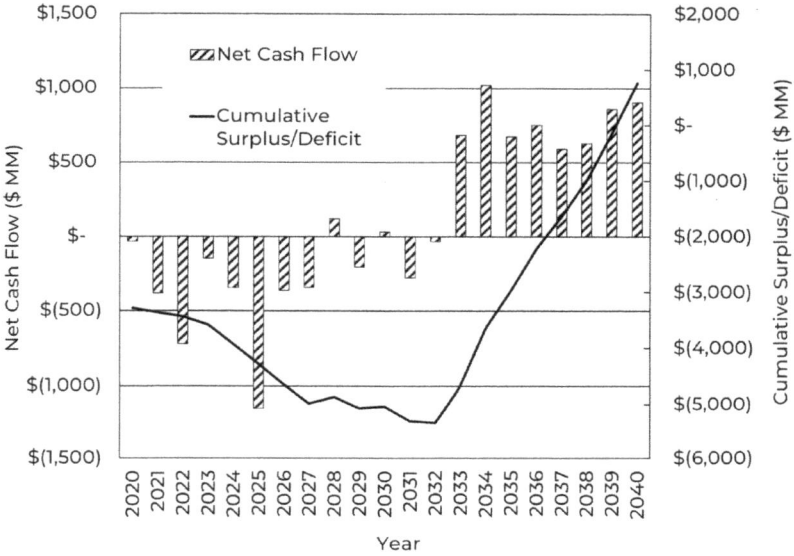

FIGURE 14 Net Cash Flow and Outstanding Debt at $40/Barrel

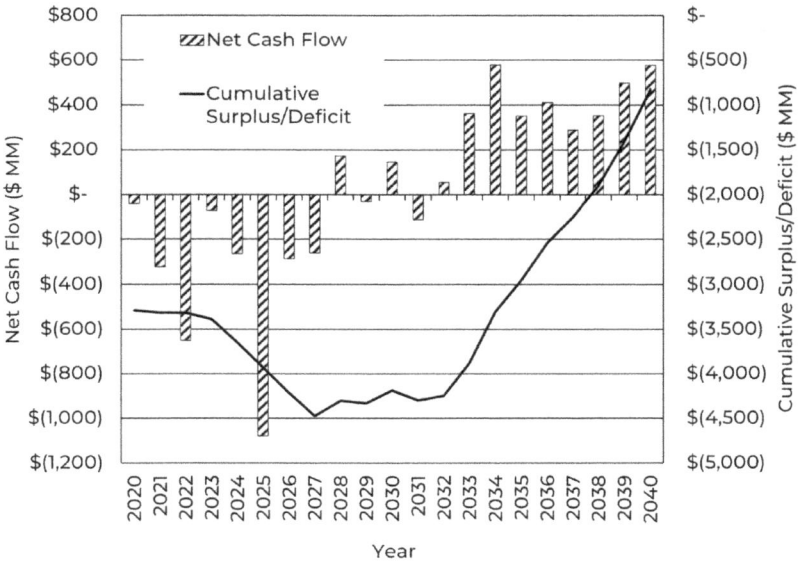

FIGURE 15: Net Cash Flow and Outstanding
Debt at $40/Barrel Reduced Scope

The key test at the low-price premise was that the firm scope could be executed, and Indie's high-graded portfolio can more than pass that test. Figure 16 shows what Indie Oil's production profile would be under this scenario—production would bottom out at about 60 Mbpd in the second half of this decade, peak just short of 120 Mbpd in the mid-2030s, and then decline from lack of investment from there.

This suggests that Indie can return cash to shareholders and pay down debt at $40 per barrel—but not profitably. Investors would make their money back, but Indie's IRR over the period would be barely positive, far short of its cost of capital. Indie would struggle to remain a viable entity in this kind of lower-for-longer price environment.

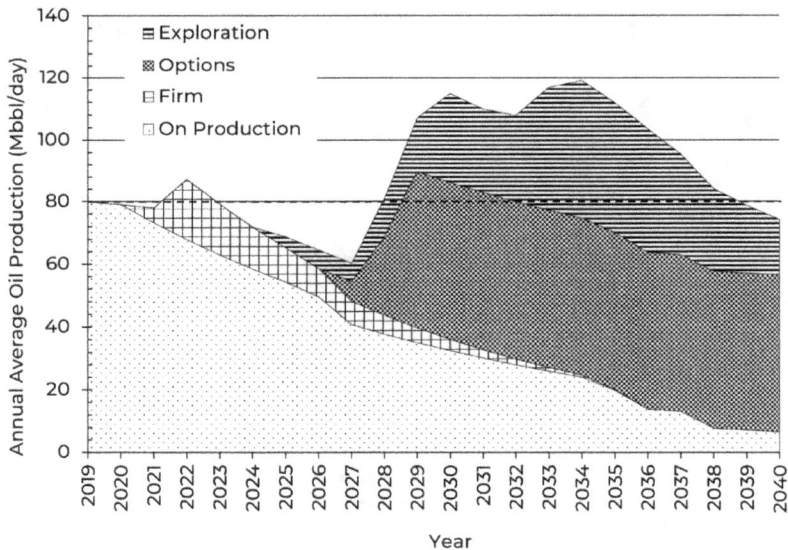

FIGURE 16: Indie Oil Production at $40/Barrel

If we look at how the portfolio performs at the reference-price premise, the entire portfolio can be delivered within the debt limit. In fact, the portfolio starts to generate very substantial surplus cash flow from the early 2030s onwards (see Figure 17), which is a signal that Indie Oil requires more options to absorb that additional cash flow and maintain production at elevated levels beyond the mid-2030s. At the same time, the chart shows that Indie's debt position is very comfortable, providing flexibility for acquisition of additional production to plug the gap in the second half of the decade. Investors would be pleased here as well, as Indie's portfolio comfortably exceeds its 14% cost of capital at this price premise.

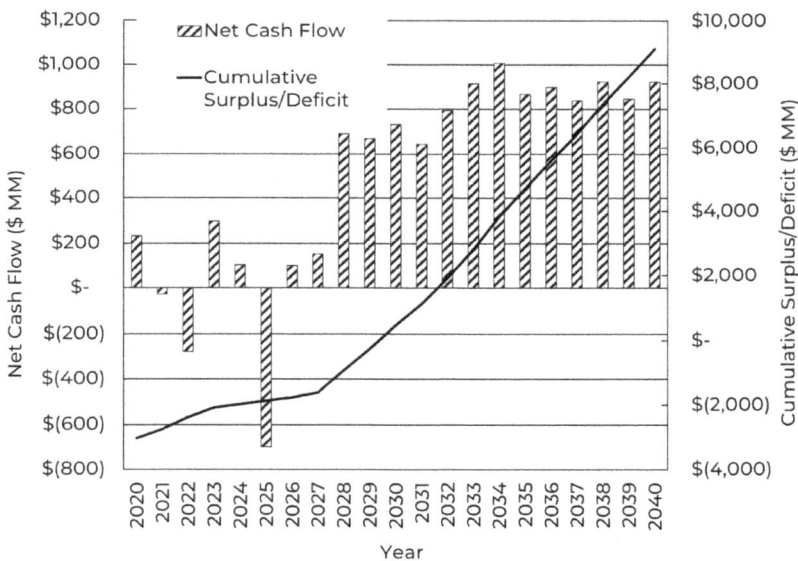

FIGURE 17: Indie Oil Net Cash Flow and
Outstanding Debt at $60/Barrel

The same exercise was then undertaken at $80/barrel, with the results shown in Figure 18. Unsurprisingly, given the results at $60/barrel, the portfolio is even more cash generative. In addition, Indie would have significant room for additional investment within the 2020s and would still stay within its debt ceiling. It is tempting, when looking at this figure, to think back to the original screening and revisit the decision to exit Roosterfish and Wahoo. After all, there is enough cash to fund them as well, and, as in the reference-price realization, Indie would need more options in the next decade. However, revisiting screening decisions because a portfolio requires more optionality is a flawed approach. The high-price premise shows what happens to corporate cash flow under that premise, but the long-term assumption is still that prices will revert to the expectation case, and investment decisions should be made on that basis. If there aren't enough options to satisfy investment criteria at the reference-price premise, the surplus should be returned to shareholders.

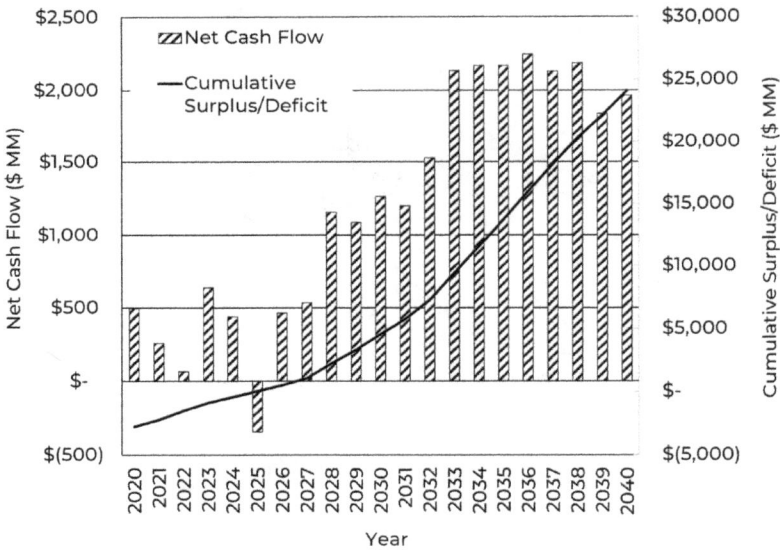

FIGURE 18: Indie Oil Net Cash Flow and Outstanding Debt at $80/Barrel

Insights

Looking back over this chapter at the analysis, we can say the following about Indie's portfolio:

- ➲ Indie can deliver the firm scope, plus the Tarpon option and some exploration, at its $40/barrel price premise.

- ⮑ Indie Oil is oil focused and would be exposed to a decline in global oil demand.
- ⮑ Indie can comfortably deliver its firm and options tranche—as well as exploration—at the reference-price premise.
- ⮑ Indie Oil is reliant on exploration success to maintain its target production levels through the next decade.
- ⮑ Indie requires additional options to continue to drive production growth through the second half of the 2030s. Indie starts generating surplus cash toward the end of the 2020s but does not have a lot of financial flexibility in the near term to make additional investments at the reference-price premise.
- ⮑ In the high-price premise, Indie generates surplus cash flow for most years of the next two decades; Indie does not have enough options in its portfolio to absorb the surplus cash.

In this section, we examined the performance of Indie's portfolio at different price points. In the next section, we will introduce scenarios that can be used to test how a portfolio will perform to sensitivities other than price.

3.7 SCENARIO ANALYSIS

In the previous section, we discussed how to analyze a portfolio at different price points to evaluate how resilient it would be to commodity-price fluctuations. In this section, we will introduce scenario analysis and show how this can be used to test the performance of a portfolio for variations in external factors other than price.

Once the portfolio has been assembled, it can be tested against a range of scenarios to understand how it will perform. This exercise can be thought of as a stress test, the objective of which is to generate insights into the strengths and weaknesses of the portfolio. This process is different from the screening and ranking processes, which focus on individual assets and are designed to flag obvious candidates for divestment and provide a picture of the relative strength of the survivors.

In thinking through which scenarios are appropriate for an individual situation, the first step is to differentiate between outcomes that are the results of corporate decisions and outcomes that are the result of events outside the corporation's control.

Sanction of an operated project is an example of an event that is within the control of the corporation, although this in itself may not be a sufficient condition for the project to move forward, as the joint-operation agreement may also require partner approval. This requirement would introduce an uncertainty into whether the project moves forward. Other examples of uncertainties are things like prevailing commodity price, long-term demand forecasts, changes in the cost of debt, project-execution performance, reservoir performance, and changes to the fiscal regime.

3.7.1 Thematic Scenarios

A scenario is a combination of decisions that can be controlled and versions of the future that cannot. In the context of this book, the decisions can be represented by a portfolio. The easiest way to think about this is as a table, with an example shown in Table 20, below.

	PORTFOLIO A	PORTFOLIO B	PORTFOLIO C
REALIZATION 1	Scenario 1A	Scenario 1B	Scenario 1C
REALIZATION 2	Scenario 2A	Scenario 2B	Scenario 2C
REALIZATION 3	Scenario 3A	Scenario 3B	Scenario 3C

TABLE 20: Scenario Table

The most effective way to build realizations is to use internally consistent themes. An internally consistent theme recognizes that certain combinations of events are unlikely to occur together. A period of sustained low oil prices is unlikely to occur at the same time as host-country governments are attempting to adjust their fiscal regimes to increase government take as during low-commodity-price periods, when host countries are forced to compete more for capital. Conversely, a theme built around sustained high commodity prices, sustained high capital and operating costs, and tighter fiscal regimes is internally consistent, as these things tend to occur in concert.

Selecting appropriate themes is very much dependent on the situation the corporation finds itself in. In a company with a large LNG business, for example, themes built around the transition from long-term contracts to a spot market and how gas-price differentials across different regions are clearly important, whereas such a theme would be irrelevant for a medium-sized oil producer. A realization built around the political situation in a single country may be the key uncertainty for a regional oil company that has most of its production in the nation but is unlikely to be significant for a globally diversified major for whom that nation would count for a few percentage points.

In building realizations, it is important to understand what the business is designed for and what is a test of impact. There will be a subset of main realization, where the business should be able to deliver the business plan, and a different subset of realizations where it will not. The purpose of the latter set is to understand how the business will perform in extreme events. One recent example would be the COVID-19 pandemic. No oil and gas company could deliver its business plan under those circumstances—the purpose of testing a realization like that is to understand how long the business could survive and what kind of measures can be taken to extend that runway. Another topical realization to test is the pace and extent of oil and gas demand through the energy transition.

Another consideration in building scenarios is whether to combine parameters. The objective is to understand how the portfolio performs under uncertainty; the risk with combining too many parameters into a single scenario is that you can't differentiate which parameter the portfolio is vulnerable to.

The final point to make in realization building is that they should test uncertainty but should not be too extreme. An example would be uncertainty over execution capability. This could be tested by building a realization where projects were delivered late, over budget, and with poor availability. However, assuming every project comes in on the P90 (worst) forecast for cost, schedule, and quality is extreme. Assuming a couple come in at P90 on all parameters and a couple more come in at P90 on a couple of the sub-parameters is more likely to reflect overall P90 project performance.

In designing the portfolios to use when scenario building, the key thing to remember is control. Where there is still control in the decision-making process, the same portfolio can be adjusted between realizations. For example, an operated option in a portfolio with a high break-even price could be excluded in a low-commodity-price realization but included in a high-commodity-price realization. The same portfolio would consist of different assets under different realizations, provided that the realizations and the degree of control are consistent.

The purpose of building scenarios is to test how the portfolio will perform under uncertainty. In contrast to screening and ranking, this process should not be expected to yield answers. Rather, the process should yield insights, such as the portfolio is exposed to poor project-execution performance, is reliant on non-operated assets to generate cash in the near term, or that there are insufficient options in the portfolio to capitalize on higher commodity prices.

3.7.2 Indie Oil

Returning to Indie Oil, there are a few scenarios that the portfolio can be tested against. Indie has a large concentration of assets in Ghana, so it would be sensitive to any fiscal-regime changes there. Indie is entirely oil focused, so it would be vulnerable to any long-term shift in demand from oil to gas. Indie is leveraged and, so, is sensitive to changes to its financing cost. Finally, Indie is dependent on two exploration programs for future growth, and it is perfectly possible that neither of those will yield commercial discoveries. Indie is a (deliberately) simple example, and its business would clearly be impacted by a fiscal-regime change in Ghana, by a decline in demand in oil, and by exploration failure, without the need to do the math. So, in the interests of brevity, we will look at financing costs.

In order to assess the impact of debt, we can start with the cash-flow model that we developed for Indie at reference-oil prices. Figure 17 shows the cash flow for Indie at $60/barrel. Indie's cash flow, with the cost of debt raised from 6% to 12%, is shown in Figure 19.

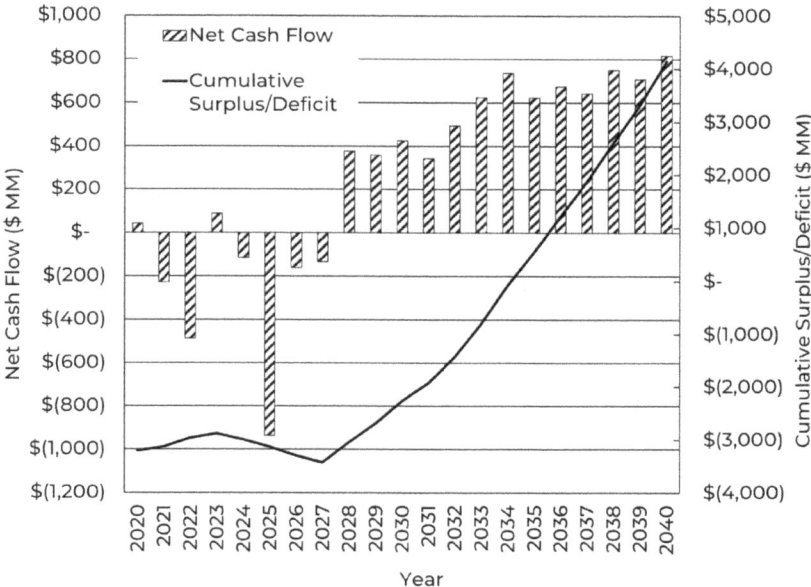

FIGURE 19: Indie Oil Net Cash Flow and Outstanding Debt at High Interest Rates

As the chart shows, under this scenario—even with the increased cost of debt service—Indie would remain within its $5 billion debt ceiling for the second half of the 2020s. However, Indie's NPV at 14% would fall from $1.6 billion to $40 million as debt-service costs ate into its revenue. From this, we can conclude that Indie Oil is sensitive to financing costs; an increase in the cost of borrowing would impact its ability to deliver its portfolio within the financial framework at the reference-price premise.

We will pick up with Indie Oil in the next chapter, when we look at capability. Next, we will turn to the two industry examples that were introduced in Chapter 1—Apache's acquisition of the Forties field and BHP's foray into shale oil.

3.8 APACHE

This section applies the methodology outlined in this chapter to Apache's acquisition of the Forties field, to see what a review of Apache's publicly available history can yield in terms of insights on the health of their portfolio and their business-development strategy.

3.8.1 History

Apache was founded in 1954 in Minneapolis, Minnesota, with $250,000 in initial capital[70]. The company was founded by Truman Anderson, Raymond Plank, and Charles Arnao, who gave their initials—A, P, A—to form the company's name. At the time, capital for oil wells was raised by promoters, who would travel around the United States. Apache introduced a more professional approach, providing a direct link between the investor and the operator of the well.

Apache drilled its first wells in Cushing, Oklahoma, in 1955 and grew quickly from there. By the late 1950s, Apache had begun to diversify into real estate, agriculture, steel, plastics, and other businesses in response to the United States' policy of proration—state restrictions on production.

Apache made its first major oil discovery in 1967, with the Fagerness well in Wyoming's Powder River Basin. Apache had held its oil and gas investments in a separate subsidiary, Apache Exploration Company, and, in 1977, Apache sold that company and reinvested the proceeds in natural-gas assets in western Oklahoma and the Texas panhandle. At this time, Apache also began the sale of its other businesses and used the proceeds to invest in oil and gas.

Apache moved offshore in the 1980s, with the acquisition of a non-operating interest in a joint venture with Shell, followed by the acquisition of an operated position from Occidental Petroleum. The 1990s saw the birth of the strategy that lay behind Apache's acquisition of the Forties field—"acquire and exploit"[71]. Apache acquired Amoco's assets in the Permian Basin in 1993, which was significant, as it changed Apache from being an 80% gas producer to more of an equal mix between oil and gas. Apache also made its first international acquisition in the Carnavon Basin with the purchase of Hadson Energy Resources in 1993.

Apache then expanded its operations in Canada through acquisition of Dekalb Energy Canada and built it out through the acquisition of Canadian assets from Shell Canada, Philips Petroleum, and Fletcher Challenge.

Apache entered Egypt in 1993, with the acquisition of a non-operating interest in the Qarun Concession, followed by acquisition of a non-operating interest in the Khalda area concessions. In 1999, Apache acquired assets from Shell, that, together with subsequent Gulf of Mexico shelf transactions from BP, Occidental Petroleum, Anadarko Petroleum, and Devon Energy, built the largest portfolio on the Gulf of Mexico shelf[72].

Apache continued both its domestic and international expansion in the early 2000s, through the acquisition of additional interests in Egypt and exploration success in China's Bohai bay.

3.8.2 Apache in 2003

Where was Apache in its run-up to the acquisition of the Forties field in 2003? The three-year period (2000 to 2002) prior to Apache's acquisition shows a company growing strongly and consistently. Apache had formulated a three-pronged growth strategy—exploitation, acquisition, and high-impact exploration—and was executing successfully. Exploitation consists of increasing production from existing fields through new investment in recompletions, and new wells and facilities. Apache had its best financial year in 2001. This period saw a consistent rise in revenues, net income, production, and reserves, as shown in Figure 20 and Figure 21, below.

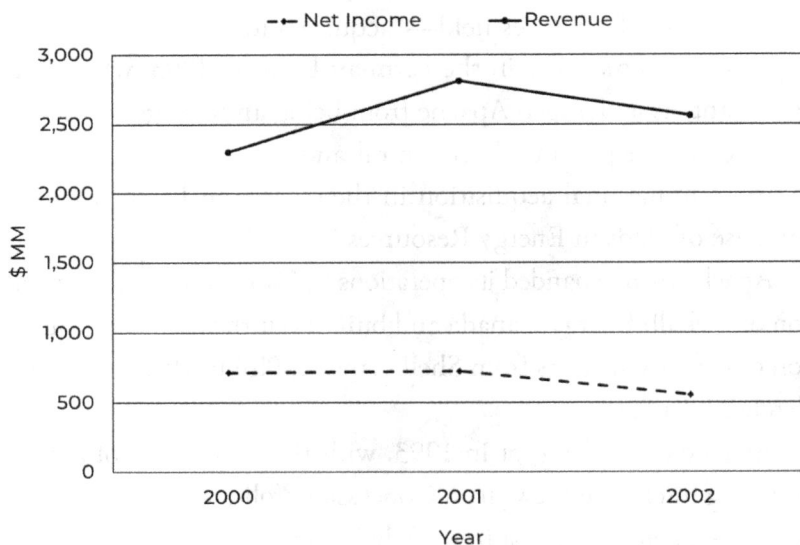

FIGURE 20: Apache Revenue and Net Income

Prior to 2002, Apache had enjoyed 24 consecutive years of production growth, with 2002 falling just short of 2001, in terms of production, while continuing to grow reserves. 2002 was also the year Apache dropped its organic investment in exploitation due to elevated drilling-rig prices and an uncertain commodity-price outlook, as well as largely suspended acquisitions due to what Apache's management considered to be elevated asset prices.[73] Apache did make two acquisitions in late 2002, without which the company's reserve-replacement ratio would have fallen below 100%.

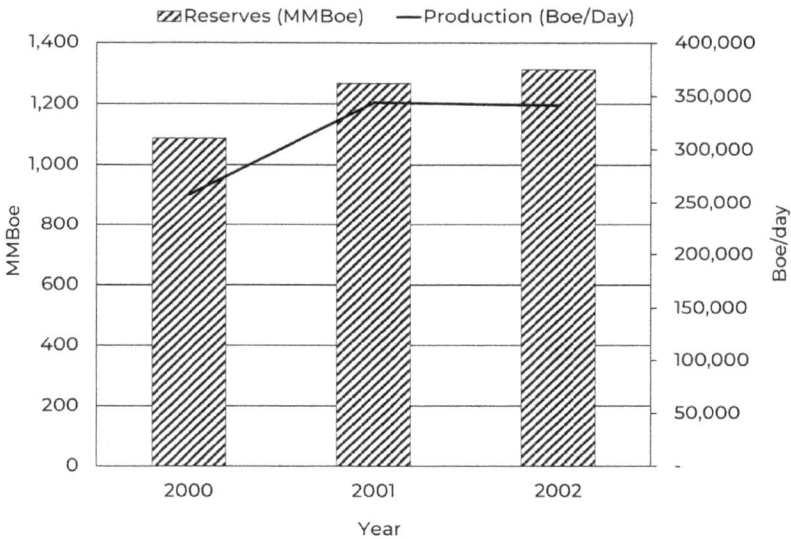

FIGURE 21: **Apache Production and Reserves (2000 to 2002)**

Throughout this period, Apache were clear, consistent, and specific in their growth strategy. Apache's acquisition strategy consisted of directly negotiated deals, with a high probability of closing, for operated positions in assets with existing production and redevelopment potential.[74] The exploration component is the least mature part of Apache's growth strategy and is focused on international, high-impact opportunities where there is scope to build a position in the basin.

3.8.3 Reserves Growth

Apache was investing heavily in proved-reserves growth for many years. 2002 was Apache's 15th consecutive year of proved-reserves growth. A summary of Apache proved-reserve additions between 2000 and 2002 is shown in Figure 22.

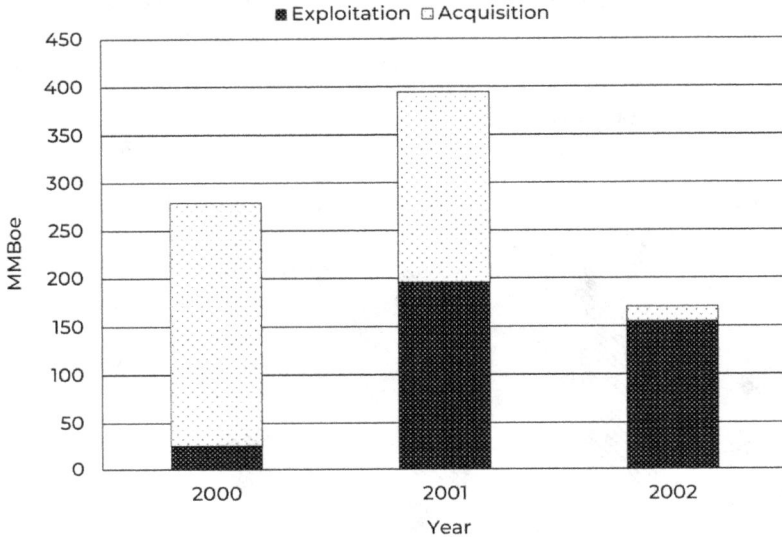

FIGURE 22: Apache Proved Reserves
Additions by Source (2000 to 2002)

Apache had been starting to add more proved reserves through exploitation of a portfolio that it had invested heavily in reloading. Reserves additions were ramping up and holding relatively steady. Business-development activity was down dramatically in 2002 due to an external-asset-price environment that Apache's management considered exorbitant but returned strongly in 2003 when Apache added 235 MMBoe of proved reserves in three acquisitions spread across three transactions.

The exploitation and acquisition components of Apache's growth strategy were working well over the period in question. The third leg, high-impact exploration, was less clear cut.

Apache's exploration activity was focused on its international acreage. Its view was that its significant positions in the USA and Canada were more mature and development focused, and that these positions would be complemented by higher-risk international-exploration positions that provided the potential for significant reserve additions. In 2000, Apache had established exploration positions in Egypt, Australia, Poland, and China.

By 2003, Apache's geographic emphasis had shifted, drilling more exploration wells and having greater exploration success, in the United States and Canada than on their international properties.[75] Apache drilled 22.9 net exploration wells in the United States and Canada in 2000 and 42.5 net exploration wells in 2002. Conversely, Apache drilled 26.8 net exploration wells in its international business in 2000 and 28.6 in 2002, with drilling focused on Egypt and Australia. Apache took an impairment charge for its exploration assets in China and Poland in 2001 and another impairment in Poland in 2002. By 2002, Apache was considering an exit from its Polish position.

Apache's position in Egypt was in many ways similar to its North American positions in that it consisted of incremental development in a proven-hydrocarbon basin rather than high-impact exploration. In contrast to its exploitation and acquisition components, Apache's international exploration business was failing to deliver a substantial pipeline of reserves.

3.8.4 Growth Strategy

On first inspection, it is tempting to think of Apache's acquisition spree as being a response to higher commodity prices—the company was generating surplus cash and needed to find somewhere to invest it. Apache's statement of cash flows, however, indicate that these acquisitions were part of a very deliberate growth strategy. Figure 23 shows the net cash flows from operating, investing, and financing activities.

As Figure 23 shows, Apache had been borrowing to fund its exploitation and acquisition program from 1998 to 2001. Apache was not flush with cash—quite the opposite. It had been issuing both equity and debt to fund its expansion.

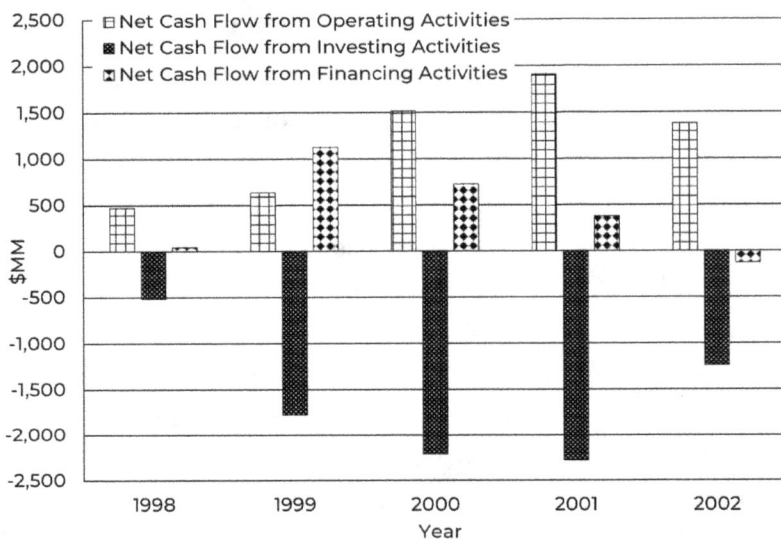

FIGURE 23: Apache Sources and Uses of Cash (1998 to 2002)

Throughout the expansion, Apache sought to maintain its debt ratio below 40% and succeeded in reducing it to 30% by the close of 2002.[76] Apache had received upgrades from both Moody's (to A3) and Standard & Poor's (to A-) in 2000 and retained those ratings through the 2003 acquisition of Forties.[77] Apache was clear in its SEC filings that maintaining financial flexibility was a key component of its growth strategy.[78] Apache stressed repeatedly in the SEC filings at the time that it was interested in pursuing assets that could be secured only through negotiation, rather than an auction, emphasizing the disciplined approach that the company took to business development.

3.8.5 Portfolio

Apache was still a large gas producer at the time of the Forties acquisition, with more than 50% of its reserve base in gas in 2000[79] and

51% natural gas in 2002.[80] The United States and Canada accounted for 66% of Apache's production and 78% of its proved reserves in 2002.[81] Its international interests included a large exploration and production position in Egypt and Australia with some small, recently acquired production in Argentina. It had a development project in China and exploration acreage in Poland. It was still very much a North American-focused company—48% of its proved reserves were in the United States, and 77% were in North America[82]—with a mix of oil and gas, and onshore and offshore production. Apache also operated 85% of its production, something that was essential for Apache if it was going to successfully work through its exploitation playbook of investing in proved undeveloped reserves.

3.8.6 Summary

Apache was a company that had been very successful at acquisition and exploitation of operated oil and gas assets in the United States and Canada, but the high-impact exploration component of the strategy was not working as well. Apache needed to acquire to continue to grow—exploitation of its current inventory wouldn't be enough to maintain a reserves-replacement ratio above 100%, but the market for the assets in the United States and Canada was becoming increasingly competitive, as commodity prices demonstrated a sustained recovery.

The business needed an acquisition that would be immediately accretive to earnings so as not to strain the balance sheet. It would have to be material, given how Apache had already grown, and there would probably be a preference for oil over gas, given the composition of the current portfolio and the uncertainty around the outlook for gas pricing in 2002. The asset would need to have running room in terms of either undeveloped reserves or exploration upside, and the position would have to be operated; both were prerequisites for Apache's exploitation playbook. Finally, Apache will consider only directly negotiated deals, so it would need to be an asset that wasn't part of a current process.

If we consider the Forties asset in the context of these requirements, then Forties provides a material operated position in an asset with redevelopment potential. It was predominantly oil, which may have been a benefit to Apache, given the company's production split at that time. It is not known whether Forties was being actively marketed at that time, but there is no evidence it was part of a public-auction process. The interesting change for Apache with Forties is that all of their other core acquisition for exploitation assets were in North America. It may have been that Forties presented an opportunity, and, while the field was not located in North America, it was located in an OECD country. Alternatively, Apache may have decided they wanted to have a new production province outside of North America, one which provided them with access to Brent as well as WTI pricing. In either case, the field seemed a good fit with their business needs at the time.

3.9 BHP EXAMPLE

Having looked at Apache, we can now apply the same methodology to BHP's United States shale-oil acquisitions.

3.9.1 History

BHP Billiton was formed by the merger of Broken Hill Proprietary (BHP) and Billiton in 2001. BHP was founded in Australia in 1885, where it began mining silver, lead, and zinc from the Broken Hill mine. Billiton was founded in 1860, following the discovery of tin in Indonesia in 1851.

BHP entered the oil and gas industry through a joint venture with Exxon in 1963 that was formed to explore for oil in the Bass Strait. This led to the discovery of gas in 1965 and then the Halibut oil field in 1967.[83] BHP expanded their oil and gas business through participation in the North West Shelf Venture in the early 1980s, a consortium of six companies that developed the oil and gas fields in the offshore Carnavon basin in Western Australia[84].

BHP acquired the United States Energy Reserves group and Monsanto's oil and gas interests in 1985, which established BHP in the United States Gulf of Mexico, with the deepwater Typhoon oil field coming on stream in 2001. This was followed by first production from the Angostura field in Trinidad and Tobago in 2005 and then first oil from Shenzi in the deepwater Gulf of Mexico in 2009.

3.9.2 BHP in 2010

BHP in 2010 was in quite a different position from Apache in 2003. BHP was a large, international mining company, with a petroleum division, as opposed to being an independent like Apache. The Petroleum division was one of nine divisions within the company, the other eight focused on minerals—principally iron ore and coal. From the period between 2008 and 2010, the Petroleum Division was the second or third most important division in terms of revenue and EBITDA, and the first or second most significant in terms of capital investment[85]. In 2010, the petroleum division contributed about 15% of BHP's total revenue, so it was a significant contributor, but not the dominant one[86].

BHP was an Australian company, but the Petroleum division had its own headquarters in Houston. By 2010, the company's production base consisted of a strong non-operated legacy position in Australia and a number of operated fields in the United States Gulf of Mexico. It also had some producing interests in the UK, Algeria, Trinidad, and Pakistan. Development projects were focused on Australia, the United States Gulf of Mexico, and Trinidad and were either facility-life extensions or small incremental developments. Core-exploration activities were in Australia and at the United States Gulf of Mexico, with some additional exploration activities in Canada, Colombia, the Falklands, India, Malaysia, the Philippines, and Vietnam.

2010 was BHP's third consecutive year of record annual production, but reserves had been essentially flat over the preceding few years, as shown in Figure 24.

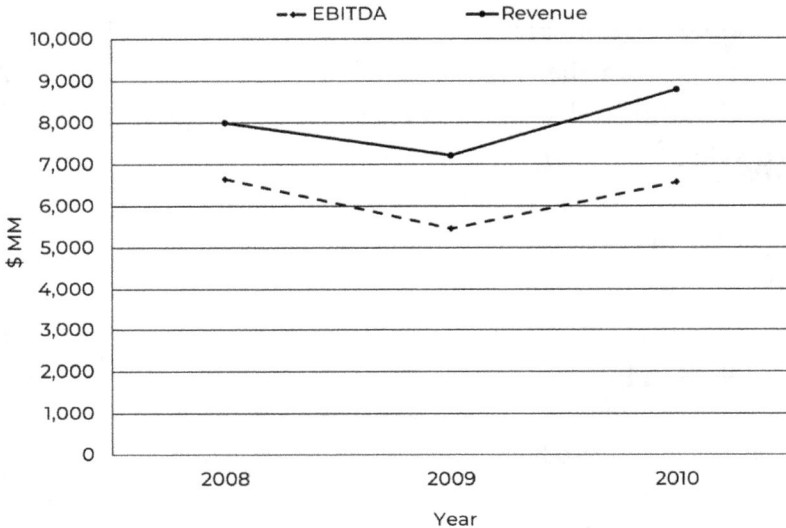

FIGURE 24: BHP Revenue and EBITDA (2008 to 2010)

BHP's corporate strategy, as summarized in their 2010 annual report,[87] was to:

"Create long-term value for shareholders through the discovery, development, and conversion of natural resources, and the provision of innovative customer and market-focused solutions."

BHP's Petroleum Customer Segment Group's strategy was as follows:

"Our Petroleum CSG comprises a base of large, long-life, low unit cost production operations that are located in six countries throughout the world. We pursue significant upstream opportunities with multiple options for growth to ensure continued success."

BHP's strategy, at the corporate and division level, was not as clearly defined or actionable as Apache's three-pronged growth strategy. Referring to the section on business strategy earlier in this chapter (section 3.2.1), this strategy was not defined with sufficient granularity to make clear choices. It is, therefore, unclear what BHP do and don't want to do with their petroleum business.

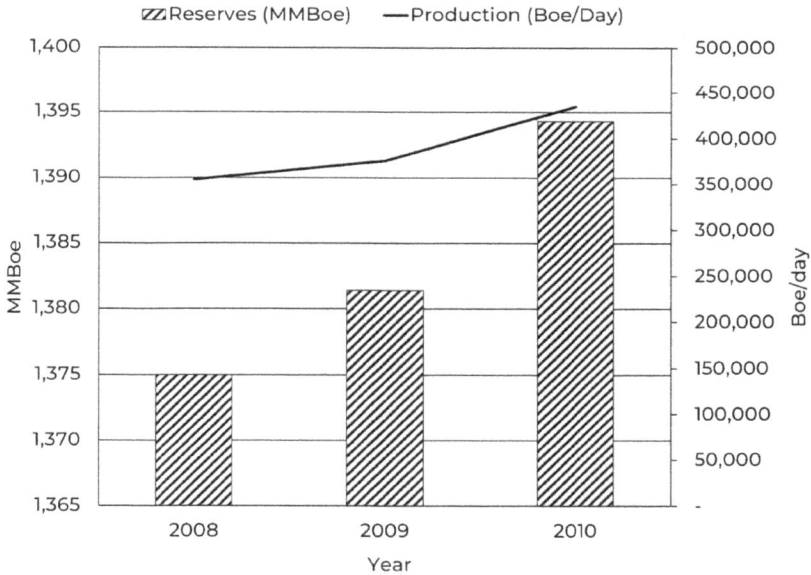

FIGURE 25: BHP Production and Reserves (2008 to 2010)

3.9.3 Reserves Growth

BHP recorded four categories of reserve addition—Improved Recovery, Revisions of Previous Estimates, Extensions and Discoveries, and Purchase and Sale. Of these, most of the additions over the period in question had come from either Revisions or Extensions and

Discoveries, with improved recovery making some contribution in each year. BHP had not added proved reserves through acquisition since 2007, when they farmed into the Genghis Khan field in the United States Gulf of Mexico.[88]

Of the 65.4 MMBoe of additional proved reserves ascribed to "Extensions and Discoveries" in 2010, all of these volumes were through proved extensions to existing fields, rather than proved reserves added through the maturation of exploration activity.[89]

While BHP was not active in acquiring producing properties, it had been active in the acquisition of exploration acreage and, by 2010, was becoming increasingly active in exploration and appraisal drilling activity.

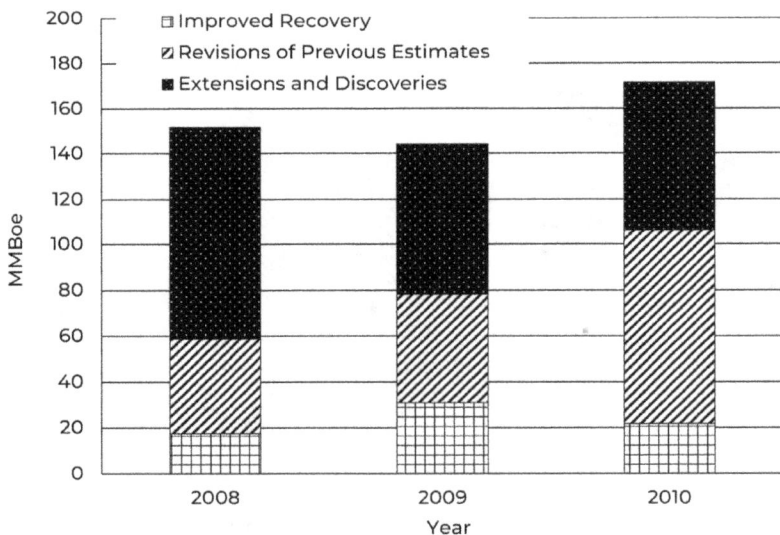

FIGURE 26: BHP Reserve Additions by Category (2008 to 2010)

By 2010, BHP had ramped up exploration activity to the point where it was spending $1 billion/year on attempting to identify new petroleum resources. There were two drawbacks to the approach that BHP had adopted. The first is that frontier exploration takes a long time to generate proved reserves—it can take five years to go from farm-in to discovery and another ten years before appraisal and development have been completed and the facility is onstream.

The second is that frontier exploration is inherently high risk. Of the nine exploration wells BHP drilled in 2010, only one was a technical discovery; the other eight were dry holes. By 2010, the BHP Petroleum division growth engine was sputtering. If resources are not being added through exploration, and the company is reaching the limited of reserves additions through improved recovery, then the only remaining option to maintain growth is acquisition.

3.9.4 BHP Petroleum Portfolio

In 2010 BHP's portfolio was still very much focused in Australia, at its legacy positions in the Bass Strait and Northwest Shelf, and its main growth engine in the United States Gulf of Mexico. It also had smaller production operations in the UK North Sea, Algeria, and Trinidad and Tobago, and a very small producing interest in Pakistan. Australia accounted for 53% of BHP's production, and the United States accounted for 29%. BHP's production was about 40% gas and 60% oil, condensate, or natural gas liquids. Significant parts of its portfolio were non-operated, and most of its production was offshore or deepwater.

3.9.5 Financial Flexibility

BHP also differed from Apache in its financial strength. By 2010 its gearing was at 6%, and it had $12.5 billion in cash sitting on the balance sheet. As discussed earlier in this chapter, excess cash can be a signal that the portfolio does not contain enough options to absorb the cash being generated by the business. The analysis is complicated in BHP's case, as it is a mining conglomerate, and there are other business lines to invest in; presumably these were also unable to absorb the cash that was building up.

3.9.6 Summary

BHP was a profitable mineral-resources conglomerate, with a petroleum division that was struggling to grow organically. The strategy that companies articulate for the petroleum division is indistinct; it is not clear how such a generic statement of intent could be used as a basis for decision-making. The company was also generating large amounts of cash but appears to have lacked sufficient options to absorb it. This is a topic that was touched on in section 3.6. An excess of cash can be a sign that a company lacks investment options, and that does seem to have been the case with BHP.

The petroleum division would have found it difficult to continue to maintain its reserve-replacement ratio through infill drilling and recalculation of existing reserve estimates. In the absence of an acquisition, it is reasonable to expect that proved reserves would have started to decline. Given this situation, the acquisition of a large, producing asset makes sense—it solves the reserve-replacement problem and provides an investment option to absorb the cash on the balance sheet.

As we will discuss in Chapter 4, whereas Apache had an ongoing acquisition program, making one or more smaller acquisitions each year, BHP had not. The public filings do not provide much insight into the thinking behind the deal, but it does appear as if they were looking for one very large acquisition to address the underlying problems they had with the health of their petroleum business.

3.10 CONCLUSION

This purpose of this chapter was to introduce the first component of developing a business-development strategy: understanding the needs of the health of the portfolio to ensure that the business-development strategy delivers the needs of the business.

We started this process from the top down, by defining the overall business strategy in sufficient detail to differentiate between investment opportunities and translating the corporate financial framework into cash-flow constraints. We then switched from a top-down description to a bottom-up description, by classifying assets into investment tranches and defining those assets to facilitate subsequent analysis.

The next step was to screen the individual assets within the portfolio—to eliminate assets that didn't satisfy investment criteria. We then ranked the assets within the portfolio to get a sense for the better-quality fields. This guides our decision on what to trim if we can't deliver the unconstrained portfolio. The next step used the unconstrained portfolio to test consistency with the financial framework. Finally, we constructed some scenarios to test how the portfolio would perform in different versions of the future. This overall approach helps us to generate insights into the strengths and weaknesses of the portfolio.

Indie Oil was used as a quantitative example of this approach throughout the chapter to try to illustrate the main points. A qualitative analysis of Apache's acquisition of the Forties field and BHP's foray into United States shale oil was then used to provide some real-world examples of where these principles had been applied successfully and where they had not.

The next chapter is focused on the second component in the creation of the business-development strategy: understanding capability, where it serves to differentiate, and when, where, and how it can be grown. We will pick up Indie Oil again in the next chapter and will continue to see how this framework can be applied by looking at Apache and BHP.

Chapter 4

ORGANIZATIONAL CAPABILITY

In the first chapter, we introduced the three components of a business-development strategy as portfolio health, organizational capability, and asset mix. In Chapter 3, we discussed portfolio health; in this chapter, we will discuss organizational capability. We will look at the different types of capability that are important in constructing a business-development strategy and where gaps can and cannot be bridged. We will also try to apply this framework to our Indie Oil example and return to the Apache and BHP examples to examine their respective organizational capabilities before and after their acquisitions.

Understanding organizational capability is a prerequisite for creating a business-development strategy. What is the organization good at? This isn't a question only for independents or smaller producers. It is true that the super-majors have tremendous capability along multiple dimensions, with a bench of personnel that seems endlessly deep, but even they cannot compete everywhere. They have struggled in the past as low-cost operators, for example, to the degree that Shell and Exxon had to spin off Aera as an independent entity with its own management system in order for it to compete. Exxon and ENI have failed to establish themselves as leading operators in the United States Gulf of Mexico, BP has no presence in Nigeria, and Shell has failed to hit the mark in Angola.

Organizational capabilities in this book are divided into first and second order. These first-order capabilities are financial, technical, and commercial. First-order capabilities are governing, in that there is no way to mitigate their absence; the only option is to develop the capability. The absence of second-order capabilities can still derail an acquisition but can be mitigated. At the margin, these may constitute a basis to select one asset over another. At the very least, the buyer should be conscious of them and develop a mitigation plan.

The discussion on organizational capability is heavily focused on technical capability. The industry has shown that it is easier to overcome obstacles if the underlying field is of high quality and very difficult to do so if it isn't. Making this determination sits firmly in the technical domain. There are examples where political or commercial challenges have prevented a high-quality field from being developed, but there are no examples where political and commercial ingenuity have made a poor-quality field profitable. Management techniques and commercial structures don't change rock properties. Having said that, the biggest constraint in a business-development strategy is financial capability, as we will discuss next.

4.1 FINANCIAL CAPABILITY

Financial capability is the single most important factor to consider in establishing a business-development strategy, as it is the most limiting, which is why most of Chapter 3 was dedicated to reconciling the portfolio against the corporate financial framework. There are a number of different facets to financial capability, beyond the obvious that the more capital you have, the more choice you have in what you can buy—the cost of that capital and access to additional equity and debt, for example. There is no typical acquisition or divestment size. Just looking at the United States market in the 3rd quarter of 2019[90], the largest deal was Hilcorp's $5.6 billion acquisition of BP's assets in Alaska. The tenth largest was a Colony Capital's farm-in to California Resource Corporation's assets in California at $320 million. The most recent year, 2020, could not be considered a normal one, given the impact of the COVID-19 pandemic; as Figure 27 shows[91], there was a substantial decline in deal value between 2019 and 2020.

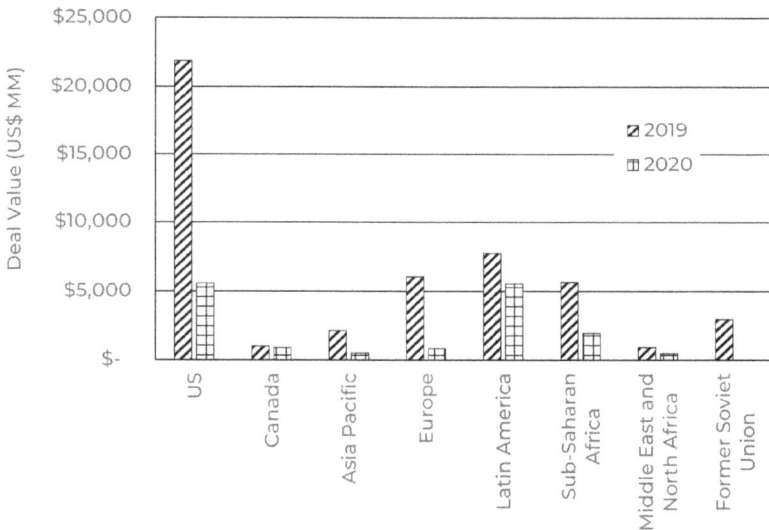

FIGURE 27: Upstream Oil and Gas Deal Value by Region

In this section, we will break Financial Capability down into its components—cost of capital, portfolio resilience, access to cash, equity and debt, and tax status.

4.1.1 Cost of Capital

The upstream oil and gas industry is capital intensive, rather than labor intensive. In a capital-intensive industry, a low cost of capital is a competitive advantage. Put simply, if a buyer's cost of capital is 5% and a seller's cost of capital is 15%, the same project is immediately worth more to the buyer than the seller, creating a value gap between the two.

Mercer undertook a study of WACC for different groups of upstream oil and gas participants in 2016 and found that the cost of capital varied, depending on their focus[92]. Their results, using the standard approach** to the calculation of the cost of debt, are replicated in Table 21, below:

CATEGORY	MINIMUM	MEAN	MAXIMUM
GLOBAL INTEGRATED	6.42%	6.89%	8.26%
GLOBAL E&P	8.37%	9.28%	9.88%
NORTH AMERICAN E&P	4.12%	7.84%	10.79%
PERMIAN	5.99%	8.52%	11.20%
MARCELLUS & UTICA	5.07%	7.11%	13.87%
BAKKEN	6.74%	8.17%	10.04%
EAGLE FORD	7.08%	8.64%	10.37%

Table 21: Estimated Weighted Average Cost of Capital by Sector

The company with the lowest WACC is a North American upstream oil and gas company, one who by Mercer's methodology has more than 90% of its production in North America, but without a concentration in any of the United States basins mentioned. The firms with the highest WACC are those concentrated in the Marcellus and Utica, a natural gas basin in the northeast United

---

** In the Mercer standard method, the current effective interest rate (which is the interest expense divided by the simple average of debt at the beginning of the last twelve months and end of period) is multiplied by one minus the company's marginal corporate tax rate.

States. The lowest-mean WACC are the Global Integrated oil companies, which is to be expected, as these are the largest private firms in the industry.

From a value-gap perspective, a Global Integrated with a median WACC would see an immediate value gap in acquiring assets from a focused Permian company with a median WACC. The implication here is that larger oil and gas companies enjoy a structural advantage because their cost of capital is usually lower, which means there will be a tendency within the industry to consolidate over time.

4.1.2 Portfolio Resilience

Portfolio resilience, the topic discussed in Chapter 3, refers to how sensitive the financial performance of the company is to future events. In section 3.7, we talked about developing scenarios built around realizations—combinations of future events that were outside the organization's control. This approach is intended to test financial resilience. A resilient portfolio allows greater risk to be taken through acquisition, as the enterprise as a whole is not reliant on the performance of a single asset.

Risk in this case can be thought of along two axes. One is uncertainty in outcome, and the second is length of time horizon. It is unfortunate that the most profitable projects are likely to have the most uncertain outcomes and the longest time horizons. A resilient portfolio positions a company to accept those risks.

The acquisition of exploration assets, for example, incorporates both uncertainty in outcome and long time horizons. Exploration assets, however, have the greatest potential upside, but clearly have the highest risk, from a technical and commercial perspective. Acquisition of an unfamiliar asset type also introduces a greater uncertainty in outcome—lack of experience is likely to make valuation more difficult, and lack of operational expertise with the asset type will increase the possibility of cost overruns, execution delays, and increased downtime. Entering a new geography introduces many of the same risks as a new asset.

A company with a resilient portfolio is able to accept those risks because failure is not terminal; it can, in fact, take a portfolio approach to higher-risk assets on the basis that some of them will play out. The company whose portfolio lacks resilience can't afford to take those risks but instead has to focus on assets with greater certainty. This is not necessarily a fatal flaw; there is nothing wrong with acquiring a string of producing assets of a familiar type and geography, but it should be recognized that it does restrict the assets under consideration and limits potential for growth.

Part of the analysis of current situation should focus on what aspects of the portfolio make the portfolio vulnerable. If the entire portfolio is vulnerable to a certain realization—if the portfolio as a whole lacks resilience—then that is a signal that it is time to transition to a different set of assets, through staged divestment, if necessary.

If only one component of the portfolio is vulnerable but the remainder is resilient, then this could indicate that that particular asset or asset group are divestment candidates.

4.1.3 Access to Cash and Cash Equivalents

Access to cash or cash equivalents, in the form of company stock, for example, provides great flexibility but also introduces its own set of risks. Having access to cash or cash equivalents speeds up the transaction process and strengthens the buyer's position during negotiations, as they are obviously qualified to close. Where the seller values certainty in the transaction, the absence of financing conditions will help close the deal.

The amount of cash or cash equivalents required should be in the context of the portfolio and operational commitments. The ideal situation is one in which there is enough cash available to cover the lease-maintenance requirements for the core portfolio under a low-oil-price premise or when credit is limited, but where there are enough options in the portfolio to soak up all of the excess cash generated by the high-oil-price premise.

If the business is generating more cash than there are portfolio options to absorb it, then this also introduces potential risks. Writing this in the first quarter of 2020, as Brent Crude flirts with $20 per barrel, the idea that having cash on the balance sheet is a potential risk seems laughable. There are, however, a number of negatives associated with it.

When upstream oil and gas companies are flush with cash, it is normally because of the commodity cycle. When commodity prices rise, it takes time for the industry to adjust to changes in demand, which means organizations tend to grow, salaries tend to rise, and service providers are able to improve their margins. In short, operating costs rise, absorbing some of the surplus cash.

The temptation, when cash begins to pile up, is to start looking for something to invest it in. Given the cyclical nature of the upstream oil and gas industry, cash is likely starting to pile up for everyone else as well, leading to asset-price inflation as all industry participants try to put it to work at the same time.

As well as testing investment discipline, a large cash surplus signals that the portfolio lacks sufficient investment options to soak up all of the cash that the business is generating. It is a signal that the portfolio should be reloaded.

A company with a well-structured portfolio should have sufficient options to invest surplus cash from operations or require the discipline to either pay down debt or return the cash to shareholders. High points in the commodity cycle are invariably bad times to buy.

4.1.4 Access to Debt
Access to debt financing is the corollary of maintaining cash on the balance sheet. When thinking through realizations to test your

portfolio, one in which you lose access to debt—or access to debt at reasonable rates—should be a case that is considered. The Indie Oil example, from section 3.7.2, used an increase in interest rates to test the resilience of Indie's portfolio.

There are a number of scenarios under which a company could suddenly lose access to financing, all of which have occurred in the last few years. In the first instance, there is a financial crisis, similar to the one that occurred globally in 2008–2009, where there is simply no cash to lend.

The second scenario involves international sanctions, something that has become increasingly common in recent years. Russian oil companies were essentially shut off from international credit markets in 2014, which had a material impact on their ability to invest in their portfolios. At the time of writing, LUKOIL, Russia's largest privately held oil company, has no debt.

Companies that rely on reserve-based lending facilities, as opposed to corporate bonds, are especially vulnerable to abrupt changes in the oil price. Reserve-based lending facilities lend against a discounted value of proved oil reserves. Abrupt declines in oil price have a twofold impact on these facilities: they reduce the value of oil reserves, and they also reduce the reserves base, as reserves are subject to commercial as well as technical tests.

In addition, with these specific risks, sectors tend to move in or out of favor depending on their perceived risk. At the time of writing, the upstream oil and gas business in general and the United States onshore shale business in particular, is out of favor with lenders due to a perceived default risk as a result of low commodity prices as well as a longer-term concern over the energy transition. As a result, most United States shale-focused oil and gas companies are essentially shut out of the debt markets and will have trouble refinancing the principal payments that fall due in the first half of the 2020s.

Project financing, either explicitly through an international development system, or implicitly, through equipment leasing, can also be considered under this category. In the international arena, lending by international development institutions usually comes with additional requirements that will burden the project administratively. Uncertainty around qualification for project financing and the disbursement of funds can also make it difficult to schedule development projects with confidence. As the upstream oil and gas industry moves out of favor politically, access to this type of lending is being tightened. Project financing plays a bigger role in gas-to-power projects, where the necessity of executing long-term gas-supply agreements and power-purchase agreements lowers the risk profile. Reliance on project financing is a worthwhile approach to pursue for portfolio options, for which it may become a prerequisite, but is not recommended for core portfolio projects.

Service providers are increasingly offering project financing to fill order books and boost their own profitability. Providers of Floating Production, Storage and Offloading vessels (FPSOs) have long provided a lease model as they typically design and operate the vessels as well. Financing through vendors of this type will typically be higher cost, as the upstream oil and gas company would normally have a lower cost of capital than the service company, who must also be compensated for taking financial risk. In some case, the upstream oil and gas company is required to guarantee the lease payments directly with the lender, in which case, the upstream oil and gas company receives no protection in the case of contractor non-performance.

An oft-cited benefit of leasing equipment is that the lease payments can be treated as an operating cost, which can flatter asset performance on internal economic metrics and, it used to be argued, was more tax efficient. The tax benefit of leasing applies only to certain, specific jurisdictions; recent changes to United States accounting rules mean that all leases in excess of one year are classified as capital leases. There is a potential cash flow benefit, but that same benefit can be realized through borrowing at the corporate level, probably at a lower rate.

There are benefits to leasing, especially in the build, own, and operate context common in the FPSO industry, but these are not financial. The commercial structure helps align risk and reward between the upstream oil and gas company and the service provider throughout design and construction. In addition, the upstream oil and gas company benefits from the operating experience and supply chain of the FPSO supplier—it is always better to operate multiple similar facilities with common design and equipment supplies than it is to operate multiple different designs with multiple equipment suppliers. The benefits of leasing should be viewed from that perspective, rather than as a form of financing.

4.1.5 Access to Equity

Public equity has historically been used to fund asset-acquisition programs, but, since 2016, the upstream oil and gas industry has fallen out of favor with public markets. The number of United States upstream oil and gas Initial Public Offerings (IPOs) fell from a peak of 67 in 2006 to 5 in 2018[93]; see Figure 28. That isn't the worst year on record—that was 2015, when there were fewer IPOs, but more capital was raised.

Follow-on offerings, where publicly listed companies raise capital by issuing additional stock, have historically been more resilient but have followed a similar pattern in recent years.

Things have not improved since 2018, when the latest edition of Haynes and Boone's borrowing base redetermination survey[94] showed that only 2% of respondents were planning to source equity from capital markets in 2020.

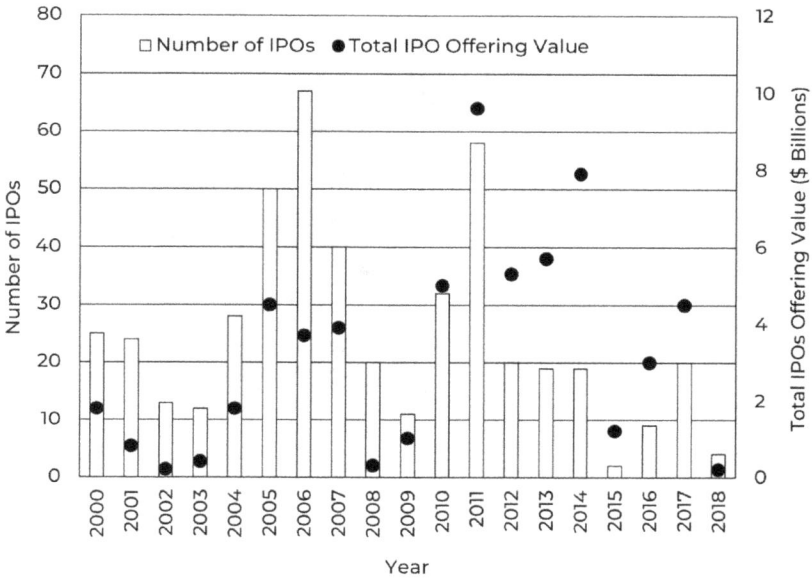

FIGURE 28: United States Upstream Oil
and Gas IPOs (2000 to 2018)

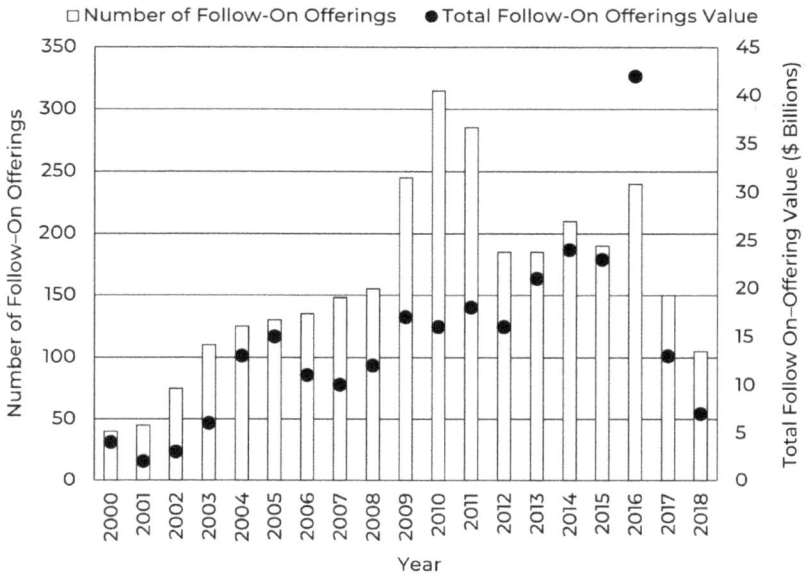

FIGURE 29: United States Follow-On Offerings (2000 to 2018)

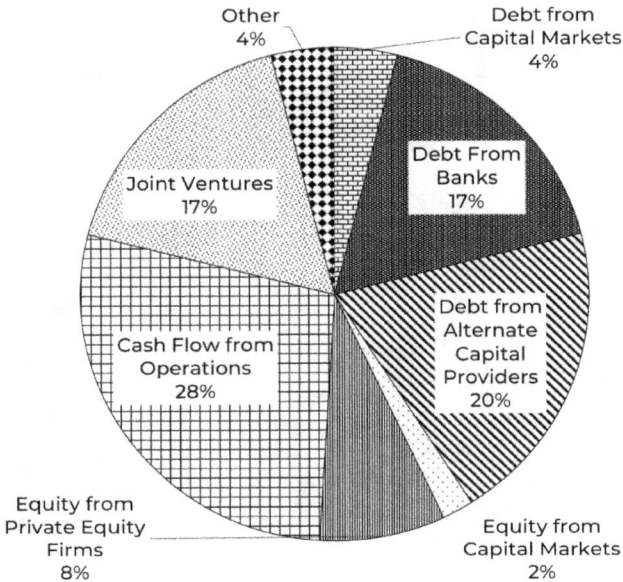

FIGURE 30: Sources of Capital

The history of the oil and gas industry in the United States has been characterized by small, independent companies financed initially through private investment, but those companies that were initially successful would tap the public markets to provide capital to scale and as an exit for their initial investors. The chilling of the public market—and the IPO market in particular—has cut off the main exit route for a private-equity investment.

Sources of private-equity investment in the oil and gas industry include dedicated private-equity firms, private firms that wish to diversify into the upstream oil and gas industry, and family offices. The largest and most sophisticated private-equity firms with energy funds—Blackstone, Carlyle, and Warburg Pincus—will invest in international assets and have billions of dollars available to deploy. There is a much larger number of smaller private-equity firms that focus on the United States onshore, where assets are more homogenous, and the risks are better understood. These are companies such as Denham Capital, Kimmeridge Energy, and Post Oak Energy Capital. The latter half of the last decade has seen a sustained decline in the funds flowing to private-equity energy investment, with 2020 being a notably bad year. The United States shale boom of the last decade was funded by private equity, and this sector has become renowned for failing to generate the promised returns. This, coupled with the difficulty in exit and growing concerns about energy transition producing stranded assets, has cast a shadow over the sector.

There are private firms that invest in oil and gas assets, either to diversify their operations or as a hedge against commodity-price fluctuations. Flint Hills resources, a subsidiary of Koch Industries, is an example of a private firm that invests in the upstream oil and gas industry at scale. Family offices will participate in private-equity funds but can also invest directly in oil and gas assets, usually in partnership with other investors.

The other alternative to raising equity is through a special purpose acquisition vehicle (SPAC), which combines the characteristics of public and private equity. A SPAC is a publicly traded company, sponsored by a private-equity fund or other financial investor, that raises acquisition funding through an IPO. The SPAC may have an acquisition target at the time of the IPO or may have a strategy to be executed on completion of the IPO. SPACs can raise substantial amounts of capital. The Silver Run Acquisition Corp II, sponsored by Riverstone and led by Jim Hackett, raised more than $1 billion at its IPO. The SPAC is something of a hybrid between public and private equity, as it is similar to a publicly listed private-equity fund, providing the retail investor with exposure to investment activities which have typically been the domain of private equity.

4.1.6 Taxation Status

Taxation status refers to the acquiring parties' tax status in the jurisdiction where the acquisition takes place. An existing taxpayer enjoys an advantage over a new entrant, as they are able to offset expenses against income immediately, boosting the value of the asset of an acquirer. The same may be true under a PSC, but care must be taken over the precise terms of the granting instrument, as costs and revenues are usually ring-fenced within the PSC.

Another form of tax-status advantage is a substantial tax-loss carry forward. In this case, the acquiring party, who is carrying forward a tax loss from prior years, is able to accelerate the use of the allowance through the acquisition of an existing producing asset. This acceleration creates a value wedge between buyer and seller, creating value for both. Premier planned to take advantage of their taxation status in this way through their acquisition of BP's Andrew, Shearwater and Tolmount working interests in 2020[95], before COVID-19 struck.

4.1.7 Conclusion

The purpose of this section was to highlight some important considerations when assessing the financial capability of an entity and the implications of this capability on an entity's ability to act. In the next section, we will look at technical capability, before rounding out the discussion on first-order capability with commercial capability.

4.2 TECHNICAL CAPABILITY

The author's first week working for an oil company was spent at a hotel in Alkmaar, a small town in the Netherlands, attending a workshop for a project that was just entering the Define phase (see section 2.7 for a description of this). The author had never seen so many people spend so much time in one room, talking. The abiding question in the author's mind was *What do all of these people do?* As the author learned over the subsequent decades, it is these people and all of that time spent talking that adds most of the value in the upstream oil and gas industry.

The technical capability of an organization is almost as important as its financial capability in determining its business-development strategy but much harder to articulate quantitatively. As discussed earlier, the upstream oil and gas industry is capital- rather than labor-intensive. It doesn't employ many people relative to any financial metric—be it capital investment, revenue, or profit. While the industry employs relatively few people, the capability of those people is very important. People in technical roles have historically been well compensated compared to equivalent industries. At the time of writing, in 2020 with oil in the low \$20s/barrel, collegechoice.net lists the best-paid college-graduate career as Petroleum Engineering[96]. Whether this is true when collegechoice.net updates their page in 2021 remains to be seen, but historically the industry has been very competitive in attracting talent.

Why is the capability of technical staff in the organization so important in determining a company's business-development strategy? It is because the roles themselves are complex, requiring capability across three dimensions—they require creativity, they require experience, and they require teamwork—over and above just having had the appropriate education and job-specific training for the role. If one of these capabilities is missing, then the organization will not perform well.

In this section, we will introduce the core technical skills required in an upstream oil and gas company and then examine each through the lens of creativity, experience, and teamwork.

4.2.1 Core Technical Skills

Core technical skills can be broadly or narrowly defined, depending on the operator in question, Table 22, below, introduces a broad and a narrow breakdown.

BROAD DEFINITION	NARROW DEFINITION
Geoscience	Geology Geophysics
Petroleum Engineering	Petrophysics Reservoir Engineering Production Technology
Wells	Drilling Completion
Facilities	Process Engineer Subsea Engineer Pipeline Engineer Civil Engineer/Structural Engineer Mechanical (Static) Engineer Mechanical (Rotating) Engineers Electrical Engineer Instrumentation Engineer
Project Management	Project Engineering Technical HSE Project Services QA/QC Supply Chain
Production Operations	Operations Operational HSE Maintenance

TABLE 22: Upstream Oil and Gas Core Technical Skills

The above table is not exhaustive, as there are sub-specialties below the narrow definition. Sedimentology is a specialist subset of geology, and flow assurance is a sub-specialty that can sit within process engineering, subsea engineering, or pipeline engineering. HSE can be managed at the corporate level; for the purposes of our description, it is split between technical and operational HSE.

Geoscience

The United States Geological Survey defines geoscience as follows:

> "Geoscience (also called Earth Science) is the study of Earth. Geoscience includes so much more than rocks and volcanoes, it studies the processes that form and shape Earth's surface, the natural resources we use, and how water and ecosystems are interconnected."

In the narrower context of the upstream oil and gas industry, the purpose of geoscience is to find oil and gas, and support reservoir modeling and well planning. Geology is the study of minerals, their distribution, formation, and erosion. Geophysics is the study of how rocks interact with sound waves and is a specialist subset of geology. Exploration and development in the oil and gas industry rely on seismic surveys, which are designed and interpreted by geophysicists.

Geoscience is one of the most academically demanding fields within the upstream oil and gas industry, and, in modern times, most entry-level geoscientists at major oil and gas companies will hold postgraduate degrees.

Petroleum Engineering

Petroleum Engineers evaluate and develop oil and gas fields—it is a discipline that exists only within the oil and gas industry. Petroleum engineering can be further subdivided into petrophysics, which is the study of rock and fluid properties, reservoir engineering, which is focused on how fluids will flow through the reservoir, and production technology, which links reservoir engineering to well and completion design and production operations. A petrophysicist will interpret log data, core data, and samples from a well to provide a description of the physical properties of the field. The reservoir engineer will use that definition with analytical or simulation models to evaluate different development plans. The production technologist will evaluate completion design and artificial lift options.

Some petroleum engineers have undergraduate or graduate degrees in that subject; many more have degrees in mechanical or chemical engineering.

Wells

Well engineers design, drill, and complete oil and gas wells. Again, it is a discipline that really exists only within the oil and gas industry. Well engineering can be further subdivided into drilling and completions. Drilling involves, as the name suggests, designing, planning, and drilling the well, whereas completions involves designing the completion—the part of the well that interfaces with the reservoir to allow hydrocarbons to flow into the well. The well and completion design and program must obviously complement one another, but these wells' disciplines also work very closely with geoscience and petroleum engineering.

Well engineering also includes a significant commercial component, as wells can constitute up to 50% of the cost of a deepwater development, and the procurement and management of rigs and services under long-term contract can have a large impact on their overall cost.

Well engineers typically have mechanical- or petroleum-engineering degrees.

Facilities

Facilities engineers design and build the facilities required to bring hydrocarbons from the well, process them, and transport them to their destination. Facility engineering has more in common with other industrial-engineering disciplines than geoscience, petroleum engineering, or wells, which are very oil- and gas-specific disciplines. There are also lots of different flavors of facilities engineers and little overlap compared with the subsurface-focused disciplines.

Process engineers are chemical—sometimes mechanical—engineers, who work closely with the subsurface team to define the process-flow scheme—how the hydrocarbons will be processed from the wellhead to the end user. Once this has been established, they will specify equipment. Process engineers are the closest to the subsurface and will usually be the only facilities engineers involved in the early stages of a project.

Subsea engineers work on offshore, wet-tree projects and design the subsea system that transports hydrocarbons from the wellhead to the processing facility. Flow assurance can be part of process engineering or subsea engineering and is focused on risks to fluid flow like asphaltene drop-out or hydrate formation during producing or upset conditions.

Pipeline engineers design, build, and install pipelines from the processing facility to the final destination; there is a significant flow-assurance component here as well.

Civil/structural engineers work on the design, installation, and construction of the onshore civil works of offshore structures. Geotechnical engineers, who execute soil surveys and design foundations, are a subset of civil/structural engineers. Naval Architects, who design floating structures, are another subset of the civil/structural group.

Mechanical (Static) engineers are mechanical engineers who are responsible for the design and fabrication of process vessels and process piping. Mechanical (Rotating) engineers are mechanical engineers who are responsible for the design and fabrication of rotating equipment such as pumps and compressors.

Electrical engineers are responsible for power generation, and distribution and instrument engineers are responsible for instrumentation and control systems.

In most cases, the engineer will have an undergraduate or graduate degree in the relevant discipline.

Project Management

Project Management is the discipline responsible for executing the project, directly and in co-ordination with the other disciplines. Project Engineers, Managers, and Directors perform an integration function at different levels of authority. A project engineer may be responsible for delivery of an individual project component that requires multidisciplinary input, a project manager runs a small project—or a component of a large project—and a project director runs large projects. In addition to integration, project managers will normally act as contract holder for the contracts that have been awarded to deliver the contract, although this responsibility can also sit with the facility engineers.

Formal project management will normally start around the Select phase, but upstream oil and gas companies are increasingly creating early-project-management roles, to bring more structure to the early phases of a project's development. These early-project managers usually have more of a background in geoscience, petroleum engineering, or wells than the traditional execution-focused project manager.

Technical HSE is focused on the quantification of risk associated with health, safety, and the environment, inputs that are key to decision-making. Project services is an emergent discipline that covers cost estimating and control, planning, and risk-identification and mitigation. These outputs are used by the project manager to help manage progress on the project.

Supply chain is responsible for pre-qualifying vendors and managing the bid and award process. Supply chain is a discipline that has been growing in importance on the back of a move within the industry toward longer-term relationships with suppliers.

Quality Assurance/Quality Control (QA/QC) develops the quality-assurance plan for the project and ensures that it is executed; it's a critical role in ensuring that you get what you pay for.

Production Operations

Upstream oil- and gas-production operations consist of operations and maintenance. Operations involves the operation of the facility, controlling the inlet, process, and export of hydrocarbons streams. Maintenance involves maintaining the facility, through schedule maintenance, planned shutdowns, and breakdown maintenance. Operational Health Safety and Environment has been included under operations, although HSE can also be part of a more centralized organization. Operational HSE focus is on things like the Permit to Work Process and tracking and reporting on the various metrics associated with HSE performance such as emissions, unsafe situations, or accidents. Production operations will become involved in the asset long before the asset comes into operation, with the best practice to have involvement from the Concept Selection phase. Operations personnel may have an engineering degree or high school diploma.

4.2.2 Creativity

While people may not think of large, technocratic firms as being a hotbed of creativity, the core function of an upstream oil and gas company, finding and developing hydrocarbons, is entirely dependent on the creativity of its staff. It starts with ideas and ends, often decades later, with the production of oil and gas. Parke A. Dickey, a prominent American geologist, summarized this aspect of the industry as follows:

> **"We usually find oil in new places with old ideas. Sometimes, also, we find oil in an old place with a new idea,**

but we seldom find much oil in an old place with an old idea. Several times in the past we have thought that we were running out of oil, whereas, actually, we were only running out of ideas."

The need to constantly generate new ideas or, at least, to identify new places in which to apply old ones, requires that these large, technocratic organizations retain their creativity. One model of the organization defines the four outcomes that it must deliver to be successful[97]:

	OUTCOME	DESCRIPTION
Traditional Outcomes	Production CapEx Opex	Outcomes that can be easily and quantifiably measured
	Psychological Engagement	Employees are engaged in the overall enterprise
	Creativity, Innovation, Organizational Citizenship	Employees are creative and voluntarily do things outside of their job description for the good of the enterprise
Non-Traditional Outcomes	Learning	The employee and the enterprise learn from their experience and employ those learnings to improve the performance of the organization.

TABLE 23: Organizational Outcomes

The author would argue that all of the roles described in this chapter require staff who are able to learn from experience and use those learnings as they move forward in their careers, albeit to varying degrees. Creativity, on the other hand, is different. Some roles require a lot of creativity; in some cases, creativity can be a handicap. This is as it should be—to be successful, the organization has to deliver against traditional and non-traditional outcomes.

This becomes significant in the context of business development, because there is no reliable test for creativity. If someone is industrious and has the necessary education and work experience, they should succeed in a proceduralized role, one delivering conventional outcomes, but how can their ability to find new reserves of oil and gas be judged? How is performance predicted and measured?

Figure 31, below, shows the different roles plotted for the requirement for creativity and ease-of-performance measurement. As this figure shows, the requirement for creativity and the ease of measuring performance is not spread evenly across technical disciplines within the upstream oil and gas industry.

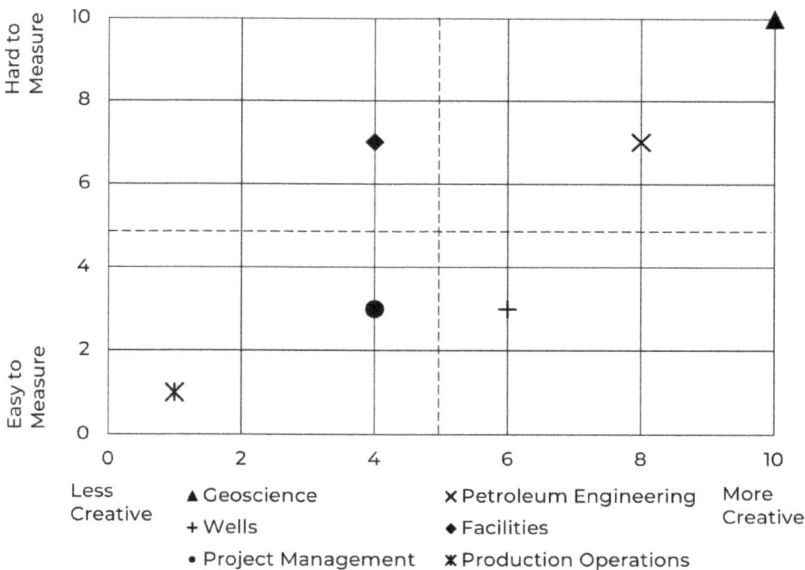

FIGURE 31: Creativity and Ease of Measurement by Role

Geoscience roles require the greatest creativity in order to generate new ideas and decode existing basins. Performance in geoscience is also the most difficult to measure, as the best-planned exploration campaign can result in no return after a string of dry wells.

Conversely, serendipity, where you accidentally find something while looking for something else, can also play a role. The advice given when it comes to measuring geoscience performance is to focus more on how the outcome compared to the range of predictions, rather than whether commercial hydrocarbons were discovered or not. As deepwater-drilling campaigns can quickly escalate into the hundreds of millions of dollars, maintaining this philosophy requires a lot of organizational discipline.

Petroleum engineering is more structured but still requires a high degree of creativity in interpreting and creating a development plan based on multiple geological realizations. Petroleum engineers also work with a lot of uncertainty, and actual outcomes may not be clear until the field has been on production for years. Again, the best approach to assessment here is to focus on inputs, not results. A petroleum engineer who acknowledges uncertainty, explores how the development plan will work under different realizations, and investigates mitigations should inspire more confidence than one who projects certainty about the proposed solution being the best.

Well engineering is even more structured than petroleum engineering, but performance is extremely easy to measure. There are databases available, like Rushmore, that allow a well operator to compare their well against the rest of the industry's in terms of both time and cost. This is not to say that drilling and completing wells is easy—it is not; it is extremely difficult. It is, however, easy to measure because it is a tightly defined activity that lends itself to comparison.

Facilities engineering, outside of frontier developments, is more codified by commonly accepted industry standards. Performance is harder to measure because each facility is different, and problems may not become apparent until the facility has been in operation for many years. It is also the activity that requires the most input from disparate disciplines, which means that it is harder to determine if the problem stems from the interaction of the team or the performance of an individual.

Project Management requires creativity in a tightly defined solution space—the capacity to work out *how* to do something, rather than *what* to do. Performance is transparent, as the project will either be hitting its schedule, CapEx, and safety targets, or it won't. While performance against plan is easy to measure, this doesn't account for the level of realism in the plan. This can make it hard to make an objective assessment of relative performance—*Was the estimate of CapEx too low or the schedule too aggressive?* But there are data providers, such as IPA, who can undertake benchmarking of projects.

Production operations, by design, are the most proceduralized components of the upstream oil and gas value chain. This is by design because of the complexity of the equipment being operated and the consequences of an accident. This is not to say that employees who work in production operations are not creative; it is to say that those roles do not require a high degree of creativity to be successful. Performance measurement is straightforward here—production, maintenance vs. plan, and controlling operating cost. Morale and culture at the site are equally important as leading indicators, but harder to gauge.

The implications of this from a business-development perspective is that a lack of technical capability introduces a greater risk for assets at the exploration and development stages, as those require the most creativity, where it is the most difficult to measure performance. A lack of expertise in certain aspects of facilities can also introduce risk, as this is also an area where it is hard to assess performance. Attempting to mitigate these risks by establishing the organizational capability is challenging: *How can you assess capability if you don't have the capability?* There are some established upstream oil and gas companies who cycle through heads of Exploration every couple of years, with each new head bringing in their own ideas and rebuilding the organization again, before they are replaced after a few disappointing wells. Is that driven by performance—or by bad luck?

Conversely, lacking production-operations capability when acquiring a producing asset does not introduce a lot of risk, as assessing the capability is relatively easy—that capability will transfer with the asset. The concern should be more that those operations staff are well managed by the new owner to ensure that satisfactory performance is maintained. Chapter 5 includes a discussion on the acquisition of an asset in the execution phase, and, while this is not recommended, acquiring an asset that will subsequently require the buyer to establish a project-execution capability is also possible.

4.2.3 Experience

The second consideration when it comes to organizational capability is experience. As touched on in 4.2.2, staff in all disciplines need to be able to learn from their experience and apply those learnings as they move forward in their careers. Upstream oil and gas is an experienced-based—as much as a skills-based—industry. The last time the author of this book updated his Shell competence profile, in 2013, he was ranked against 201 distinct competencies. That was not an exhaustive list of competencies, rather the ones that applied to his role at the time. Simply put, it just takes time to do all of the things that need to be done to establish these competencies. David Greer, the Project Director of Sakhalin II, one of the largest and most complex integrated oil and gas projects of all time, joked that Shell required him to have 100 years of experience to be considered competent for his role.

The importance of experience falls differently across disciplines; in some cases, it is play- or basin-specific; in some cases, it is less linked to a specific play type or setting. Starting with geoscience, it can take years to become familiar with a basin, to really understand how it functions and to become effective in describing it. Kerr McGee drilled the first well out of sight of land in the United States Gulf of Mexico in 1947[98]. Sixty-three years later, in 2010, Shell discovered the Appomattox field in the United States Gulf of Mexico, in Jurassic-age sandstones in a play known as the Norphlet[99]. The industry today continues to seek out new plays in this basin.

The implication here for business-development activity is that entry into a new basin will impose a lead time on the organization while it develops an understanding. It is not realistic to expect a successful switch quickly from one basin to the next.

Petroleum Engineers accumulate experience over time, but that experience is more readily transferred from field to field, providing the underlying hydrocarbon type and geology are consistent. It will take a year or so for a petroleum engineer who has been working in an oil field to become fully conversant with a gas-condensate field, or shale, for example, but only a few months to move from one oil field to the next.

The experience curve for well engineers is similar to that for reservoir engineers. Changing from shale to deepwater is a major change that will take a year or more of training, but switching between different fields with the same hydrocarbon type will take only a few months.

The implication here from a business-development perspective is that petroleum and well engineers can adapt quickly to the same type of field but will take much longer to adjust to a different-play type of setting. Once again, this will impose a lead time on the organization.

Facilities engineers also accumulate experience in their discipline over time but can apply it readily in a new setting. Compressors are more or less the same, no matter where they are located. The challenge with facilities comes when moving from onshore to shelf, or shelf to deepwater, or some other environment which is outside the experience base of the organization. Moving from shelf to deepwater, from wet trees to dry trees, for example, introduces a whole new discipline in subsea engineering, which has to be integrated into the organization.

Project Managers and Production Operations staff improve with experience and are able to move between projects or assets, with a few months required to get up to speed. The only note of caution here is that a new setting can create blind spots—the consequences of delayed start-up between an oil project and an LNG project can be very different, for example.

For a company that doesn't have the experience to manage the asset, or execute the project that they are considering for acquisition, the options are to buy it or grow it. The experience can't be rented—there are no companies out there that do what oil companies do except oil companies. As discussed in the previous section, buying expertise in certain disciplines introduces risk because of difficulty in assessing performance. In addition, buying experience is uncertain because of the time and expense required to resource an organization and the difficulty in imbuing it with a common culture. People tend to import the working cultures that they grew up in, and these may or may not be compatible. Even among the majors, there is no consensus on how assets should be matured. There is not even consensus on whether oil should be red or green on a map, or whether the P10 case is high or low, never mind the far-less-visible differences in the way people are expected to interact. Does the balance of power in decision-making sit with the project manager or with the technical experts? It depends on which culture you grew up in.

Growing the expertise is a sounder approach but requires the upstream oil and gas company to think in terms of maturing a portfolio over a multi-year time horizon and make investments for strategic as well as financial reasons.

4.2.4 Teamwork

Lack of a common culture makes the teamwork required to mature these assets even more challenging. Each of the disciplines identified earlier in this section work together on every phase of an oil- and gas-field development. The emphasis shifts as the project moves from one phase to the next, but each stage is truly a team effort. The Exploration stage is dominated by Geoscience, with some input from Petroleum Engineering, Facilities, and Wells.

In the Appraisal phase, geoscience still dominates, but Petroleum Engineering has a bigger role, as more location-specific data becomes available. Wells, once more, is required for the appraisal wells themselves.

As the asset moves into Concept Selection, Petroleum Engineering takes center stage, with Geoscience and Wells moving into a supporting role. Facilities become more heavily involved, albeit at the conceptual building-block stage, Production Operations will start to get involved, and a Project Manager will be appointed. Once the asset moves to the Define phase, the Facilities engineers take center stage, with Project Management and Wells taking over after sanction. They will lead the project through execution, with all of the other disciplines still participating to a greater or lesser extent, until it is ready for handover, and Production Operations takes the reins.

Learning to function as a team takes time. The National Transportation Safety Board found that 73% of incidents took place on a crew's first day of flying together and that 44% took place on their first flight[100]. The reason was that the crews had not yet had time to learn how to work with each other.

The interdisciplinary interdependence required to mature oil and gas assets goes beyond what is normally considered teamwork because each of the participants of the team, has, at best, only a vague idea of what the other members of the team actually do.

Geoscience is as much art as science, whereas the other disciplines are really sciences. Geoscience is qualitative, whereas the other disciplines are quantitative. Geoscience, Petroleum Engineering, and Wells are focused on what happens below the mudline; everyone else is focused on what happens above it. Geoscientists and Petroleum are focused on what *could be*; everyone else is thinking about what *is*. Geoscience, Petroleum Engineering, and Wells think of the world in terms of ranges of outcomes; everyone else wants a single number for everything, one that doesn't change, so they can size their facilities for exactly that number. The list goes on, and this is just the technical team, let alone when you start to introduce economics, finance, marketing, legal, and so on. Major oil and gas companies have developed processes and created roles to try to ease this interaction, but the best solution remains experience, both individually and working together. That, of course, takes time to build.

4.2.5 The Challenge

As this section has attempted to illustrate, an upstream oil and gas company's technical staff really are their most important asset. Establishing and maintaining technical capability creates an enduring competitive advantage because it takes so much time for a competitor to attempt to replicate it. There aren't really any mitigations here, only a reduced selection of lower-risk acquisition alternatives.

The most obvious alternative is to negate the need for organizational capability by acquiring producing assets, as the operations team will normally transfer with them. This is viable, although you still require the technical capability to assess the asset in the first place. The other drawback here is that producing assets are usually fully priced and have the least potential upside.

Another potential bridge is to focus on acquiring a non-operating interest in an asset and using that as a bridge to learn. Non-operator strategies are valid and addressed later in this text, but you are still restricted as non-operator. If you don't have technical capability, how do you decide what to buy? How do you know what *good* looks like? A company with financial capability but no technical capability risks becoming a buyer with a lot of money and not a lot of taste. That is not where you want to be.

The key to understanding technical capability is to think about how big a jump can realistically be made while being clear on what is required to make the transition successful. An onshore operator with deep roots in a single country would be stretching to acquire an offshore operated asset in another country, as it combines a new regulatory environment, with new geology, with a new setting. A position as an onshore operator in a new country or a non-operated position in an offshore asset would be more realistic.

4.2.6 Conclusion

This section was intended to highlight different technical functions within the upstream oil and gas industry and where thought is required in formulating a business-development strategy. The next section also covers human resources, but in this case, it is focused on commercial rather than technical capability.

4.3 COMMERCIAL CAPABILITY

This section discusses the commercial capability required for the acquisition, operation, and divestment of upstream oil and gas assets, rather than the commercial functions that a company requires in general. Consequently, internal functions, such as finance, are not addressed here, although competence in this area is clearly required for corporate success. Competence in supply-chain management is considered in section 4.2 as part of Project Management.

Commercial capability in this context consists of the ability to create and execute business-development strategy, originate and execute the transaction, integrate and manage the asset effectively, and sell the produced hydrocarbons competitively. The level of capability varies with the maturity of the asset, the hydrocarbon type, joint-venture structure and whether it is operated or non-operated.

4.3.1 The Business Development Process

The business-development process starts with strategy and ends with integration of the asset into the buyer's operations, the integration of a new partner into existing operations, or the exit from those operations. The following initial steps need to be undertaken:

- ⮑ Create a business-development strategy, for which the author recommends following the guidelines in this book.
- ⮑ Use the asset archetypes, described in Chapter 6, to develop a coveted-asset list.
- ⮑ Identify qualified buyers for your divestment targets.
- ⮑ Run an asset-acquisition or marketing campaign.
- ⮑ Negotiate commercial agreements, or prepare license-round submissions.
- ⮑ Close out conditions precedent.
- ⮑ Integrate the asset.

These steps can be undertaken using your internal business-development resources or in conjunction with external consultants and bankers. An important consideration here is how you incentivize behavior, internally as well as with external resources. If incentives are structured to reward transactions, there will be transactions, but not necessarily good transactions. If incentives are structured to reward advice, then there will be advice, but not necessarily any transactions.

When divesting an existing producing asset, there will be a fairly limited valuation range that the seller will understand well. Under these circumstances, it may be better to incentivize for transactions, with a reasonable reserve price. On the buy side, the calculation is different, as the buyer has less information, and the consequences of a poor acquisition can be far more damaging. In this case, it is better to incentivize for advice, as it is better to have no transaction than a bad transaction.

The choice of how to run the asset-acquisition or marketing campaign will also depend on role and circumstance. Many buyers, outside of participation in exploration-acreage auctions, are reluctant to participate in auctions, and for good reason, aside from as a means to gain competitive intelligence. Auction formats provide limited degrees of freedom, meaning that it's difficult to structure an agreement that allows the buyer to pay his best price, and are designed to find a winner who is willing to overpay. In some jurisdictions, however, auction processes are mandatory, as with the sale of Petrobras assets in Brazil.

A similar set of considerations face the seller. Many buyers won't participate, or they will participate only to allow you to educate them. The format could prevent you from finding the best overall value transaction, as it is hard to incorporate different arrangements within an auction format. If you are farming down, rather than out, then you will lose a lot of control over selection of your future partner. The auction process is either staff-time intensive or expensive, depending on whether you plan to run it yourself or outsource it. It will, however, provide price discovery. It is probably best reserved for exits of package sales, where it provides a way of exiting something that may otherwise be a difficult sale.

The commercial agreements and close-out of conditions will be time consuming and likely require some specialist external resources, particularly tax and legal. The simplest thing to agree on is the architecture of the deal, the price, the assets, and the phasing. Converting that into an executable Farm-Out, Joint Operating Agreement (JOA), and Marketing Agreement is complex and time consuming, and where a myriad of other considerations that come up during negotiation can derail things. Conditions precedent, which may require buyer to close on financing or the buyer or seller to obtain host-country government clearance or approvals are all points that require careful planning and management.

There will also be a requirement to integrate the acquisition into your existing systems or shepherd a divestment out of them. This typically involves functions such as finance, human resources, and information technology. Smooth execution here is key to maximize value from the transition and limit potential liabilities; it is likely that some integration support will be required from consultants to augment your internal capability.

4.3.2 Credibility and Relationships

One way to think about how to approach business development successfully is to think about what a counterparty looks for. The immediate thought is a drunken sailor, who has just discovered a chest filled with gold, the embodiment of indiscipline, flush with money, critical faculties impaired. But is that really the case? For one thing, drunken sailors aren't educated, which means their counterparty has to invest the time and resources in educating them, an effort they may well not be receptive to. Drunken sailors are unpredictable; this casts doubt on whether any deal will close or on what kind of timeline.

The drunken sailor is not the counterparty of choice; instead, it is the reliable partner, someone who is educated, who moves expeditiously toward closing, and who places as much emphasis on the longer-term relationship. A reliable partner will be credible as a buyer or seller, will cultivate relationships and will maintain a presence in their active markets.

Credibility starts with understanding what you are looking for in either an acquisition or divestment, being educated in the area of interest, and being aligned with internal and external stakeholders. In short, developing a business-development strategy, as outlined in this book. The process of developing the strategy defines the target assets, but it also provides the explanation of why the action is being taken. How much of the "why" is then shared is tactical, but being able to supply some explanation of why the corporation has selected a certain course of action is an important part of being credible. The process of developing the strategy will educate the participants on salient issues, and the process of approving the strategy will ensure internal and external alignment.

Maintaining credibility involves being clear about what you plan to do and then doing it. A counterparty's biggest concern is that they will squander time, money, and resources—and potentially forgo alternatives—in a process that will never close. The best way to assuage this is to be clear on what you can and can't do and on how you will move forward—and then stick to that plan. In the course of looking at either assets or potential buyers, new information can emerge as the process moves along that undercuts the value proposition for the transaction. At this stage, it is perfectly understandable to explain the situation, provide the counterparty with an opportunity to remedy it, and terminate the process if there is no solution. This is quite different from arbitrarily terminating a process because opinions have changed; that is something that people will remember.

Credibility is also important as a seller, something which is perhaps best illustrated by this example. A number of years ago, an IOC decided to divest some of its United States Gulf of Mexico assets. The mechanism that it chose was to parcel them up in a subsidiary and sell off minority interests in the subsidiary, with its U.S. office forming the subsidiary's management team. This structure was new to the United States Gulf of Mexico, but the same company had used it successfully in West Africa. One of the pre-conditions was that participants had to abandon their own exploration programs in the Gulf of Mexico, because of the potential conflict with their access to data from the subsidiary. They invited everyone currently active in the Gulf of Mexico to participate in a data room, including Shell, Chevron, and BP, who at the time were the biggest producers in the basin and held the most exploration acreage. All three pointed out that they had no intention of abandoning their exploration programs but would still be happy to visit the data room, a position which the seller accepted. Quite where they thought this would go isn't clear, but allowing access without receiving the required concessions only served to undermine their credibility. They were unable to find a buyer and abandoned the process.

This is a good point to move the discussion from credibility to relationships. Relationships are important in every walk of life, but they are particularly important in the upstream oil and gas industry, and particularly in business development, because the community is so small. The cornerstone of a professional relationship is credibility. Developing a reputation as an individual or at a corporate level of being difficult to deal with, unreliable, or unrealistic will limit the opportunities that you have access to. Conversely, investing time in building and maintaining a positive reputation will maximize those opportunities. Needless to say, the more opportunities you are exposed to, the higher the chance that you will come across something consistent with your business-development strategy.

A focus on relationships is important because many transactions involve an ongoing relationship, and, even in those that don't, a repeat transaction is more likely with a counterparty where a transaction has been successfully completed. LUKOIL, for example, developed a long-term relationship with Chevron following LUKOIL's participation in the Tengiz project; while Chevron was the operator, LUKOIL was an active participant in its execution.

Since then, retired Chevron executives have served on LUKOIL's board, and some of LUKOIL's largest overseas investments have been in Chevron assets.

Having built those relationships, maintaining them requires that you establish and maintain some form of presence. A personal professional relationship, a lunch or dinner, or regular attendance at industry or host-country events are all great ways to maintain those relationships and remind people of the kind of assets you are in the market for. Establishing and maintaining a presence shouldn't be random, and it shouldn't be ubiquitous; it should be structured and targeted based on your areas of interest. It should be *structured* in the sense that it should cover all the likely counterparties and other stakeholders, such as government agencies, within the bounds of what is ethical, if required at several different levels. It should be *targeted* in the sense that this engagement should focus on the areas of activity, the country or basin, and potential counterparties for the country or region that you are pursuing.

There is nothing in crafting a business-development capability that is usually challenging, but, in common with the development of technical capability, it does take time, discipline, and consistency—and there really is no alternative. Each company and asset is unique, and there really is no way to outsource the function; there is no alternative to investing the time in developing this capability.

4.3.3 Asset Management

Once an acquisition has been successfully completed, the asset has to be managed to deliver its potential value to the owners. Successful asset management requires a competent asset manager with commercial and legal support, as well as a finance function. The asset manager will require additional support, depending on the maturity of the asset—an exploration prospect has a very different asset-team footprint compared to a producing asset.

The key considerations in determining how the asset will be managed are whether this is a new-country entry, asset maturity, joint-venture structure, the maturity of the host-country regulatory stability, and operator status. The first four sections are written from the perspective of the operator, with the final section revisiting the previous issues from the perspective of the non-operator.

New-Country Entry

In a new-country entry, the asset manager will normally have a dual role—they will be responsible for managing the asset, and they will also be the parent company's most senior in-country representative. The country-manager role is significant and brings with it an additional diplomatic workload which requires political skill on behalf of the incumbent. In addition, in a new-country entry, the amount of in-country representation in an upstream oil and gas company's workforce is likely to be little to none. It is good practice, where possible, for the senior local representative to have lived and worked in the country for years, to have built relationships, and to understand the business culture, but in a new-country entry, this may not be possible. It is more important that the local representative has a track record and strong relationships in the upstream oil and gas company, as the asset manager will need to draw on those relationships to function effectively.

Developing local talent becomes a priority in a new-country entry, and it becomes important to imbue the local employees with a sense of the values and purpose of the parent company as quickly as possible. In many cases, a lot of core upstream oil and gas skills may simply not exist in-country, requiring technical skills to be imported or the work executed remotely. It is more likely that more universal functions such as finance, legal, and supply chain are initially available locally. As these individuals have local knowledge but lack corporate knowledge, there will need to be some duplication in functions.

The practical outcome of this is that asset teams for new-country entries need to be larger than in existing assets of similar materiality and maturity; a lot more money should be invested in the development of local staff early on. Staff development can involve things like a residential training course at the upstream oil and gas company's head office but should include a higher level of early expatriation opportunities, so that local staff have the opportunity to work in the company's head office. Once the asset has become established, sponsoring study-abroad schemes or local-university courses in key disciplines is a way to create a pipeline of local talent that will allow the upstream oil and gas company to reduce expatriation levels over time.

If the asset is in a country where the upstream oil and gas company already has established operations, the cost and complexity of entry can be a lot lower. If the new asset is just another unincorporated joint venture, then the asset manager is a much-less-prominent figure. These kinds of roles provide a great opportunity for developing the company's future senior executives. If existing operations in-country are in the form of an incorporated joint venture, then the asset team will need to be stand-alone. The learning curve is not as steep as for a new-country entry, but there will still need to be substantial additional investment in building a stand-alone organization. If the upstream oil and gas company has two or more assets in a country in the form of an incorporated joint venture, then the upstream oil and gas company would be well advised to create a separate role for the country manager. The asset managers running an incorporated joint venture have a fiduciary duty to the joint venture, not the company that they are seconded from. The interests of an individual asset may diverge from each other, or, indeed, from the parent company. The creation of a separate country-manager role with a supporting administration helps to eliminate these conflicts.

Asset Maturity

The maturity of the asset has broad implications for management. In the exploration and appraisal phase, before the asset is declared commercial, the bulk of the staff technical work will probably be completed at the upstream oil and gas company's head office—for large companies, at some kind of center for excellence. Some form of in-country footprint will be required to establish and maintain relationships with the host-country government and regulator, to procure and manage local contracts, to hire and manage staff, to ensure legal compliance, and to pay bills and taxes. At this stage, that the bulk of the work will be done outside of the country and near-term exit are real possibilities. Thus, long-term financial commitments should be limited. There is a worthwhile debate at this stage in where the asset team should be located—in-country or at headquarters. As a default, the head-office location will be more efficient, but with some countries that have a "high-touch" business culture or value physical presence in developing trust, it may make more sense to locate the asset team in-country from the start. The location of joint-venture-partner teams is also a consideration here, as proximity can help manage those relationships. There will be travel, but with the bulk of the work undertaken at the head office, this is the best location for the asset team in those early stages, with an asset representative located in the host country, as this minimizes travel.

Once the asset has matured to the Select and Define stages, the balance changes, and, while the bulk of the technical work will still be undertaken at the upstream oil and gas company's headquarters, there is much greater need for interaction with the host-country government and regulator. Moving from the exploration and appraisal to select phase usually involves some form of declaration of commerciality, and, so, the probability that the asset will eventually be developed has increased substantially. At this stage, it is appropriate to begin to make longer-term in-country commitments and establish a larger local presence. The asset manager may well change at this point as well, from someone with more of an exploration background to someone with more of a development focus, and a full-time execution project manager or director should have been appointed. One approach is to split the top two roles, with the asset manager located in-country and the project manager located in the upstream oil and gas company's head office. The core subsurface team may re-locate to the host country at this point. Interaction between the upstream oil and gas company, host-country government, host-country regulator, and joint-venture partners will ramp up substantially in this phase, and the in-country organization will need to be augmented with commercial and legal staff to manage those interactions.

In-country activity will peak during the execute phase, as the commercial functions move more to reporting and compliance with the terms of the granting instrument and dispute resolution rather than negotiation. There is less focus on joint-venture management during this phase unless there are significant delays or budget over-runs. During this stage, the entire asset organization, plus the in-country component of the project organization, will be in-country. This can place a strain on local relationships, something that the asset manager and his supporting organization should be careful to manage.

The start-up of the asset will see the project organization ramp down as the asset organization ramps up to its final shape. Host-country government and joint-venture-management activity will be limited to closing out any disputes from the prior phases; once this is complete, the workload for this function may decline to the point where it could be provided on an ad-hoc basis by head office. As production starts, the role of the finance function—and, particularly, tax—rises substantially. There is also a residual requirement to maintain compliance with the terms of the granting instrument, which will require a small team to monitor and engage with the regulator.

As you move through the life cycle of an asset, the level of commercial support and the skills required for the roles evolve. Heads of incorporated joint ventures can be very high-profile roles. The General Director of Tengizchevroil, for example, who has historically been a Chevron secondee, ran what was for many years the largest energy company in Kazakhstan.

Joint Venture Structure

Most upstream oil and gas industry assets are owned by joint ventures rather than individual upstream oil and gas companies. Joint ventures come in two types—Incorporated Joint Ventures and Unincorporated Joint Ventures. In an Incorporated Joint Venture, the granting instrument is held by a legal entity, with joint-venture partners acting as shareholders. In an Unincorporated Joint Venture, ownership in the asset is governed through your working interest in a granting instrument—a PSC, License, or Concession, which is conferred by the host-country government. The operation of the Joint Venture is governed by a JOA, a contract which confers rights and responsibilities on each of the joint-venture partners.

There is more than an abstract legal distinction between the two structures, as, at a practical level, they function very differently. In the context of commercial capability, the incorporated joint venture, once established, is probably the easier of the two to manage. The participants appoint their directors, who then vote on decisions in accordance with the articles of incorporation or equivalent that govern its operation. The entity has its own processes, and all partners have equal access to its work products and opinions.

In an unincorporated joint venture, decisions are taken in accordance with the terms of the joint-operating agreement. The JOA requires active management, commercially and legally, from all sides. In addition, not all work products will be shared with all joint-venture partners; the operator may consider some to be proprietary. There are some key assumptions, such as oil price, that cannot be shared, and functions such as marketing may not be common, with each partner required to make their own arrangements. The negotiation of common midstream agreements forms a commercial workstream all its own. The asset manager will spend a substantial amount of their time actively managing the JOA.

Host-Country Regulatory Stability

The degree to which host-country regulatory regimes are established and provide a consistent operating environment is another factor in determining the degree of commercial capability required for success. A stable regulatory regime is very easy to deal with and requires little commercial or legal input. At the other extreme, a regulatory regime in which the regulator routinely over-lifts production, disputes cost-recovery claims, or cannot fulfill its own obligations under the granting instrument requires a far-greater degree of commercial capability. Where the regulator is subject to political appointment, the direction of the regulatory agency can change every few years with a new election, which obviously presents challenges to projects that are matured over multi-year time horizons.

Because it takes time for institutions to mature, many of the most promising oil and gas provinces have relatively immature regulatory regimes. In some cases, an established oil and gas province may struggle to regulate a project in a new setting. In the Russian Federation at the time of the execution of the Sakhalin II project, for example, there was no regulatory regime in place for new-build offshore platforms, because there had been no new-build offshore platforms in the country prior to that. It just wasn't clear what they were classified as and, thus, which regulatory agencies were responsible for their regulation. This lack of clarity creates a huge commercial and legal challenge.

There is no real answer to this, other than to make an appropriate cost, schedule, and resource allowance, and work through it. Different IOCs have differing philosophies on how to approach these issues. One approach is to identify issues but continue to invest and make progress while they are negotiated. This demonstrates goodwill but yields potential leverage. At the other extreme, some companies insist on the application of the letter of the contract and will suspend work until the issue is addressed to their satisfaction. This approach demonstrates no goodwill but has the advantage of maintaining leverage.

Non-Operated Partners

The prior sections have been written from the perspective of an operator; a non-operated partner still requires commercial capability to be successful.

Under the new-country-entry scenario, participation as a non-operated partner alleviates the heavy lifting involved in establishing a relationship with the regulator and host-country government. The asset manager and commercial team can remain in the upstream oil and gas company's headquarters until the asset nears production. At that point, it will be necessary to establish a local office to interact with the operator on a regular basis and to handle marketing and tax issues.

In an unincorporated joint venture, the joint-venture partner really needs to be as commercially active in managing the joint venture as the operator. The non-operated partner will need to manage through the JOA and will have just as much of a role in transportation and marketing discussions. While the operator will be managing the relationship with the host-country regulator, the non-operated party will have to, as a minimum, understand the situation.

Conclusion

As illustrated above, the importance and dimensions of the asset manager's role can vary from a basic administrative function at one end of the spectrum, to a Fortune 500-equivalent CEO at the other. This, together with the location and composition of the asset team, should be given due consideration when deciding if you have the commercial capability to successfully execute an asset acquisition. As with technical capability, there is no shortcut to developing this capability, and, aside from adopting a non-operated strategy, there is no way to outsource to a third party. It is important for an organization to internalize that this is not just about individuals—there must be an institutional appetite to make asset integration work.

4.3.4 Marketing

For the purposes of this discussion, marketing covers the sale, lifting, transportation, and delivery of hydrocarbons as well as any financial products used to mitigate price risk. Lifting, transportation, and delivery involve taking custody of the hydrocarbons, transporting them, and selling them to the customer. In unincorporated joint ventures, most working-interest partners will take title and are responsible for lifting their own product, whether they operate the field or not. This is important from a legal perspective, as it protects non-operated partners from having their hydrocarbons seized to satisfy an operator's creditors but introduces logistical difficulties.

Oil

Both operators and non-operators require a marketing function early in the maturation life cycle, to advise on the development concept as well as to identify optimal export routes and negotiate pipeline contracts for transportation. Oil is typically quite straightforward, as it is a fungible liquid, but even with oil, provision must be made for associated gas. Outside established regions, associated gas requires dedicated pipelines and long-term supply contracts—which often run at a loss.

Once stabilized, oil is easy to transport and store. It can be transported by train, truck, pipeline, or tanker. The futures market for oil allows a producer to hedge some of their biggest risk, which is price. A hedging strategy may be desirable, particularly for a small producer, but small producers are least likely to have access to their own trading group. In this case, banks, trading houses, or specialist consultants can be retained to develop and execute those strategies.

Gas

Gas-condensate, dry-gas, and LNG projects are the most complex commercially, as discussed in more detail in section 5.2.2. There is a regional market for gas in Europe and the United States, so in these geographies, dry-gas and gas-condensate developments can be progressed in the same way as an oil development.

Outside Europe and the United States, the situation is different. A long-term buyer must be found for the gas before the project can move forward. A gas development in these circumstances requires an extra level of certainty for both the buyer and the seller. From the seller's perspective, the pipeline only moves the gas to one place. He cannot market it to anyone else, so he needs a long-term guarantee of sales volume and price. The buyer needs to know there is enough gas available for his needs, which means the seller must invest more in delineating his field before moving forward.

In some cases, a local market for the gas does not exist. In these cases, development hinges not only on a gas-supply agreement but also downstream agreements that govern whatever facilities are constructed to utilize the gas. These can be power plants or chemical plants that produce methanol or fertilizer. This introduces a chain of guarantees—someone must guarantee the power-purchase agreement, on adequate terms to fund the power plant, so that the owner of the power plant can guarantee the gas-supply agreement that is required to support development of the gas field. It is not unusual to see large gas fields, discovered decades ago, that have never been brought into service because of difficulties in establishing this gas market.

The net effect of this is that gas developments outside the United States and Europe are commercial projects first and technical projects second. When contemplating dry-gas or gas-condensate assets, you need to have enough commercial sophistication within your organization to mature them effectively.

One recent development in this market is the emergence of small, leased LNG facilities. Golar LNG is a company that provides leased, floating FLNG facilities with long-term contracts. At the time of writing, Golar has one operating vessel, leased to Perenco in Cameroon, with a second vessel due to be delivered to BP in 2022. This model still requires the operator to market the LNG but could open LNG as an option for smaller, previously stranded gas fields.

Large-Scale LNG

LNG solves the problem of guaranteeing a gas-sales agreement, by providing the owner of a gas field with access to multiple buyers—but with its own commercial complexities and at a very substantial capital cost. There is a large materiality threshold for large-scale LNG; the field will need to be able to produce at least 4 trillion cubic feet (tcf) of gas or more, depending on the complexity of the setting. More certainty is required by both the buyer and seller for project sanction, and, so, these projects again are commercially led. There is also a myriad of different commercial models that LNG facilities can adopt—long-term contracts tied to oil or other indices, spot-market sales, tolling models—and combinations thereof that require a high degree of sophistication to design and execute predictably and profitably. LNG really is a specialized commercial area that is evolving rapidly. When considering LNG-based assets, you either require or plan to assemble that specialist capability or find a joint-venture partner who has it.

4.3.5 Conclusion

This section covered the commercial capabilities that are required to create a business-development strategy, originate and conduct a transaction, and then successfully integrate and operate the asset. In the next section, we will look at some second-order considerations, things that are important but whose absence can be mitigated.

4.4 SECOND-ORDER CONSIDERATIONS

The prior three sections of this chapter covered first-order organizational requirements, capabilities that the author believes an organization would require in order to be successful. In this section, we look at second-order considerations, which are important for success but where a deficiency can be mitigated. These are ESG capability, political capability, organizational and cultural alignment, organizational risk appetite, and non-operated capability.

4.4.1 ESG Exposure

Environmental, Social, and Governance (ESG) considerations are top of mind for most industry executives at the time of writing. The author has classified these as second-order considerations because everyone in the upstream oil and gas industry is, by definition, already taking ESG risk. The primary question is mitigation. There is currently an active discussion on whether the oil and gas industry has, or should have, a long-term future, as both oil and gas contribute to climate change when used as intended.

While the industry works to reduce emissions from the production of hydrocarbons, their combustion will result in the emission of CO_2. Some fields have higher emissions than others, either because of the nature of the production process or as a result of operational decisions. Oil sands and heavy oil will typically have higher CO_2 emissions because of the energy intensity required in the production process. These also use large amounts of water, which must be treated and disposed of. In the peak oil world of the early 2000s, these investments made sense, but, more recently, these types of fields—which also have some of the highest operating costs—have fallen from favor.

In general, evaluation of any field should include an economic assessment of the impact of CO_2. A lot of conventional fields elect to flare associated gas rather than sell or re-inject it, and these fields could be particularly sensitive to changes in legislation, which are difficult to foresee.

United States shale oil is another potentially sensitive area for environmental concerns due to its water use, the prevalence of flaring of associated gas, groundwater-contamination concerns, and the links between hydraulic fracturing and earthquakes. More mundane considerations—such as excessive traffic on local roads and the impact of a transient workforce on local communities—also require due consideration.

This starts to trend into societal considerations, which have resulted in some of the most severe project derailments of the last couple of decades. Onshore production, the least challenging technical-development type, is the most vulnerable to this form of risk.

Assessing and managing ESG risks is of prime importance to understanding the value of the potential transaction. This is classified as a second-order organizational capability, because this is expertise that can be hired from one of the many ESG consultants, such as ERM. It is important to have this type of assessment in hand before proceeding too far with a transaction.

4.4.2 Political Capability and Relationships

The oil and gas industry is inherently political, as, outside parts of the United States and Canada, it deals with the development of a nationally owned natural resource. This reality is commonly given more priority in emerging market economies but is true universally. Witness the amount spent on lobbying by energy companies in Washington: oil and gas companies spent $125 million on lobbying in the United States in 2019[101]. A key consideration in asset acquisition and divestment is your political capability, specific to the host-country setting.

As the recently elected Biden administration has shown, political risk cannot be avoided by focusing investment on OECD countries. Energy companies that are based in some oil-producing regions will find it difficult to do business in many OECD countries, due to formal sanctions or the relationships between the respective nations. Conversely, there are close historic ties between some nations, including, in some cases, common language, industry practices, or legal systems that can make an entry far easier.

Some historic examples are British companies in the Middle East and French companies working in Africa. More recently, Galp, a small Portuguese integrated energy company, has expanded successfully into Brazil and Angola, while LUKOIL has done the same in parts of the former Soviet Union, sharing not only a common language but also a distinct approach to field development.

The best way to build these political relationships is to establish an entity in the host nation and start working with the regulator, other government agencies, and contractors. Acquiring a Non-Operated Working Interest is a good way to do this, as it will be seen as a real commitment and provides something concrete to discuss. This requires a blend of local staff, to provide local context and relationships, and home-country staff, to provide the link back to the mothership. Both sides will end up translating.

Another source of potential access is relationships with other energy companies that operate in the host country. If you have partners in an established joint venture and the relationship is healthy, then partnering elsewhere can mitigate many joint-venture risks. You are already familiar with each other, and there will be personal relationships at the executive level that can help smooth the joint venture over the inevitable bumps. Working as a non-operator is an exercise in picking a good partner more than anything else, so there is a clear advantage to picking a partner that you have already worked with. Sometimes these arrangements can be formalized—defining an area of mutual interest, for example.

4.4.3 Organizational and Cultural Alignment

Incompatible culture and language can present difficulties in working with an acquired asset. This may seem strange in an era that is dominated by talk of artificial intelligence and big data, but working with people who don't speak the same language is still surprisingly difficult. Language differences make everyday transactions hard, but they make explaining complex commercial, legal, or technical issues, often in a charged environment, especially so.

The same is true of culture. International business cultures differ, even between countries that share a common history and language, such as the United States and the UK. Bribery and corruption—of staff and government officials—is endemic in many of the societies that produce oil and gas and is viewed in many of those societies as being entirely normal. For an investor from an OECD country, it's important to be aware of that and have a plan to address it.

Cultural issues also apply to non-OECD countries investing in the OECD. Staff in the United States will speak freely, work off their own initiative, and leave the company if they are punished for it, regardless of home-country norms. This may be incompatible with the acquirer's home-country business culture, but attempting to re-educate the workforce is not going to change it. Even global multinationals can be surprisingly tribal when push comes to shove, with staff on the working level frequently ascribing investment decisions, promotions, and layoffs to national origin in the first instance.

The best remedy for addressing cultural differences is to work together, to build teams that include members from both the home and the host countries. In a non-operated setting, seconding staff into operating companies can also help bridge these gaps.

4.4.4 Organizational Risk Appetite and Loci

It is important to establish an understanding of the type and degree of risk that the organization is sensitive to. In theory, it really shouldn't make any difference. Risk is risk and can be quantified and mitigated, but, for some reason, perhaps as a result of their own organizational evolution, companies tend to approach risk differently. Some companies are extremely sensitive to technical risk but are much more comfortable working in opaque environments. Some companies, on the other hand, are willing to invest billions in projects that are based purely on science but won't move forward unless all the commercial agreements have been completed. Some are in the middle.

If an organization struggles to understand why reserves estimates, project costs, or schedules change, then producing assets, or development assets with a lot of producing analogs, are going to be a better acquisition fit. Investment in United States shale, with predictable costs and production performance, would be a good fit for a company with that predilection. If the organization is uncomfortable with complex political environments, then the OECD is probably a better market.

4.4.5 Non-Operated Capability

The decision on whether to operate a field or invest as a non-operator is a decision that comes up frequently in this text. Operating a field clearly requires organizational capability, but a successful non-operated partner also requires a distinct organizational capability.

The role of a non-operator varies considerably from phase to phase. The non-operator can see substantial involvement in the Exploration, Appraisal, and Select phases, less involvement in the Define phase, and little to no involvement in the Execute and Operate phases.

The first job of a non-operated partner in the early phases is to avoid preventing the operator from operating. This means that the non-operator must have a clear definition of the information that they require to make decisions, the capability to execute their own work when the operator will not provide the deliverable, and a clear decision process that conforms to the timeline in the JOA.

Once this has been established, the non-operated partner can focus on influencing and learning from the asset. The best non-operated partners can act like shadow operators, steering the direction of a joint venture without requiring the technical capability to execute the work or commit resources for the benefit of the joint venture. This doesn't happen by accident—the companies that have the best non-operated capability employ formal training in the role.

Thus, for an oil company new to a region and without a non-operated infrastructure, farming into an operating asset as a non-operated partner is a low-risk place to start. The same operator farming in to an asset in the exploration phase would be a much higher risk.

4.4.6 Conclusion

The purpose of this section was to provide a summary of organizational-capability considerations that are important in the creation of a business-development strategy but are not governing. The next two sections of this chapter return to our Apache and BHP examples, applying the framework outlined in this chapter.

4.5 ORGANIZATIONAL CAPABILITY—INDIE OIL

Indie Oil is a fictional company, which means it is rather too easy to portray organizational capabilities that conveniently highlight the point that the author is trying to make. With that disclaimer out of the way, how would we describe Indie Oil's capability using the framework outlined in this chapter?

Financial capability and the financial framework were fairly well covered in Chapter 3, so we start by looking at technical capability. Indie Oil is, at its core, an explorer that added development and operations capability as that became necessary to realize value from its discoveries. Indie Oil has a strong exploration capability, with a long track record in sub-Saharan Africa and Latin America.

Indie does a lot of exploration-acreage-type transactions and farm-outs but has less experience farming into discovered acreage. It is used to new-country entries, again in sub-Saharan Africa, but does not have experience in Europe, North America, the Middle East, or the former Soviet Union. Indie doesn't have expertise in gas marketing or LNG.

Indie is comfortable taking technical risk and a moderate degree of political risk. It has very limited non-operated experience and has yet to execute an onshore development; it has limited experience dealing with host-country communities.

4.6 ORGANIZATIONAL CAPABILITY—APACHE

This section takes the framework that we have introduced in the first four sections of this chapter and applies it to the Apache acquisition of the Forties field that was introduced earlier in the book. What would an assessment of organizational capability of Apache look like at the time of the Forties acquisition?

4.6.1 Financial Capability

Apache had an A credit rating at the time of the acquisition, with gearing at 26%.[102] The company was solvent and had access to both equity and debt markets on reasonable terms. Average book leverage for the upstream oil and gas industry over the period 2002 to 2004 was 17% to 22%, and average United States upstream oil and gas leverage over the period 1997 to 2014 was 27%[103]. Apache carried a normal level of debt for an upstream oil and gas company at the time. At the time, BP had an Aa1 (Moody's) and AA+ (Standard & Poor's) credit rating and also had gearing at 26%[104]. BP, as a larger company with a stronger credit rating, would likely have had a lower cost of capital, and, so, Apache did not have an advantage here.

Apache's 2003 annual report provides a discussion on the resilience of its portfolio and how the Forties acquisition complements it. Apache aimed to construct a portfolio that was diversified by hydrocarbon type, geology, and geography. The portfolio consisted of producing assets in mature regions, which provided steady cash flow, and some development potential (mainly in the United States), producing assets with large-acreage positions that provided more substantial running room and frontier exploration. The Forties acquisition provided diversification in geology and geography and added a large producing asset with substantial running room.

Apache used a combination of cash flow from operations, new equity issuance, and debt to finance the acquisition. Forties was not the only acquisition that Apache made that year; they also closed on substantial United States Gulf of Mexico assets from Shell and BP. Apache had access to both equity and debt markets, and tapped both to finance the acquisition. Apache issued 19.8 million shares, raising $554 million and $350 million of 12-year senior unsecured notes at 4.375%.[105]

Apache was a newcomer to the North Sea and, therefore, did not have any prior losses to accelerate. The acquisition of a producing asset did, however, provide immediate taxpayer status, against which future-exploration activities and other expenses could be offset.

4.6.2 Technical Capability

Apache had no experience in the basin but was acquiring a producing asset with nearly 30 years of production history, so, geological and petrophysical parameters were well defined. There was very little subsurface risk left with Forties. Apache had experience with offshore operations in the United States Gulf of Mexico and had acquired older facilities from other operators in the past. So, while it did not have North Sea operating experience, it had a good analog.

One interesting aspect of the transaction was that Apache inherited the Forties team from BP[106]—that is, the technical team as well as the offshore logistics, operations, and maintenance teams. This transfer of personnel did a great deal to accelerate Apache's ability to get to work on Forties. It also provided a springboard for Apache's subsequent infrastructure-led exploration program.

4.6.3 Commercial Capability

Apache's 10K filings of the late '90s and early 2000s prominently articulated a very clear business-development strategy. Apache has developed a well-documented "acquire and exploit" strategy, where assets with development potential were acquired and then exploited, and executed the strategy successfully over several successive years. They were clear on how this strategy linked to the requirements of their portfolio, as discussed above, and how it should be executed—they would not participate in auctions and would pursue only assets where they could engage in direct negotiation with the seller. They were also disciplined and patient, with the annual reports making repeated references to passing on opportunities due to elevated asset prices.

Apache had been executing acquisitions like Forties for several years and, so, had developed an institutional capability to identify, execute, and integrate these kinds of opportunities. The Forties acquisition was the largest single acquisition to date, but Apache were also able to undertake two other major transactions—a United States Gulf of Mexico acquisition from BP and a United States Gulf of Mexico acquisition from Shell—in the same year.

At the time of purchase, Forties was a medium-sized producer but was technically complex and high profile. As this was a new region, the Forties asset manager was essentially Apache's UK country manager and would have been the most senior executive for Apache in Europe. Apache selected a senior, long-term Apache executive for the role. John Crum had been Apache's Executive Vice President of Eurasia and New Ventures for the prior two years and would have been familiar with both the transaction and the region.

One area where Apache could have struggled as a newcomer is in marketing. They addressed this cleverly by striking a side deal with BP to market all their production for the following two years, essentially transferring the risk until they had had time to develop their own regional marketing capability. They also hedged a proportion of their production, to ensure a minimal level of cash flow in the period immediately following the transaction. They hedged 25,000 barrels/day through the end of January 2004 and a full 40,000 barrels/day from then until the end of 2004—nearly 90% of production at the time of acquisition. Forties contributed the lowest realized oil price in their portfolio in 2003, at $25/barrel.

4.6.4 Other Considerations

While Apache did not have prior operations in the North Sea, the North Sea oil industry had been working with United States companies for decades, and, so, Apache were following a well-trodden path. Aberdeen, the home of the North Sea oil industry, owes that industry its prosperity, and, so, as expected, welcomed anyone who was willing to invest.

United States and UK business cultures are not identical but are similar, and, notwithstanding jokes about nations separated by a common language and the distinct Doric dialect of Aberdeenshire, there would be minimal communication issues.

The key risk was probably organization, with Apache imposing an Apache leader on an ex-BP workforce, but that risk in itself mitigated the technical risk of Apache assuming operations of the field.

From an ESG perspective, the key concern at that time would have been the integrity of the facilities, but, as discussed earlier, this is a risk that Apache had prior experience in managing.

4.6.5 Conclusion

Apache were very well prepared to acquire Forties. They clearly understood what they were looking for and how it would enhance their existing portfolio, they had the commercial capability to identify and execute the transaction, and they were able to finance it. In the handful of areas where they had shortfalls—marketing, technical capability—they identified and applied mitigations in the form of marketing agreements of staff transfers.

4.7 ORGANIZATIONAL CAPABILITY—BHP

Returning to BHP's Haynesville and Petrohawk acquisitions, we can go through a similar exercise, although we are hampered to a degree as the disclosures are not as detailed as Forties'.

4.7.1 Financial Capability

BHP had an A1 (Moody's) or A+ (Standard and Poor's) credit rating at the time of the acquisition, and gearing was at 9% following the Haynesville acquisition, rising to 26% with the Petrohawk acquisition[107]. BHP was solvent and had access to debt markets on reasonable terms, and presumable equity markets as well, although this was not tested in the course of the transaction. Average book leverage for the upstream oil and gas industry over the period 2010 to 2013 was 13% to 20%, and average United States upstream oil and gas leverage over the period 1997 to 2014 was 27%.[108]

BHP's annual report makes reference to a diversified portfolio of large, Tier 1 assets that can deliver growth and margins throughout the cycle. BHP is a minerals conglomerate, rather than a focused upstream oil and gas company, so, by its very nature, its portfolio is diversified. BHP does not define the properties of Tier 1 assets, but we can infer from the name that they are considered premier assets. The published documentation does not provide a discussion on how either the Haynesville or Petrohawk was classified as Tier 1 or how their acquisition would impact the portfolio. Shale does have different characteristics: it is shorter cycle and requires continuous investment to maintain production, so this would impact the composition of BHP's portfolio.

BHP did take on additional debt at the time of the Petrohawk acquisition but not specifically to support that transaction. BHP took on $8 billion in debt directly and $3.8 billion indirectly in assuming debt from Petrohawk. BHP made a total of $32 billion in investments in that year, of which the largest single item was the $12 billion acquisition of Petrohawk. Multiple notes were issued throughout the year, with maturities running out through 2042 and rates of between 1% and 4.125%.

BHP had existing operations in the United States and, so, was a taxpayer but did not have any prior year's losses to accelerate.

4.7.2 Technical Capability

BHP had no experience with either shale oil or gas, at the time of the transaction, shale oil and gas were still niche, and few of the larger firms had any experience with it. Both the Haynesville and Petrohawk acquisitions were new plays that were being opened and lacked a track record within the industry.

BHP had onshore operations in Algeria and Pakistan but no onshore operations in the United States or other OECD countries. As such, their training systems and standards would not be applicable to the new acquisition. The BHP annual reports and other publications do not detail how BHP integrated and managed either of the acquisitions. As the Petrohawk acquisition was corporate, Petrohawk executives and employees presumably transferred with the assets, which provided BHP with at least operational capability.

4.7.3 Commercial Capability

BHP did not have a history of making acquisitions, it had not executed any acquisitions for a number of years, and Petrohawk represented the largest single petroleum acquisition in its history. While the firm's business-development strategy may have been clear internally, it did not articulate the strategy in its published documents, other than general statements about large, Tier 1 assets.

BHP had no U.S. shale expertise; in fact, shale was a new play at that time. It is not clear how BHP evaluated either the Haynesville or Petrohawk transaction, given it had no prior experience in U.S. shale. BHP does not disclose the organizational structure of the units that it acquired, and, so, it is not possible to comment on the arrangements that were made to manage the assets.

BHP does not provide any information on how it markets product from the Haynesville or Petrohawk transactions, other than to note that most of its marketing is undertaken through a central hub in Singapore.

4.7.4 Other Considerations

BHP was already established in the United States as an operator but in the deepwater Gulf of Mexico rather than onshore. The early shale pioneers were proud of being small and nimble, whereas BHP was closer to a supermajor in terms of decision-making and work processes. BHP seems historically to have been more comfortable with technical risk, focusing on challenging plays in the OECD, so this was in line with its risk preference. U.S. shale oil, in particular, increased BHP's ESG exposure due to concerns about fracking causing earthquakes and polluting groundwater, as well as flaring from wells without gas infrastructure and methane leaks from pipelines.

4.7.5 Conclusions

BHP is less transparent than Apache about its strategy and the execution of the transaction, which makes a definitive conclusion difficult. The Petrohawk acquisition, in particular, constituted a big bet on a play type where they had no operation experience and no way to really evaluate what they were buying. Given this uncertainty, it would have made more sense to make some smaller acquisitions or try to grow the business organically—to learn the play, rather than make a huge acquisition of this type. Joint ventures could also have been deployed—again as a way to develop understanding of how the play type performs.

4.8 CONCLUSION

This purpose of this chapter was to introduce the second component of creating a business-development strategy—understanding organizational capability. This section started by looking at first-order organizational capability—financial, technical, and commercial—describing what is important under each category. It then introduced some subsidiary considerations—things whose absence can be mitigated.

We then looked at Apache's acquisition of the Forties field and BHP's shale assets, using this framework. This exercise concluded that, in terms of organizational capability, Apache were much better positioned to capitalize on their acquisition than BHP were.

The next chapter is focused on the third component in the creation of the business-development strategy; asset mix, where we look at how to create asset archetypes that reflect the characteristics that we are looking to build into our portfolios. Again, we will see how this framework can be applied by looking at Apache and BHP.

Chapter 5

ASSET MIX

The THIRD COMPONENT of a business-development strategy, together with portfolio health and organizational capability, is asset mix. Assessing asset mix involves describing assets by their constituent characteristics, so that they can be grouped into similar asset types. This particular part of the process tends to weigh more heavily on acquisition than divestment decisions, although, in selecting the assets that you choose to exit, then it is important to think about the characteristics of those assets and how that exit will impact your portfolio.

Referring back to the discussion in section 1.1, particular care is required in the acquisition of oil and gas assets, as they are commodities; the owner has limited ability to improve their performance. As commodities, the owner has no control over price, and, as the underlying characteristics can't be changed, the owner has limited control over the cost of extraction. Timelines—for acquisition, development, and divestment—are also long, meaning missteps cannot be easily rectified. Each asset is unique (one of the things that make our industry fascinating), but there are some common characteristics that are useful to consider.

The approach taken in this chapter is to break an asset down by considering certain generic asset characteristics—oil or gas, materiality, setting, maturity, geography, joint-venture structure, and some other parameters. This approach helps to describe an asset by type; when we move on to crafting a business-development strategy in Chapter 6, we will construct notional portfolios built up from asset types, rather than specific assets. The advantage of defining assets by type is that it results in a long, rather than a short, list, as assets that would perform the same function in a portfolio. The approach provides maximum flexibility through the acquisition and divestment processes. The chapter then outlines the implications of a business-development strategy for each. This chapter makes several references to the concepts introduced in Chapter 2.

5.1 OIL

This section explains why it is necessary to differentiate between oil and gas. Section 2.2 contains a more detailed discussion on the different types of oil and gas fields, and, as that section illustrates, there is a continuum in oil and gas content across the different field types. While there is a natural continuum in oil and gas fields, the processing, transportation, and marketing of oil and gas are very different. In this section, the focus is on the business implications of the methods used in processing, transportation, and marketing of oil. There is a discussion on the energy transition, long-term oil demand, and tactics for mitigating demand decline. Gas is discussed separately in section 5.2, but we will start by explaining the key differences between the two.

5.1.1 Key Differences Between Oil and Gas

The most obvious difference is that oil is a liquid at atmospheric temperature and pressure, while gas is a gas. This phase difference means that oil and gas are processed, transported, and stored differently, with oil being the simpler of the two fuels. Simpler processing reduces facilities cost, and ease of transportation, storage, and global trading means that oil fields are less sensitive to location and market access than gas fields, although development and transportation are still more expensive in remote or challenging environments.

This fundamental physical difference drives differences in their application. Oil is primarily a transportation fuel and petrochemical feedstock. It is also used as a heating fuel and for power generation in certain circumstances, although most OECD countries transitioned from oil-fired to gas- or coal-fired power stations during the oil shocks of the 1970s. Gas is used for power generation, heating, cooking, and petrochemicals.

The physical and product differences between the two fuels have resulted in differences in how they are marketed—gas markets are primarily local or regional, whereas oil markets are global.

These differences are also reflected in the relative value of the two fuels. The United States, which has both a functioning oil market and a functioning gas market, is one of the regions where a direct cost comparison can be made on an energy-equivalent basis. On a given day in 2020, West Texas Intermediate was trading at $41.05/barrel, the equivalent of $7.20/MMBtu, whereas gas at Henry Hub was trading at $2.62/MMBtu. Over the previous 12-month period, West Texas Intermediate had been as high as $65.65/barrel, the equivalent of $11.50/MMBtu, whereas the highest natural-gas price over the same period had been $2.96/MMBtu. This isn't a good period to look at low prices, as, during this period, one West Texas Intermediate crude futures contract had turned negative for the first time in history, as traders who were not in a position to take physical delivery struggled to offload their contracts on settlement day. There are examples of effective negative gas prices as well; in some sub-regions of the United States, the Permian, for example, transportation and processing capacity for gas had failed to keep pace with production, resulting in operators paying midstream companies to take their gas. In general, oil is a more expensive fuel than gas on an energy-equivalent basis; all else being equal, from the upstream-development perspective, it can be thought of as more valuable. As we discuss in this section, all else is not equal, which tilts the value equation further in the direction of oil.

5.1.2 Oil Processing, Storage, and Transportation

Oil is processed in two stages—in the first stage it is processed at the production site, in the second it is refined into oil products. Producing and processing oil is referred to in the oil and gas industry as Upstream. Transportation and storage of processed oil is a Midstream activity. Refining processed oil is known in the oil and gas industry as Downstream. In this section, we will look at Upstream and Midstream requirements, as Midstream has a direct bearing on Upstream activities.

Crude-oil processing is a lot simpler than gas. Crude oil from an oil well, known as the well stream, is routed into a series of pressurized tanks, known as separators, each one at lower pressure than the last, designed to separate oil, gas, and water. In oil production, the purpose of this process is to remove water and other impurities, stabilize the oil for storage and transportation, and maximize extraction of hydrocarbons.

Water is produced as part of the wellstream and can promote corrosion in storage, transportation, and refining. As the oil producer pays for storage and transportation by volume and produced water has no value, there is also an economic incentive to remove as much water from the well stream as possible. Produced water is either injected back into the reservoir for pressure maintenance—or just for disposal—or, if the regulatory regime allows, disposed of overboard. The maximum amount of water allowed for storage or transportation is specified as a percentage volume. Impurities such as salt and hydrogen sulfide must be reduced to threshold levels. Stabilization involves reducing the amount of gas that the crude oil will release at a given pressure and temperature, specified as the "vapor pressure" of the crude. The purpose of oil processing is to bring these parameters within the specified ranges for storage or transportation.

Once oil has been processed, it can be stored on location in a tank farm or floating storage unit, or it can be transported by pipeline, rail car, truck, or tanker. Over long distances, tankers are the most efficient mode of transport, and, so, most large field development will aim to bring the crude oil to a deepwater port. As discussed in section 2.2, oil production will always involve a degree of associated gas production, and, so, commercialization or disposal of associated gas is a further consideration. Gas can be used for fuel, reinjected, or processed and sold, or some combination of all three. In some field developments, gas is re-injected into the main oil reservoir or into a separate structure and produced and sold later. As discussed in section 2.3, gas can be injected to improve oil recovery as well as for temporary storage; these additional benefits should be considered in the analysis of options. Handling small amounts of associated gas can often be an additional cost rather than a benefit—this is why associated gas is still often flared in many parts of the world. Given the increasing societal focus on climate change, flaring of gas for economic reasons is something that will become increasingly difficult to justify.

5.1.3 Oil Marketing

Oil is priced off global, or in the case of the United States, regional, benchmarks at a premium or discount, depending on its quality. The United States regional benchmark, West Texas Intermediate, emerged in 1981, when the United States government ended price controls and from then until 2011 traded at a premium to Brent, the international benchmark. WTI, as a grade, is sweeter and lighter than Brent, and, so, a premium would be expected based on fundamentals. From 2011 onward, it traded at a discount, as increasing United States shale production exhausted storage capacity in Cushing, Oklahoma, and a lack of national pipeline infrastructure meant it was difficult to move the crude to refineries around the country. As United States shale production continued to rise through the first half of the decade, the differential between WTI and Brent Crude widened, until, in 2016, the United States Congress lifted a forty-year ban on crude-oil exports. This narrowed the Brent premium, but it began to widen again in the second half of the decade, as the United States continued to struggle with the logistics of transporting domestic crude to refineries around the country.

Heavier oil, which has a higher proportion of long hydrocarbons, is typically less valuable than lighter oil, because it yields lower proportions of higher-value products when refined. Oil that contains sulfur also sells at a discount, as the sulfur must be removed prior to refining.

The extent of the differential in the discount or premium of a given grade varies with geography and time. The United States Gulf Coast refining system has historically imported heavy, sour grades from Venezuela and Mexico, and has refineries that are configured for these grades. As United States shale-oil production, which is light and sweet, increased, and Mexican and Venezuelan production declined, the discount for their heavy, sour grades narrowed as those grades became increasingly sought after to blend with the new shale production. These changes will impact project economics at the margins, but there are some crudes that make development prohibitive. Crude with a high total acid number or crudes that contain high proportions of heavy metals[109] introduce a very significant discount over the marker crude, to the extent that the development of these fields may never be economically viable.

Oil fields are generally more attractive than gas fields, with a higher-value product and less of the commercial complexity that comes with gas or gas-condensate fields. Gas has two major benefits over oil. Gas is still sometimes sold under long-term contracts, and, so, there can be less price volatility, although many long-term contracts are indexed to oil. The second is that the combustion of gas emits less CO_2 than the combustion of oil. As climate change moves up the social and political agenda of an increasing number of governments, the carbon intensity of a fuel becomes an increasingly important consideration.

Gas is a more economic and environmentally friendly solution than oil for power generation, heating, and cooking and, so, has displaced oil in those applications. There are, of course, other even more environmentally friendly solutions to power generation than gas, such as wind and solar, but the general view is that gas will continue to have a future in power generation because of its flexibility, as discussed in more detail in section 5.2. Oil still has the advantage as a mobility fuel and in certain petrochemical applications, but both of these markets are under threat—from the transition to electric vehicles and from another societal trend toward a reduction in the use of plastics.

5.1.4 Long-Term Oil Demand

These challenges call into question the long-term trajectory of oil demand and introduce the threat that part of the upstream oil and gas companies' portfolios may become stranded—the resource exists, but it cannot be economically recovered.

There is little consensus on the direction of long-term oil demand. According to some forecasts, it has already peaked, whereas other forecasters believe that it will continue to grow at about 50% of the annual rate of GDP growth for decades to come. In 2019, the world consumed almost 100 million barrels of oil per day. When discussing oil demand, this is crude oil plus natural gas liquids.

Figure 32 shows a comparison of long-term oil demand forecasts[110,111,112,113].

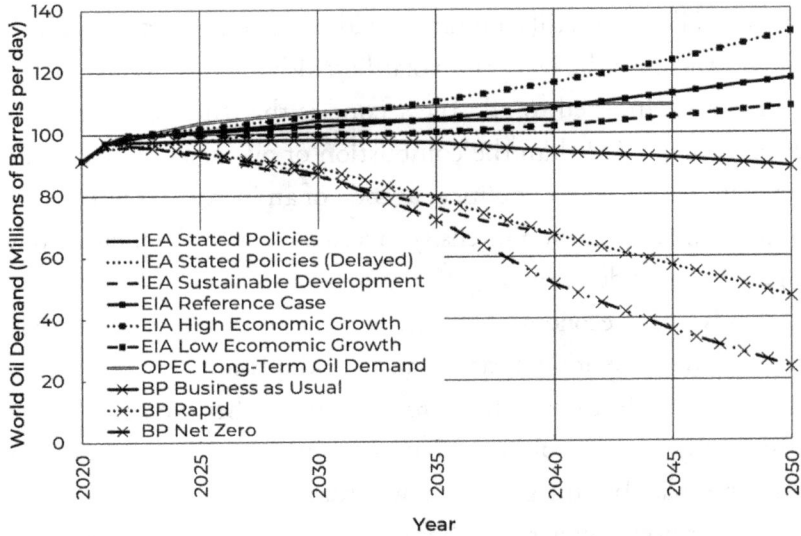

FIGURE 32: Comparison of Long-Term Oil Demand Forecasts

According to some forecasts, oil demand has already peaked, while others see it continuing to grow for decades to come. The only conclusion that can really be drawn from this chart is that the future of oil demand is highly uncertain, a major obstacle for a capital-intensive industry. As oil is a commodity, declining demand will depress prices until the marginal producer is forced out of the market.

There are three basic strategies for mitigating this risk:

➲ Diversify
➲ Limit Cycle Time
➲ Minimize Break-Even Price

Diversification

Diversification involves increasing investment in gas, or even renewables, rather than oil. As discussed later in this chapter, estimates of future gas demand are generally more optimistic than those for oil, and, as a result, there is less concern about demand destruction and the creation of stranded assets. In some markets, traditional gas developments offer some protection from demand destruction, as gas is normally sold under long-term contracts, and the producer and user of gas are physically tied together by infrastructure. Highly developed gas markets—like the United States—or LNG, which can be traded globally, do not offer these kinds of protections.

Figure 33, below, shows the relative proportion of oil and gas production for the major IOCs for 2019[114,115,116,117,118,119]. The IOCs fall in a surprisingly narrow band, with oil production between 50% and 60% of their overall production, with the two United States-headquartered companies, Exxon and Chevron, at the oilier end.

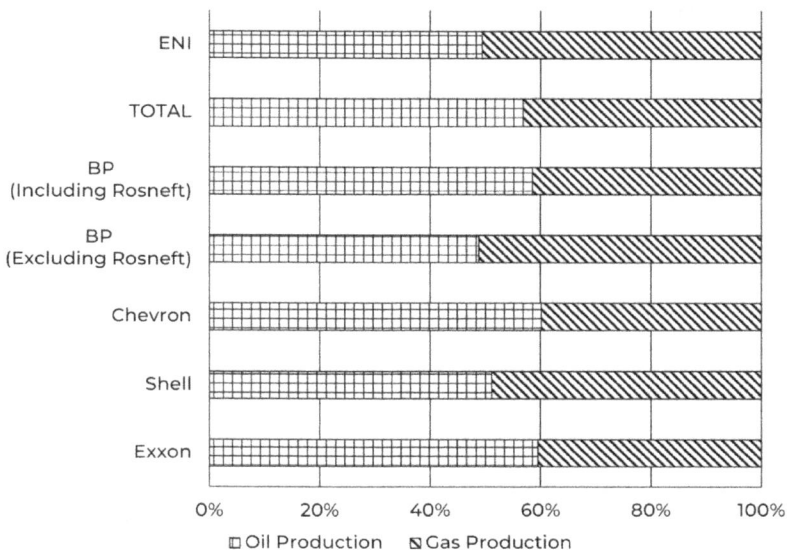

FIGURE 33: IOC Relative Oil and Gas Production 2019

Diversification, especially by the largest IOCs, has increasingly come to mean investment in renewable technologies such as wind, solar, hydrogen, and biofuels, and the transmission and delivery of electricity. Diversification into these areas is a more certain way to eliminate the risk of demand erosion, but a transition to renewables is not explored in this book for two reasons. The first is that, while both involve energy, renewables and upstream oil and gas don't have a lot in common. As such, the sections of this book dealing with portfolio design, organizational capability, and asset characteristics would be completely different for renewables-focused businesses. The second is that there is still a question mark over whether an upstream oil, gas, and renewables firm is really a viable business model. There are already established companies that generate electricity from renewable, hydrocarbon, and nuclear sources—utilities. It is not clear why an oil and gas company would be better at this than the present incumbents. Oil and gas companies have attempted to diversify in this way in the past. Shell entered both the nuclear (energy) and mining (extractive) industries, only to exit both again after poor performance, refocusing on oil and gas.

Limit Cycle Time

The second mitigation against demand destruction is to compress cycle times—that is, to reduce the amount of time required to discover, develop, and produce from the field. The industry has been focused on this issue for at least two decades and has tried a number of approaches, with varying success. In deepwater exploration, for example, pre-planning contingent appraisal wells allows the drilling rig to move straight from exploration to appraisal, depending on the results of the initial well. This approach has successfully reduced the exploration and appraisal cycle.

Attempts to compress the decision-making phases—concept selection and concept definition—by standardizing on subsea-system design and host type have seen some success on super-giant fields such as the Brazilian pre-salt or the more recent discoveries offshore Guyana. In these cases, the fields will ultimately require multiple hosts to develop, and, so, there is little optimization required and much value to be gained in accelerating production. Attempts to standardize on host and subsea designs across individual hub-class fields have been less successful. The idea here is to reduce the number of decisions that need to be made and options that should be considered. There is also a perceived benefit that flows over into the design and construction phases—in theory, detail design drawings can be re-used, and a fabricator should improve with experience. In practice, these benefits are rarely recognized—fields are too different to accept standard solutions. Given the low number of projects and advances in design codes, detail design is still repeated, and contractors have proven resistant to providing a fabrication discount.

Different contracting strategies have been used, again with varying degrees of success. Frame agreements avoid the need to renegotiate terms and conditions but limit the operator's commercial freedom. They can work well for simple things, like line pipe, where quality and terms can be easily specified but become exponentially more difficult as complexity increases.

The author had successful experience exercising a contract option on simple offshore tie-back; in this case, it was for a third, unmanned facility that did not include any processing. There was no time-saving in terms of design and construction, but the tendering and award process was accelerated by as much as six months, and a cost saving in staff time was realized over that period. The author also had experience of an attempt to negotiate a frame agreement for an FPSO; in this case, there was no cost or time saving in any phase; this was a step too far in terms of complexity.

The common and consistent refrain from the contractor community is that they can add value and reduce cycle times if they are engaged earlier in the process. The author has yet to see any evidence that this is the case, as the contractors who execute projects have little understanding or expertise in the front-end process, dominated as it is by subsurface disciplines. The upstream oil and gas industry has been notoriously successful at commoditizing its contractor base, and this kind of early engagement is more likely to be an attempt to reduce their clients' commercial options and improve their margins.

These are all examples of things that can be done to compress cycle times, but these are all things that result in small improvements, and they are not without risk. Research on the subject has shown that ultimate project value—as well as execution schedule—is improved by spending more time on front-end definition: going slow to go fast.[120]

There is one field type where this guideline doesn't hold, and that is shale oil. Shale oil, particularly in the United States, has some unusual characteristics that result in very short cycle times. First, while there is variability in reservoir productivity, there is no uncertainty as to reservoir presence, and, so, there is no exploration or appraisal risk, or phase. Development planning and definition are simple and standardized, equipment consists of stock items, and execution contractors are readily available. This resource type naturally lends itself to phasing. This compresses lead time from initial investment to production. On the production side, shale-oil wells exhibit such aggressive declines as a result of fracture stimulation that half of the economic value of the well can be delivered in the first year of production. While the well will continue to produce at low rates for many years, that initial year is of critical importance to the overall success of the well. This allows a substantial proportion of production to be hedged, at the point in time where the decision is made to proceed with the investment. Shale oil does offer a genuine way to limit cycle times and, so, can form an important part of a diversified portfolio.

Minimize Break-Even Price

The third strategy that can be adopted to mitigate the risk of declining oil demand is to aim to have the lowest break-even prices. The theory here is that, as oil is a commodity, the highest-cost producers will be forced from the market first as demand declines. This makes intuitive sense but requires some more examination.

The first thing to consider is the definition of "break-even price." Is that life cycle or point forward? Is it for an individual well, an entire asset, or the company as a whole? Is it discounted, and, if so, at what rate? Is this an expectation case or a low-price-premise case?

Investment decisions should be taken on a life-cycle basis but will, in practice, be taken on a point-forward basis. Existing production may have a higher break-even than a new project on a life-cycle basis, but on a point-forward basis, it will almost always be lower, as the capital outlay is a sunk cost. Take the example of a deepwater hub-class development approaching Final Investment Decision. The field has a very competitive break-even of $30/barrel on a life-cycle basis, compared to the $100/barrel life-cycle break-even cost for oil-sands projects. On a life-cycle basis, production from the new deepwater hub should displace production from the existing oil-sands project. However, the capital for that oil-sands project is already a sunk cost, and its ongoing operating cost is only $7/barrel. It is that cost, the go-forward cost of $7 per barrel, against which the new deepwater hub will have to compete. There will be no displacement, just additional, excess production, which pushes down the price. This example is intended to illustrate that, while demand continues to rise, life-cycle break-even prices can be less important than investment timing and operating cost.

Once oil demand does begin to decline, then the investment dynamic will shift dramatically. There are *almost* no new developments that can compete with existing production on break-even price. As illustrated above, break-even means life cycle for pre-FID projects, whereas it means operating cost for post-FID projects. The word *almost* is used because, as usual, there are exceptions. There will be fields in the Middle East whose life-cycle cost will be lower than the operating costs of some existing fields, but those exceptions aside, the kind of long-term exploration and development that has characterized the industry to date will be difficult to sustain.

Looking at individual-well or project-break-even prices can be informative as a useful point of comparison, but what really matters is the corporate break-even, and what really matters there is undiscounted cash flow. If the corporate base case is a scenario in which oil demand is in sustained decline, then it is hard to see the case for further investment, as even the best new products will struggle to compete with existing production. At this point, the concept of break-even prices becomes irrelevant, as there are no investment decisions to be made. Existing production will decline until individual fields are sub-economic, at which point, they will be abandoned.

If the corporate base case is continued demand growth or even stable demand, then demand destruction should be tested, as a scenario, as outlined in Chapter 3. It isn't a primary decision-making criterion; it's a stress test on the entire organization: *How low can the price go before the corporation risks insolvency?* Therefore, it is the corporate perspective that is important. Undiscounted cash flow, rather than an economic metric like NPV, should be considered.

5.1.5 Conclusion

Oil is generally the more valuable commodity than gas, as it is easier to process, store, and transport; global spot and futures markets are well established. It is the world's preeminent mobility fuel and has fewer potential substitutes in mobility than gas has in power generation. The long-term-demand outlook for oil is, however, uncertain, and there are no copper-bottomed strategies for mitigating stranded-asset risk once demand does peak and decline. Next, we will look at gas, with natural gas liquids and LNG included in the gas section.

5.2 GAS

What do we mean when we talk about gas fields? In the same way that oil fields contain varying amounts of gas, gas fields contain varying amounts of oil, or liquid hydrocarbons. This continuum is described in section 2.2, and with reference to that section, when we talk about gas fields here, we are talking about:

- Dry-gas fields
- Wet-gas fields
- Retrograde-condensate fields

Gas fields are more commercially complex than oil fields, and viability is dependent on some additional factors—size, productivity, composition, setting, and geography—coming together in the right way. In this section, we will talk first about why and how gas is processed and then about how it is transported and marketed in its different components or forms. Finally, as with oil, we will look at long-term gas demand and strategies for stranded-asset mitigation.

5.2.1 Gas Processing

Gas processing is the term used to describe the treatment of well-stream gas. Gas processing has four main objectives:

- To mitigate flow-assurance risks.
- To meet export-pipeline, LNG, or customer specifications.
- To maximize the value of the product.
- To facilitate field development.

The type and extent of gas processing can vary, depending on the objective.

When gas is transported from the wellhead to a processing facility, storage, or an end user, the gas has to be treated to mitigate flow-assurance risks—these are, typically, slugging caused by water, hydrocarbons condensing in a line, hydrate formation caused by entrained water in the gas, and corrosion caused by wellstream impurities.

Gas transportation and sales specifications will typically include limits on water and impurities such as mercury, sulfur, and CO_2. They will also include a composition range expressed as a heating value in British Thermal Units (Btu) per standard cubic feet (scf), which is used to describe the richness of the gas.

As discussed in section 2.2, the liquids associated with production from wet or rich gas can be more valuable than the gas stream itself. In these circumstances, it is sometimes worth additional investment in processing equipment to separate these streams—to strip out natural gas liquids or increase the condensate yield, as the sum of the revenue from these individual streams can exceed the value of selling the gas stream, even accounting for the increased capital cost.

Finally, there are circumstances in which gas-processing requirements are dictated by the overall field-development plan. One example of this would be where the development of the field has run ahead of the development of gas infrastructure. In this case, the gas stream can be stripped of liquids and reinjected for storage, until the gas infrastructure is available, and the field can switch over to gas export. Another example of this would be where gas is stripped of liquids and processed and re-injected to maintain pressure and maximize liquid yield. As in the first example, gas can then be produced and exported at the tail end of field life.

Gas processing is usually undertaken in two phases. There is an initial field-processing phase, where associated gas from the oil separator or the wellstream gas is prepared for transportation, and a gas-processing phase, where the gas is processed to sales specification. Field processing involves the removal of water, some impurities, and liquid hydrocarbons. The first stage uses separation, like the separators employed in oil processing. This removes the heavier oil fractions and free water. In addition to this first stage of separation, the water vapor that exists in solution with natural gas must be removed. This involves a process known as dehydration, which relies on chemicals such as glycol or desiccants to remove this water vapor from the gas stream. Finally, natural gas liquids are removed, using either chemical or cryogenic processes, discussed in more detail later in this section.

The split between field processing and gas processing is dependent on the gas source and transportation and sales specifications. A remote offshore gas field, supplying a single customer, would have to process gas to meet that customer's specification. This could involve offshore field processing, to facilitate transportation, and onshore processing to sales specification, as many of the technologies involved in removing natural gas liquids, in particular, are very expensive to bring offshore. On the other hand, a gas field, or associated gas from an oil field, in the United States Gulf of Mexico, may require only limited field processing to meet third-party transportation requirements. There are a number of specialist midstream companies, such as Enbridge, who operate their own gas-gathering, transportation, and processing systems along the United States Gulf Coast. They will either buy the gas directly from the operator or charge gathering, transportation, and processing fees to deliver gas to sales specification.

5.2.2 Gas Transportation and Marketing

Whereas oil marketing is global, gas transportation and marketing is regional or local. Gas does not sell at a premium or discount based on quality in the same away that oil does; rather, gas typically has a delivery specification. Gas is either sold under long-term contact, sometimes with an index to oil prices, or is priced off regional gas benchmarks. The best example is Henry Hub in the United States, which is a natural-gas pipeline in Louisiana that serves as the official delivery location for gas futures contracts on the New York Mercantile Exchange (NYMEX). There are also other international pricing points in the UK, Europe, and Asia.

Generally speaking, in North America, gas is transported via pipeline at spot prices. North America is an LNG exporter, and there is no scope for LNG import. The European market is mainly pipeline based, with most gas now sold at spot prices—in 2018, 75% of gas was sold in this way[121]. There is some scope for LNG import at the margin, but these must compete with pipeline gas on an economic basis. In contrast, the Asian market is dominated by LNG, with long-term contracts still making up 66% of LNG deliveries.[122] Africa is a large gas supplier of gas, but there is little domestic market. Some parts of the Middle East, like Qatar and Iran, are gas rich, while Saudi Arabia has long sought to find domestic gas supplies and burns crude oil for power generation instead.

Like processing, gas transportation is very setting-dependent. Very large gas fields close to demand centers—Western Europe or the United States, for example—can be developed via pipeline. Until recently, development of these gas fields would have required the producer to enter into long-term sales contracts, but both Western Europe and the United States have developed active spot and futures markets for gas sales. Gronigen is an example of a dry-gas field that was fortuitously located, next to a major population and industrial center. The need to secure a right of way for the pipeline is also a consideration here.

There are local as well as regional gas markets. This is where the gas is used locally for power generation, cooking, heating, or petrochemicals. In these cases, the producer is captive to their customer, which requires that appropriate payment guarantees are in place before either the upstream or downstream projects can proceed. This one of the reasons why these projects often take many years to move forward or fail to move forward at all.

The regional and local nature of gas markets drive gas-marketing decisions. A gas field in North America can be commercialized easily, but prices are very low. A gas field in Europe is easier to commercialize and will provide better margins. Very large gas fields—or smaller gas fields with access to LNG-export facilities, as in Nigeria—can target the Asian market. Smaller fields outside North America and Europe will need to find or develop a domestic buyer for their gas.

For smaller gas fields, location near a demand center is critical. Gas fields that have not been developed because of their distance from market are referred to as *stranded* gas fields. Gas fields in the United States or western Europe have a ready source of demand. Small gas fields in other locations where export is not a realistic option may require a complementary investment in power generation or petrochemicals, to create demand for the gas. Such an arrangement would need to be underpinned by long-term contracts. The commercial complexity associated with gas development means that their development timelines are typically longer than for oil. Most fiscal regimes have been designed to accommodate this, allowing longer license periods in each phase.

Large-scale LNG requires a source of recoverable gas of at least 4 trillion cubic feet and, so, is applicable only at scale. The industry has converged on a standard size for a liquefaction plant of about 5 million tonnes per annum or LNG, which is about 600 million cubic feet per day of gas. Each of these liquefaction plants is known as a train, and an LNG development usually consists of multiple trains, allowing for phasing of development and flexibility in future expansion.

LNG will necessitate the removal of LPGs and other impurities, prior to liquefaction, but as LNG requires scale for economic viability, those LPG yields should be material. In addition to liquefaction facilities, LNG requires specially designed LNG carriers and the regasification terminal on the receiving end. LNG carriers can be built and owned or leased, and there is now an extensive secondary market in short-term LNG carrier charters. LNG regasification terminals are widespread and normally owned by energy companies, local governments or utilities, or some combination thereof through a joint venture.

Small scale and merchant LNG—leasing small LNG vessels—was an emerging technology some years ago. The idea is to use a small, floating LNG facility that can be relocated from field to field to develop stranded gas fields. The technology is established, but the economics of this approach have yet to be proven. In addition to losing economies of scale, the cost of gas processing on a small scale can be prohibitive.

LNG has traditionally been sold under long-term contracts, indexed to oil. Given the scale of the investment required and the lack of an international market, this is the only way that these kinds of projects could receive financing. Over recent years, this has started to change. Initially, this was driven by traditional providers selling surplus cargoes, but the abundance of North American gas, driven by United States shale-oil development, created a class of merchant LNG suppliers such as Cheniere, who traded on gas-price differentials between North America, Europe, and Asia, using Henry Hub-linked formulas and fees to trade natural gas.

An integrated gas field and LNG development are at the upper end of the spectrum for capital intensity and technical and commercial complexity; they require a substantial balance sheet and organizational capability. If the organization does not have LNG experience, then this is an example of when farming down to bring in expertise or developing expertise through farming into a new project would be beneficial.

5.2.3 Natural Gas Liquids

Natural Gas Liquids (NGLs) is a term used to describe a group of hydrocarbon molecules from ethanes to pentanes. Many of the supply and demand issues associated with NGLs were addressed in section 5.1, but NGLs have some distinct characteristics that warrant discussion. Figure 34 conforms to the definition provided by the International Gas Union's Natural Gas Conversion Guide[123] and provides a good overview of the overlap in application and terminologies of the different molecules that are collectively classified as NGLs.

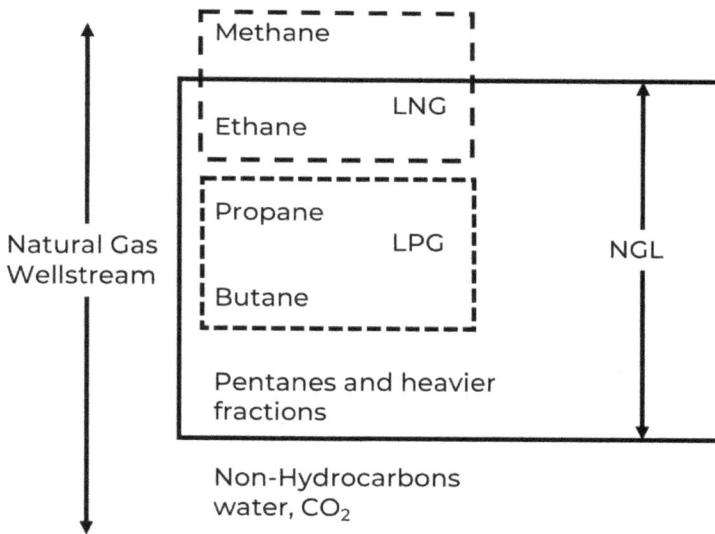

FIGURE 34: Wet Gas Components

LNG consists primarily of methane, with some ethane. Richer LNG cargoes such as those from Libya and Abu Dhabi are up to 13% ethane.[124] LNG also includes heavier NGLs, but in small proportions—less than 5% propane and less than 1.5% C4+. The higher the proportion of heavier molecules, the higher the calorific value of the LNG.

In addition to LNG, ethane can be used to create ethylene, which is a feedstock for the petrochemical industry. One of the side effects of the surge in United States shale production, which results in the production of large amounts of gas as well as oil, was a huge expansion of ethylene-production capacity along the United States Gulf Coast.

Liquified Petroleum Gas (LPG) is used as a cooking and heating fuel as well as a transport fuel. LPG is transported in pressurized tanks by road, rail, boat, or pipeline. Condensate consists of the C5+ fractions removed from a natural gas stream, primarily pentane and hexane. Condensate is usually liquid at ambient conditions and, so, is treated like a light crude oil. It can be transported in bulk in oil tankers rather than chemical or product tankers. Condensate is often blended with heavy crudes to raise the API and thus the value of the crude stream.

NGLs add value to a gas development but also introduce costs in processing complexity, transportation, and marketing. In addition to NGL extraction, more consideration must be given to processing wet gas close to the wellhead, to prevent flow-assurance issues caused by liquid drop-out in pipelines.

In traditional, smaller-scale developments, condensate can be removed easily and treated as a high-value oil stream, but ethane and LPGs can be more problematic in small volumes. The gas will have to meet a sales specification that may require the removal of LPGs and reduction in ethane. If the specification can be met untreated and the volumes are small, it may be more economic to remove condensate but leave the other NGLs in the gas stream. If not, then NGL removal through absorption, cryogenic expansion, and fractionation will be required, which yields valuable product streams but at the expense of additional processing complexity and cost.

Acquisition or divestment of a field with NGLs requires a careful assessment of the costs and benefits of the different product streams in the context of the local market. In a region where there are existing ethylene plants and a market for LPG as a heating or cooking fuel, then small-scale development is viable. In a gas-to-power project, where the gas specification of the power station is undefined, it may make more economic sense to specify a richer gas for the plant and minimize processing. A large field may be able to support investment in an ethylene plant on a stand-alone basis, an investment that would also be politically astute, as it retains a value-adding activity within country. NGLs need careful consideration, given the specific circumstance of the asset.

5.2.4 Long-Term Gas Demand

Natural gas is the cleanest-burning fossil fuel and has the lowest carbon footprint. The future for global gas demand is less divergent than the forecasts for oil, with most institutions predicting demand growth through to 2030 and many predicting continued growth beyond. A selection of long-term gas-demand forecasts is shown in Figure 35, below[125,126,127]. Gas is often discussed as a transition fuel, and displacing coal-fired with gas-fired power generation is one of the most cost-effective ways to reduce carbon-dioxide emissions[128]. There is also an emerging school of thought that gas should not be considered as an energy-transition bridge fuel, and that, instead, society should jump straight to renewables. As gas is used for power generation, heating, and cooking, there are more substitutes available than for a mobility fuel like oil.

The outlook for LNG should track the global outlook for gas, and, in general, demand should increase. The picture is a little more complex, though, as the construction of new LNG liquefaction capacity is lumpier than the introduction of new gas fields. Heavy recent investment in liquification capability along the United States Gulf Coast, combined with a decline in demand caused by COVID-19, sees the global supply of LNG outstripping supply. Existing capacity and capacity under construction are expected to outstrip demand through the rest of the decade, but beyond

2030, continued strong-demand growth will require investment in additional capacity[129].

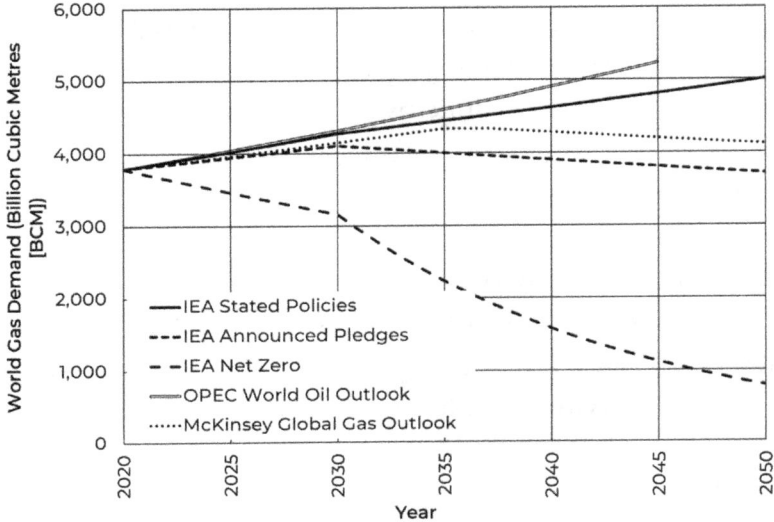

FIGURE 35: Long-Term Gas Demand

In piped gas markets, the gas source is physically linked to the customer, and, whether that gas is used for power generation, heating, or cooking, the customer has invested in the equipment compatible with that gas supply. It is costly for the customer to switch to a substitute energy source or a different gas supplier. Even with spot market pricing, this sort of mutually beneficial relationship insulates the gas producer from stranded-asset risk to a greater degree than the oil producer. LNG is a little closer to the oil market, with suppliers at greater risk. Here, the mitigations discussed in section 5.1.4 are applicable.

5.2.5 Conclusion
Gas is generally less valuable and more commercially complex to develop than oil. It is, however, cleaner, and demand should continue

to grow well into the second half of the century. The difficulties in storing and transporting gas also serve to insulate it, to a degree, from stranded asset risk.

5.3 MATERIALITY

The third characteristic to consider is the materiality of the asset; in other words, *How large is it relative to your existing portfolio?* This is a primary consideration for three reasons. In the first instance, holding all other characteristics equal, price will roughly correlate with materiality. Thus, materiality, in conjunction with the other desired characteristics, can provide a quick, rough first cut at a coveted asset list.

The second consideration is that all upstream oil- and gas-asset transactions are large, and, so, the difference in corporate band-width required to execute a small upstream oil and gas transaction is similar to that required to execute a large upstream oil and gas transaction. It is not the case that twenty $100 million transactions take the same time and effort as a $2 billion transaction; each one probably takes half as much. Therefore, it is more efficient in terms of time and resources to focus on a few, more material, transactions than on a large number of smaller ones.

The same consideration is at work for a seller. A common reason for a large company to divest an asset is that it is no longer mate-rial. An asset producing a few thousand barrels a day absorbs the same kind of staff and management attentions as one producing fifty thousand barrels per day. At some point, it is more efficient for a large organization to reallocate its management focus and staff resources to more significant assets. This creates a market in high-quality assets for smaller buyers.

The third consideration when it comes to materiality is the impact of the acquisition on support functions, something that is linked to the geography, maturity, and operating structure. The acquisition of an asset in a new geography introduces additional SG&A costs disproportionate to the size of the acquisition. Acquisition in a new geography usually requires the buyer to establish a local office, which will introduce some inefficiencies through replication of corporate capability and additional integration and reporting requirements. Corporate functions such as finance, legal, HR, IT, HSE, and security will have to expand their capacity to accommodate the additional geography, something that is discussed in more detail in section 5.6. The extent of this expansion is, to a degree, dependent on the maturity and operating structure of the acquisition. A Non-Operated Working Interest in an exploration opportunity does not normally require the participant to create an in-country presence and will provide some additional workload only to finance and legal, in addition to the technical team. At the other end of the spectrum, an Operated Working Interest in a producing asset will require a substantial in-country presence and a significant increase in workload across all ancillary functions.

The same consideration comes into play with a divestment. The operational cost reduction achieved by a country exit goes far beyond the operational cost reduction of divesting the asset alone. Therefore, a full country exit can be more impactful in simplifying the business and lowering costs than exiting assets across a number of countries. This simplification must be balanced against the inherent benefit of geographical diversity.

What constitutes materiality is difficult to define; it's a little like the famous judicial definition of obscenity—that you will know it when you see it. Production is one metric, if the asset is producing; acreage and resources are others. A company with production of 200,000 barrels/day of production that acquired a non-operating interest in a field that yielded net production of 2,000 barrels/day would not be material. But 20,000 barrels/day would be material, and 50,000 barrels/day would be transformational.

Not all acquisition or divestment needs to be material, provided that there is another strategic reason for their execution—developing expertise in new technology, entering a new geography, or acquiring a new commercial skill. Under such circumstances, there are good reasons to proceed with an acquisition or divestment even if they are not material. In fact, if the primary aim is to expand organizational capability, then it may be preferable to make the investment immaterial.

5.4 MATURITY

The maturity of an asset is an important consideration for both buyers and sellers. Not only does maturity have a direct impact on portfolio composition, but, given the way in which hydrocarbons are matured, acquiring or divesting at different stages means stepping into or out of different risks. The international oil and gas industry has adopted a relatively uniform description for the maturity of assets; this system is discussed in section 5.4 of this book. This section discusses considerations associated with each stage in the context of acquisition and divestment activity.

5.4.1 Exploration

The exploration phase is where oil and gas are discovered and the most value is added. This is where the variance in both view and outcome are the greatest.

Exploration-phase assets can be accessed either directly from a host-country government or through farming into a lease that has already been awarded. The process by which leases are auctioned varies from country to country. The more established basins will typically hold regular auctions—the United States Gulf of Mexico or the UK North Sea (UKNS)—while countries that do not yet have an established industry may have a system of open application—Greenland, for example. Where leases are awarded at auction, the host-country government will define the biddable components. These could be a signature bonus and work program or, in some cases, components of the fiscal regime—royalty, for example. The more prospective the basin, the more competitive the bidding.

In most cases, the winner of a lease at auction will seek to farm-down some of their working interest in order to spread risk. This farm-down is normally structured as either a swap or a promote, with companies seeking to spread their risk over a number of prospects.

Unless it is infrastructure-led, exploration is a long-term commitment, requiring years of work and investment to understand a basin, a real possibility of failure, and years before any production will be realized, even in the success case. Exploration should form part of every oil company's portfolio, but it is a long-term commitment that relies on both a portfolio and a campaign approach.

A portfolio approach is required in terms of selecting the basins that you are going to target. A mix of high-impact, high-risk wells—the Frontier or Emerging play types discussed in chapter 2—needs to be balanced with lower-impact, lower-risk wells—the Maturing or Mature play types. The statistics referenced in section 2.7.1 suggest that the best approach to exploration is to focus on emerging plays, but this ignores the benefit of a more mature oil province that may have a more mature regulatory regime and developed infrastructure. This established capability shortens cycle times, keeping basins relevant in your portfolio as they mature.

There are still examples of oil companies drilling an exploration well in a new basin and striking oil, but this should not be the expectation. A company must drill nine independent wells to have a 50% probability of making one or more commercial discoveries in a frontier play.[130] While the odds are not as bad for emerging, maturing, and mature plays, it takes time for a company to develop basin-specific skills, and latecomers will be at a comparative disadvantage to early entrants. Thus, a campaign approach is required in each basin. A campaign approach means a multiple-well commitment, with a well sequence designed to gather the most information for the lowest cost, rather than striking oil immediately.

From an acquisition perspective, this means that joint ventures must be employed to spread financial and technical resources across the greatest number of wells. Where you have differentiated expertise in a basin, you should aim to operate wells and bring in partners to help fund. Where you believe you have transferable technical skills, those are the Frontier plays that you want to focus on. Where you lack technical skills or are late to the game, that is where you want to pursue non-operated positions.

In the case of exploration, divestment will be as active as acquisition. It is inevitable that blocks will rise and fall in perceived value as the exploration campaign reveals itself; a decision will have to be taken about which blocks to relinquish. Being able to anticipate which work-program commitments will not be met allows more time to bring in a partner to carry a well, retain optionality, or divest or swap the block before it is forfeit. The very worst time to start looking for a partner is when an upcoming work-program commitment puts your lease at risk.

5.4.2 Appraisal

Fields in the appraisal phase are those that have been discovered but have not yet been fully delineated. Appraisal-phase acreage is more valuable than exploration acreage as hydrocarbon presence is proven, but there is usually still uncertainty about economic viability.

Some operators look to farm-out during the appraisal period because they need to raise capital to complete their work program. This is a difficult phase for anyone looking to farm-in. Hydrocarbons have been discovered, but there is still substantial doubt over whether the field can ever be developed economically. As hydrocarbons have been discovered, the price will be higher than in the exploration phase—the seller may well be looking for the buyer to fund some or all of the appraisal phase work program. It is also a period of pronounced information asymmetry, as there will not have been a lot of work done that a buyer can look at; the knowledge is in the heads of the seller's staff.

Why would a company farm-down at this point? Some oil companies farm-down fields at this point because, while it is a discovery, it doesn't rank in their portfolio, and they wouldn't get funding for an appraisal campaign otherwise. Other companies simply can't afford to fund appraisal. Some very small operators can pick up relinquished acreage with a discovery well on it for next to nothing and then set about trying to raise capital to fund appraisal. It could also be that, while the exploration well discovered hydrocarbons, some other data point indicated that the field will never ultimately be viable, and they want to recover as much as possible.

Should a company ever farm-in in a situation like this? It depends. If they have no expertise or presence in the basin, it is hard to evaluate, and so it's probably better to wait until it is appraised. On the other hand, it is a relatively low-cost way to enter. If they are already working in the basin, are comfortable with the geology, understand their field, and, crucially, know why they are really farming-out, then it could work. If there is some reason why a deal could be attractive—if you have or will have production facilities, or if you have spare capacity on a rig in the region that could accelerate appraisal, then it might make a lot of sense.

5.4.3 Selection

Selection is the phase where a field has been declared commercial, but work is ongoing to determine the best way to develop it. The end of the selection phase is marked by submission and approval of the Field Development Plan (how the field should be developed) and the Concept Selection Report (why the field should be developed this way). The definition of "best" could be the subject of a book by itself, but this can be an attractive time to farm-in to a field.

At this stage, the field has been declared commercial and is highly likely, though not certain, to move through to production. At this stage, the buyer, as either operator or non-operator, will have the ability to influence the shape of the development—capital cost, schedule, and production—but has not yet actually committed to fund the project. These barrels will be more expensive than in the appraisal phase but cheaper than producing barrels.

If the operator is farming-down at this point, they probably need to raise capital to move forward with the project or to fund projects elsewhere. They may also be looking for a strategic partner that brings some capability that they do not have—experience with the regulator, or technical or commercial expertise. This is the point where many independent exploration-focused companies choose to monetize their investment. If this is a gas or LNG project, the operator may want to sell a portion of their working interest to their customers to help align incentives.

If a non-operator is more likely to farm-out than farm-down at this stage, they may have decided that they don't want exposure to this region or play type anymore, that they have better opportunities elsewhere, or that the execution risk is too high. There are a lot of legitimate reasons that make these good assets to look at.

If a company farms-in as operator at this stage, then they need to consider their existing capability in the location and the play type. Even if they have existing regulatory relationships and a team in place, it is inevitable that there will be a degree of recycle that will push back the development program. If this is a new entry, and they need to establish relationships and understanding of the regulatory regime and technology, then they should assume a longer delay to the phase. This is a good entry point for a non-operator, as there is still an opportunity to influence the outcome and the potential to build capability in the location.

5.4.4 Definition (FEED)

During this phase, the operator will be completing Front End Engineering (FEED) and obtaining bids from contractors to finalize the cost and schedule estimate for Final Investment Decision. This phase will typically run for around 6 months on small projects and 12 to 18 months on major projects.

This is not a stage where the operator should consider farming-out of a field, and, if they do, you should not consider farming-in. An operator who is trying to transfer control of a project, while at the same time completing FEED and preparing a joint venture for a Final Investment Decision (FID) is not going to satisfy all their objectives, the best-case scenario here being a long delay. Operators may consider farming-down some of their working interest, and non-operators may consider farming-out or farming-down. At this stage, the project will be well defined, and either operator or non-operator may choose to farm-down to limit their capital commitment.

This is not an optimal time to consider farming-in to a field development. At this stage, the project has not been sanctioned, but with an approved FDP, the scope has been locked. This means that, absent a long and costly recycle, the scope has been finalized, but the CapEx cost of the project is still unconfirmed. CapEx estimates can be very wrong; the uniqueness of the project can provide some guide to the level of risk here.

The other issue associated with farming-in at this point concerns the degree of control, where there are two separate considerations. As a non-operated partner at this stage, the only remaining control point is Final Investment Decision. Your working interest may be enough to block FID, depending on the JOA, but blocking FID can cause a great deal of damage to the asset. In the best case, the project will need to recycle, wasting tens of millions of dollars and years of work, and, in the worst case, may constitute a failure to fulfill contractual obligations with the government and result in the loss of the asset.

Relationships with joint-venture partners will also be strained by this type of action. The other consideration is the time from completion of the deal to the point at which ownership transfers—transfer or working interest is a government process and can often take in excess of a year. While the acquired working interest may theoretically be sufficient to block an FID, in practice, it may not have transferred prior to FID, preventing exercise of the blocking option.

5.4.5 Execution

During this phase, the operator will be executing the project, and joint-venture partners will have no real influence in its direction. At this stage, the operator should have a good grasp on the cost and schedule of the project, and the buyer should be able to establish an accurate picture of the final outcome. The key uncertainty in this phase is reservoir performance, and, in gauging the potential impact of this, the buyer should consider the maturity of the play and the availability of analog data. In some frontier areas, this can still constitute a substantial risk.

A buyer should never consider assuming operatorship during the execution phase of a project. The track record for major capital-project success, even with premium operators and modern systems, is poor. Stepping in the middle and assuming the existing, partially executed contracts, with a new team, unfamiliar with the project, would prove disastrous.

The execution phase for a major project will typically run for three or more years. It is a period of exposure where the buyer is making payments, but title has yet to transfer; however, it is not significant, as a non-operated partner will have no ability to influence during this phase in any case. Given the speed at which things will move on a project in execution and the timeline for negotiating and closing a deal, both buyer and seller may find it challenging to agree to terms.

5.4.6 Operation

The operations phase follows completion of execution and start-up, and can run for decades. Farming-in to a field that is currently in operation is the lowest risk but also the lowest reward. As the field has been de-risked, the seller will be able to demand a high price for the asset. In addition, as capital has already been spent to develop the field, the buyer cannot use the more tax-efficient "carry" structure and must pay for the asset in cash, unless they can arrange some type of swap. The exception to this is in the case of redevelopment of the field, where use of a carry structure would be dependent on the local tax regime.

Acquisition of fields in operation is suitable for both operator and non-operator. In the operator's case, acquisition of a producing field can make sense if they have other nearby fields in operation and can consolidate support functions. Another case is where the acquiring company has a lower-cost structure than the seller, which allows them to realize additional value from late-life fields. A good example of this is Apache's entry into the North Sea with their purchase of BP's iconic Forties field. Apache, as a smaller company than BP, has a structurally lower operating cost. Forties was more competitive in Apache's portfolio, and, so, they continued to invest.

The case for farming-in to a producing asset on a non-operating basis is less clear. There is the possibility that, due to some combination of circumstances, the seller has to sell, and the buyer gets a great deal. This, however, is where preemption rights come in, as, if the deal is that good, then any other partners are likely to want to take it for themselves and will have the option to do so.

The other reason to farm-in to a producing field as a non-operator is to establish yourself in the region and learn from the operator. This is an expensive and inefficient way to learn, however. There is not a lot of interaction between operator and non-operator during the production phase. Joint-operating teams are not the norm in the same way that joint-development teams are, and there are unlikely to be opportunities for secondment. This approach requires the buyer to establish a side agreement with the operator to facilitate some form of knowledge transfer.

There are some circumstances where it does make sense to take a Non-Operated Working Interest in a producing asset. One situation was where an oil company already had Non-Operated Working Interests in two assets at different stages of development in a country where they had no presence, but which were difficult to manage remotely. They had the opportunity to purchase a special-purpose vehicle, which held non-operating interests in producing assets in that country but also came with an established in-country management subsidiary and management team. The acquisition provided in-country expertise and existing relationships which would have taken many years to build.

5.4.7 Conclusion

As this section highlights, asset maturity is an important consideration when developing an acquisition-and-divestment strategy. Whether a field in one phase or another is a good target for acquisition or divestment is often dependent on the circumstances and role of the buyer and the seller, but it is fair to say that you should never try to take over operatorship of a field in the execution phase.

5.5 SETTING

Setting in this context describes the physical circumstances of the asset and is distinct from geography, which is described in section 5.6. Consideration should be given to physical setting in the acquisition of an asset because it governs many of the key characteristics in the development of an oil and gas field. It governs the cycle time from exploration through development and production, the degree of capital intensity, the technical complexity, and the degree of operator experience required. Setting can be broken down into onshore, shale-oil, shelf, deepwater, and Arctic.

5.5.1 Onshore

Onshore, be it conventional or shale, is straightforward from a technical perspective. Drilling and completions are inexpensive, facilities are simple and low cost, with a diverse contractor base. There is a lot more scope to build production incrementally in an onshore environment, which shortens cycle time and allows a joint venture to achieve break-even quickly.

The complexity with an onshore field is in the relationship with the host community. Whereas other field settings are remote from people, onshore fields may be required to operate with communities around them. Securing a method to export oil or gas, or dispose of water can also present a challenge. Pipelines require right of ways, which may be hard to obtain across a patchwork of privately held land, and transporting by truck or train requires infrastructure—burdening the existing local infrastructure is a sure way to antagonize a local community.

Onshore developments have the least onerous pre-qualification commitments, both technical and financial, even for an operator. The constant contact and critical relationships with the host community mean that an operator must be competent in managing those aspects of the business, as well as in building and maintaining relationships at local-government levels and with the regulator. Onshore developments place a premium on the type of political capability described in section 4.4.2.

The other key consideration with onshore field development in some locations is security. The great benefit of onshore locations is ease of access; the great problem with onshore locations is also ease of access. In some parts of the world, these problems are limited to members of the local community who may inadvertently enter an operational area. Further along the scale, environmental or political activists may attempt to disrupt operations. At an extreme, oil and gas facilities can become targets of organized crime through either oil theft, kidnapping, or ransom and extortion.

While onshore developments are the most straightforward, it would be wrong to think of them as being without risk. Once an operator has fallen foul of a host community, it is much harder to undo that damage than it is to address offshore technical issues. Corrib, which was delayed for the best part of a decade in execution due to a host-community dispute that became a national one, is one of many examples of how badly things can go wrong if these risks are not managed appropriately.

5.5.2 Shale Oil

Many considerations that applied to an onshore environment can apply to shale oil, but shale oil has some distinctive characteristics that deserve a separate discussion. The technical differences are covered in section 2.7.8, and these technical differences drive different development approaches which distinguish shale from other onshore assets.

There are no technical exploration risks with shale oil, although there is a still a commercial-development risk. The absence of exploration risk automatically moves shale-oil fields to the Appraisal phase, greatly reducing financial risk.

With other oil and gas assets, the unit of development is the reservoir or the field; with shale oil, the unit of development is the well. This greatly simplifies the planning process for shale-oil fields, as you need to plan only the well or wells, not the whole field. It greatly reduces cycle time, as not only is the planning process truncated, but the well can be brought onstream as soon as the well is drilled and completed.

A shale-oil well's production is front-loaded—there is high initial production and steep declines. This means that well performance can be assessed quickly—over a few months rather than years—which means appraisal can be completed quickly, and it is quick and easy to test different drilling- and completion-design programs. This front-loaded production, spread across a large number of wells, also means that production can be hedged, largely mitigating price risk.

The absence of technical exploration risk, phased development approach, short cycle times, and ability to hedge make shale oil unique as an asset type in the upstream oil and gas industry. It is the only asset type where investment can be raised and lowered easily in response to an abundance or a shortage of capital.

Shale oil does have some challenges. While there is no technical exploration risk, there is commercial-development risk, and outside of sweet spots, a lot of shale-oil basins require higher-than-average oil prices to make a decent return on capital. Shale oil requires a sophisticated oil field-services industry to make these developments possible—this is where the U.S. has a real advantage. There are also ESG considerations. Flaring from shale wells is common, as, while the well-by-well approach can work with oil, it is harder to apply to gas processing and transportation facilities, so associated gas is often flared. The hydraulic fracturing used to unlock the rock requires a lot of water, which must be sourced and disposed of. There are emerging societal concerns around groundwater contamination and earthquakes that may or may not be linked to hydraulic fracturing.

Despite these concerns, shale retains different characteristics from other asset types, and that makes it valuable as part of any portfolio of assets.

5.5.3 Shelf

The oil industry began onshore and then moved to what is now considered the shallow offshore. There are a lot of definitions of the difference between shelf and deepwater, but there are only two that are really important.

The first is technical and concerns the transition from jack-up drilling to semi-submersible or drill-ship drilling. This transition occurs at about 500 feet water depth, give or take, depending on soil and metocean environment. Fields in less than 500 feet of water depth can be developed from fixed-jacket structures with dry trees and wells drilled from a jack-up. Fixed-jacket structures are cheap and easy to fabricate and install, with facilities around the world. Dry trees avoid the complexity of subsea trees, the specialized fabrication and installation contractors, high costs of subsea equipment, and flow-assurance requirements. Jack-up rigs are far cheaper than semi-submersibles or drill ships and are available around the world. It should be noted that, just because dry trees are possible in this water depth, they are not a requirement. There are still valid reasons for selecting subsea trees on shelf projects.

In more than 500 feet, there is a "transition zone," where fields have been developed using large jackets or concrete gravity-based structures with integrated drilling rigs. These are still dry-tree developments, while the technology of this is different from true deepwater, there is no less technical complexity, and, so, this is classified as deepwater for that reason. Beyond about 1000 feet is true deepwater, with floating production systems and wet trees. Once you have adopted floating production systems and wet trees, water depth is not really relevant. For these reasons, the definition of shelf for the purpose of this discussion is a water depth of less than 500 feet.

A second definition of the difference between offshore and deep-water is in the definitions provided by a host-country regulator. Most countries have different pre-qualification requirements for onshore, shelf, and deepwater, and different fiscal regimes. The differences can be quite stark. In Brazil, for example, an operator can qualify for shallow water (which ANP defines as below 400 meters or approximately 1200 feet), on the basis of the experience of their management team. To pre-qualify as a deepwater operator (which the ANP defines as more than 400 meters water depth), their parent company must have a track record of deepwater production in another country. This is a substantial hurdle and one that a relatively small proportion of oil companies can satisfy.

Technical and regulatory requirements are often misaligned. Again, if we take the example of Brazil, there are numerous fields that are classified as shallow water but which use deepwater production technology—Bauna, for example.

Shelf fields occupy a bit of a sweet spot, as they are remote from host communities, and, as they are difficult to reach, they are naturally more secure. The offshore setting does increase cycle times as offshore requires more planning and is less suited to incremental investment. Shelf-field developments will be quicker than deepwater, but it will still take at least a year to execute, and they are not as well suited to incremental investment, as more planning is required for each subsequent phase than is the case onshore. Capital intensity is a lot lower than deepwater; field developments can be executed from the hundreds of millions to the low billions of dollars. Technology and service providers are available globally.

If we set aside political risk, it is fair to say that today, a company with existing onshore operations or an experienced management team with some financial backing should be able to execute a shelf development with the expectation of success.

5.5.4 Deepwater

The distinction between shelf and deepwater developments was discussed in the prior section. Deepwater represents a step change in technical complexity, cycle time, and capital intensity from shelf production. The industry is supported by a few, very specialized contractors who drill and complete the wells and provide design, fabrication, installation, hook-up, and commissioning of the subsea equipment, floating production, and export systems. Even in the current depressed market, deepwater developments start in the low billions of dollars and can run up to twenty billion.

Deepwater development requires more technical capability from an operator, but it also requires more commercial sophistication, as the supplier market is limited, and the range of commercial solutions is broader. Long-term lease arrangements with third-party operators of floating production systems, who may also operate the facilities, are commonplace. These require a different approach through tendering and a different contractual structure to ensure alignment between operator and contractor.

There are numerous examples of small companies or management teams with financial backing who have executed successful deepwater exploration programs. The list of small companies or management teams who have successfully executed a deepwater development is a lot shorter—really only Tullow with Jubilee. There are always exceptions, but, in general, deepwater requires a deep technical bench, deep pockets, and patience. If a company is not already there, there are three routes to entry.

Exploration-led

An exploration-led approach to deepwater consists of securing deepwater exploration acreage and executing an exploration campaign and, if successful, an appraisal campaign. The successful operator then has a couple of choices. It can either attempt to move forward with a deepwater development on its own, or, more commonly, it can farm-down and bring in an experienced deepwater operator as a partner to operate the development and operation phases.

The approach relies on the difference in technical complexity, capital intensity, and regulatory requirements among the different phases. Planning, permitting, and drilling a single exploration well is a lot simpler than a full deepwater field development. It requires oversight of a single activity, with a limited number of contractors. Given that an operator has access to the technical expertise to explore the basin and can fund a multi-well campaign, it is possible for a small company to explore successfully. Cobalt is an example of a company that acted as a serial explorer and one which failed when it tried to develop as well as discover fields.

This route can also address such regulatory requirements as in-country presence, and a track record of sea-exploration activity can allow a company to qualify as a deepwater operator where, strictly speaking, it lacks the advertised credentials.

Non-Operated Working Interest

Taking a Non-Operated Working Interest in deepwater development, with a well-structured experience-transfer commitment, is an excellent approach to developing deepwater capability and requires little in the way of existing expertise, other than the ability to evaluate the field. This approach works in jurisdictions where there are regulatory hurdles to assigning operatorship. As with all non-operated ventures, success is as much about picking the partner as anything else. If the primary intent is knowledge transfer, then it is important that expectations on both sides are realistic and clear. It is not realistic for a non-operated partner to expect participation in the operator's business outside of that specific field, for example.

Operated Working Interest

Acquiring an Operated Working Interest in a producing deepwater asset is also a viable approach if the regulatory regime allows. As the facility is already in operation, there are few decisions to be made. The focus for the acquiring party should be on a gap analysis of their operational capability with a focus on things like personal and technical safety, and environmental systems and logistics. The acquiring party should attempt to secure the transfer of onshore support personally as well as offshore personnel, and then focus on adapting previous or integrating new systems.

5.5.5 Arctic

Arctic fields offer a different set of challenges from deepwater, but the overall level of complexity is comparable. The Arctic is a harsh environment, but not because of water depth, wave height, or extreme currents. Instead, the technical challenges stem from low temperature and ice. Low temperature has an obvious impact on the workforce, but it can also affect equipment; a lot of the electronics used in the industry are more susceptible to failure at low temperature. Steel specifications are much tighter, limiting the potential vendor base. The risk of pack or drifting ice introduces its own problems for the design of structures, pipelines, and wellheads.

The second set of challenges are logistical, as with deepwater, but for different reasons. Arctic fields are remote, and building and maintaining an infrastructure to execute and operate them is a mega-project in itself. Access can also be restricted by season, either by shifting ice or melting permafrost, meaning short work windows and long delays to timelines if missed. Spares inventories need to be large, and there needs to be local provision for the repair of large pieces of equipment.

One of the most significant concerns with Arctic projects, perhaps more so even than with deepwater, is the impact of the project on the environment. Careful planning and execution are required to avoid damage to pristine environments. The environment itself also hampers the typical industry response to environmental incidents. Access can be difficult or impossible at certain times of the year, and an oil spill under ice couldn't be contained with conventional measures.

Despite all this, the industry has continued to move further and further into development of Arctic fields in recent years.

5.5.6 Conclusion

The settings outlined here can be seen as a sliding scale of cost and complexity—from onshore, to shelf, to deepwater, to Arctic, costs and complexity rise. This is not to say, however, that onshore development is easy. It requires a certain skill set and the highest commitment to close relations with the host community.

5.6 GEOGRAPHY

Geography is linked to a number of the issues already identified in this section—we have already discussed the additional operational requirements of entering a new jurisdiction, and geography is inevitably linked to fiscal regime and setting. There are some geographical considerations over and above these that we will discuss in this section.

5.6.1 Political Stability

Oil and gas developments are always sensitive to domestic politics. The industry deals in extraction of a valuable, finite natural resource, and, so, the question of ownership of that resource is always a delicate one, especially when administrations transition. The nature of the industry involves investing large amounts of capital in a fixed asset, an asset that cannot be relocated and which will usually take many decades to pay out. While the industry deploys a lot of capital, it does not employ a lot of people; it does not have a natural constituency to defend it. Finally, even with the best ESG policies, host-country communities will inevitably suffer a degree of disruption, even if it is only some price inflation and congestion.

All of these considerations make the political stability of the host country of paramount importance. There are legal mechanisms that can be employed to protect investment—stabilization clauses, choice of law, and agreement to international arbitration—but these are remedial measures rather than mitigations. One consideration is a host country's track record of maintaining a consistent policy regarding energy investment within and between government administrations. Some countries, like Brazil, have developed a track record of stability, whereas Mexico opened to international investment and then started to reverse those changes following the election of Andrés Manuel López Obrador in 2018[131]. In some cases, the employees in the industry regulator may change each time a new administration comes into power. This usually results in recycle, as settled decisions are revisited by new officials. In this case, the development program must reflect the political calendar in order to move forward. In countries where the administration has not changed for many years, extra caution is required. Nobody can rule forever, and, without a transition, there is no way to tell how national institutions will perform.

5.6.2 Language, Culture, and Systems

Having a common language or shared history is a great advantage when entering a new geography. Language differences slow communication and exacerbate misunderstanding. As a native English speaker, this author still had to remind himself that most people don't naturally think in English. Language colors every interaction. Translation, even simultaneous translation, slows conversation and drains both speakers. Written presentations or reports take days to translate and, if translated by a third party, are often robbed of context at key points. Beyond the mechanics of using different words and sentence structures, there are differences in how direct the conversation is, or whether the speaker stresses opinions or facts.

Moving on with language into culture, there are also differences about respect for hierarchy and the tone of a meeting. In some cultures, open disagreement is seen as impolite, whereas, in others, shouting is seen as strong leadership.

Common systems are also a great benefit. The former Soviet Union developed a distinct oil and gas industry-governance system, which has survived the fall of the Soviet Union itself. The industry was split between asset owners who operated assets and design institutes that undertook development work and were responsible for the integrity of the design. Familiarity with this way of working is a great advantage for Russian companies working in places like Azerbaijan and Kazakhstan.

The list is long, and the problems are not insurmountable, but in looking at new areas, an allowance must be made for these softer issues, and consideration must be given to how the gaps will be bridged and what type of people will be required to do the bridging.

5.6.3 Logistics

Logistics fits in with a number of other considerations, such as how the joint venture will be structured and the extent of the local presence. In this context, we are thinking about the practicalities of getting to and from wherever it is, maintaining a presence there, and bringing in whatever equipment and supplies are required to do the work.

Some locations are notably difficult to reach from others, and time differences can make daily communication difficult. Some countries, such as Iraq, require multiple flights and additional security measures in-country to be workable. While most people will be willing to go into the office at 3 a.m. for the occasional videoconference, most people aren't willing to do it for an extended period or in perpetuity. Remoteness and difficulty of access push for a larger local presence.

At the same time, the oil and gas industry is moving away from high levels of expatriation. Host-country governments are understandably keen that as many high-quality jobs as possible are filled by local people, and it is harder to convince professional families that one of them has to put their career on hold for a few years at least.

5.6.4 Home Country vs Host Country Relations

The primary geographical concern that has not been covered elsewhere is the political relationship between home- and host-country governments. This definition spans a range from general soft power to formal sanctions. At the soft-power end of the spectrum, Shell has very skillfully used its mixed ownership and historically autonomous United States arm to present itself as a British, Dutch, or American company, one which would be greeted most warmly by the prospective host. LUKOIL was able to farm-in to the Tengiz Chevroil joint venture on the strength of its relationships and knowledge of the industry in the former Soviet Union.

Conversely, Exxon wrote off $200 million and lost access to a valuable discovery in the Kara Sea when United States sanctions, applied following Russia's invasion of the Crimea, made a joint venture with Rosneft legally impossible[132]. There is less industry experience with international sanctions than with the more traditional political risks. The nature of the sanctions imposed on Russia following the invasion of the Crimea were targeted at organizations and individuals and were very specific. The sanctions imposed on LUKOIL following the Russian invasion of the Crimea in 2014 prevented United States persons from providing technology that would assist LUKOIL in developing unconventional, Arctic, or deepwater fields inside Russia. As LUKOIL did not have any unconventional fields in Russia and was ineligible for Arctic or deepwater acreage because of its designation as a private company, these restrictions were, in practice, not very onerous. However, once they were broadened in 2016 to include unconventional, Arctic, and deepwater fields anywhere in the world, they became a great deal more restrictive.

5.6.5 Conclusion

Geography will inevitably play a major role in shaping a company's business-development strategy, for the reasons outlined in this section. By virtue of history, culture, or language, some companies will simply find it easier to work in certain geographies or enter new ones. In most cases, however, companies can overcome these challenges once they have recognized them and thought about how best to mitigate them.

5.7 JOINT-VENTURE STRUCTURE

Any field that you choose to farm-in to or acquire will almost certainly be some form of joint venture. These come in two forms—incorporated joint ventures and unincorporated joint ventures. While this may seem a legal detail, these two structures work very differently, which can impact your ability to function effectively within them. Understanding and being able to manage through the terms of your operating agreements, however organized, will help extract maximum value from your assets.

5.7.1 Unincorporated Joint Venture

The unincorporated joint venture is the most common international form of joint venture. Ownership in the asset is governed through a working interest in a lease or granting instrument—a PSC, License, or Concession, which is conferred by the host-country government. The operation of the joint venture is governed by a JOA, a contract which confers rights and responsibilities on each of the joint-venture partners.

The JOA defines how the partners will work together, appointment and duties of the operator, and voting thresholds for decision-making at each phase. The operator is a participant in the joint venture who is appointed to operate the asset. The operator is the only participant with the right to propose joint operations and engage with the regulator and contractors. There are standard JOA forms—both the Association of International Petroleum Negotiators (AIPN) and the American Association of Professional Landmen

(AAPL) have published versions—but these constitute more a jumping-off point than a standard and vary in implementation from country to country.

Operated Assets

From an operated perspective, the JOA allows a company to run the project in accordance with their own internal standards and procedures, although these must be adapted to conform to the decision thresholds and timelines specified in the JOA. The principal benefit to being the operator is control—the operator controls the pace and direction of development. Depending on their working interest, non-operated partners may be able to *block* progress but cannot *force* progress.

Operatorship also allows recovery of costs for the work that the operator undertakes on behalf of the joint venture. Most joint ventures in the exploration through execution phase include an integrated project team (IPT), with members drawn from each of the joint-venture partners. The IPT is at the discretion of the operator and includes only technical positions. Secondees to the IPT remain employees of their employer, and, so, their fiduciary duty remains to their employer. Unless negotiated under the JOA, the operator is under no obligation to offer any positions to secondees or accept any proposed secondees. Nor is the operator required to provide unfettered access to their facilities, data, or resources—in fact, it is important that certain data is not shared, as this would constitute an anti-trust violation under some jurisdictions.

Joint-venture partners receive a share of production and are liable for a share of their operating costs. In most cases, joint-venture partners are also responsible for the transportation and marketing of their production, which should be a consideration during the acquisition process. Depending on the circumstances, it may be beneficial to negotiate a joint-marketing agreement, either as part of the farm-in or prior to FID, as joint marketing of product may be the best approach.

Non-Operated Assets

Things are more nuanced from a non-operated perspective. An effective non-operated partner can influence the joint venture while building relationships with the operator and other joint-venture partners. Working successfully as a non-operator deserves a book in itself, but there are a couple of key differences in an unincorporated joint venture.

One common reason for taking a non-operated position in the joint venture is to learn, and the non-operated partner will receive the work products, except where deemed proprietary, and will have some opportunity to place secondees, but only in technical roles. Farming-in to an unincorporated joint venture in the expectation that you will be able to second people into finance, strategy, and HR roles—and thus exert a degree of control—is not a realistic expectation.

The second is decision-making. An unincorporated joint venture requires the non-operated partner to run their own maturation process in parallel with the operator, managing the joint venture through the terms of the JOA. Some companies do a great deal of their own work, and some do very little. The operator of the joint venture will be using their own management systems, and, so, the operator will not necessarily generate the work products the non-operated partner requires at the time they require them. A gap analysis is required, and the non-operated partner will be expected to fill any gap with their own technical work, without the option of recovering costs for it. Thus, the non-operated partner must have a sufficient budget and organizational capacity to complete the work. Some thought should also be given to how this work is undertaken, to ensure that the non-operated party can claim the cost appropriately for tax purposes.

5.7.2 Incorporated Joint Ventures

Incorporated joint ventures are used extensively, but not exclusively, in the former Soviet Union. In an incorporated joint venture, the granting instrument is held by a legal entity, with joint-venture partners holding a share of that entity.

Incorporated joint ventures differ from unincorporated joint ventures in that they have their own business processes and staff. The board of directors and key staff positions are normally filled by secondees from their joint-venture partners, often in proportion to their shareholding. All staff within an incorporated joint venture, including secondees, owe their fiduciary duty to the joint venture, as opposed to their parent company. This can place secondees in a difficult situation and requires careful management.

Decision-making is governed by a vote at board level in accordance with the articles of incorporation or equivalent document. There is no longer an operator, but, in some cases, one of the shareholders will have a disproportionate role in staffing the joint venture—Shell filled almost all of Sakhalin Energy's project, technical, and commercial roles during the execution of Sakhalin II, for example. NAM was staffed entirely with Shell and NAM staff, despite Exxon holding a share. This can be disorienting for the secondees, as they are working within an organization that *looks* like their parent company but isn't. The incorporated joint venture will have its own systems, culture, and staff; it may also have staff and directors from competitors. Because of this, conversations are less free, and more care must be taken when using information from the parent company.

An incorporated joint venture can provide more insight—and potentially more influence—for the smaller shareholder. Seconding staff into functions like human resources or finance is possible and can help companies from low-trust cultures become comfortable with the investment. Having board representation ensures that the incorporated joint venture will provide the work products that they need to their own, internal decision-making as shareholders; this eliminates the need for joint-venture partners to execute their own work.

5.7.3 Conclusion

Whether a joint venture is incorporated or unincorporated is not really an issue of one being better than the other. The issue is more that the acquiring party understands the distinction and is organized to manage its acquisition appropriately.

5.8 OTHER ISSUES

This section covers several other considerations that don't fit neatly under the headings above, when compiling a list of coveted assets. These are typical things to look out for.

5.8.1 Government Approval

Unless the landowner also owns the mineral rights, then your transaction will require government approval to close. Even then, if the acquisition involves foreign investment, there may be government-approval requirements. Although this represents the finish line of your transaction, it is important to establish whether approval will be an issue prior to approaching potential sellers. Likewise, for sellers, it is wise to assess whether government approval may be a barrier before investing too much time in a potential buyer. The bar for operators will clearly be higher than the bar for non-operators, but, even there, the government will want to ensure that any investor has capital, is willing and able to establish an entity and pay taxes, and will not introduce political difficulties.

Some countries have a formal review of foreign investments—the Committee on Foreign Investments in the United States (CFIUS), for example. This inter-agency committee has the power to block, modify, or unwind transactions, on national-security grounds, involving the acquisition of a United States asset by a foreign person.

In order to avoid surprises later in the transaction, it is prudent to establish the decision-maker, the decision process, and the entities that are consulted in the decision—the regulator or national oil company, for example—early in the process. There can be other requirements. For example, Petrobras is required, by law, to run all divestments through an extended open-auction process. There are some provisions that allow for a negotiated transaction, but these could be subject to legal challenge, which adds uncertainty to closing. There may be additional requirements for the acquiring party to post some form of security at time of acquisition to cover future liabilities. Again, it is recommended to establish a clear picture of this early, as things which threaten a buyer's ability to close on a transaction can make one jurisdiction materially less attractive than another. Careful preparation does not guarantee that government approval will be forthcoming; international events like Russia's invasion of Ukraine can derail any investment, but it is the best way to mitigate the risk.

5.8.2 Unitization

Forced unitization occurs in some jurisdictions where fields extend across lease lines with different ownerships. The field itself becomes a separate unit, with the owners of the licenses the field lies on assuming a working interest in the unit. The process of determining what proportion of the field belongs to each owner is complex and uncertain, given that it is based on interpretations of the best available data and the best available technology. Both data and technology will mature over time, and, depending on the settlement, interests can shift over time. Troll, one of the largest oil and gas fields in the North Sea, excluded the oil rim from the initial equity determination on the basis that it was too thin to produce[133]. Norske Hydro subsequently pioneered the horizontal drilling technology that unlocked the oil rim, transforming Troll into a large oil as well as gas producer, resulting in an equity redetermination.

Unitization is forced in many jurisdictions. In some, such as the United States Gulf of Mexico, unitization is not compulsory. The United States applies the right of capture, which allows each license holder to complete wells within 100 feet of their lease line and produce whatever they can, regardless of which side of the lease line the molecules come from. If the crest of a neighboring field lies within your lease, then this can present an opportunity, but, given the practicalities of development and the very small lease blocks offered—9 square miles—voluntary unitization is common.

Acquiring a field during a forced-unitization process introduces difficulty in valuation and uncertainty over the development timeline. As a general rule, it is better to focus on other opportunities. Acquiring a field that has been unitized also introduces risk to the buyer. Each unit participant holds their working interest through their own license. Those licenses may have been issued with different fiscal terms and license-expiration dates. Other activities in some of the licenses may prevent the unit from moving forward. This complexity results in delay, which erodes value. As a result, fields that are subject to complex unitization agreements should see their value discounted. One current example is Zama, in Mexico, where there is a unitization dispute between Talos Energy and PEMEX. Premier Oil, prior to its acquisition by Harbor, was marketing its Non-Operated Working Interest in Zama but was unable to attract interest.

5.8.3 Preferential Rights
Preferential rights refer to a partner's pre-existing right of first refusal to take the working interest that is being sold on the terms agreed. Assets that have only a single participant are not subject to preferential rights, making them relatively more attractive. Almost all

joint-venture agreements grant existing partners preferential rights. Partners will exercise these to keep a partner that they do not want involved out of the joint venture, or because they like the deal and want to increase their own working interest.

The only way around the first point is to present as a competent, qualified buyer and partner, to remove the concern about letting you in. There is no way to mitigate the risk that other partners wish to increase their working interest. The only way to minimize your risk is to secure a preferential-rights waiver in the farm-in agreement. If you suspect that they are keen to increase their working interest or that they are reluctant to execute a waiver, then you should focus your efforts on other opportunities.

5.8.4 Local-Content Requirements

As we observed earlier, the upstream oil and gas industry is capital- rather than labor-intensive, and, so, the benefits have a tendency to bypass the communities that see the greatest impacts. Local-content requirements are intended to address this by spurring development in supporting industries by requiring companies to spend a propor- tion of their CapEx in-country.

There is substantial scope for discussion on the relative benefits of different approaches to local content, but it is important when considering an acquisition because it impacts asset economics in the same way as the fiscal regime, but with less transparency. It does this in two ways. In the first instance, local-content requirements tend to increase cost or extend schedules. If they didn't—if the local option was already the most cost efficient—there would be no need for the requirement.

In the second, they introduce uncertainty in CapEx estimating, which can result in multiyear delays to projects. CapEx estimates are built from analogs, and, so, even if the field development is the twentieth field development in the country, if it is the first to be executed under new local-content rules, then your estimates can be very wrong—billions of dollars out on a large project—and the first sign of this will be contractor pricing at the end of the FEED stage. At best, this results in recycle—returning to an earlier stage in the project cycle—which is at best a delay of several years and at worst a field that is never developed. Both outcomes erode the economic value of the field, which prevents the buyer from realizing the value they had projected at farm-in.

Brazil serves as an example of the unintended consequences that ambitious local-content requirements can have on oil and gas development[134]. Starting in 2007, with the Round 7, through to 2016, Brazil imposed increasingly onerous local-content requirements on the industry, reaching 90% for specific items. The intent was laudable—to leverage Brazil's natural endowment to drive development of a domestic oil and gas manufacturing base. This manufacturing base could not grow quickly enough to support the industry, which meant oil and gas companies were left with a choice between manufacturing in-country and accepting schedule delays or paying fines; in many cases, it made sense to simply pay the fines. From 2016, local-content rules were relaxed to align requirements with domestic supply-chain capacity. The impact of this was to raise Brazil's projected sustainable-production capacity from 3.7 million to 5 million barrels/day by the mid-2020s, boosting royalty collection and job creation.

5.8.5 Access

The method of access is also a consideration. Assets are typically sold through either direct negotiation or some form of structured sale process, which usually follows an auction format. From a buyer's perspective, the best approach is direct negotiation, for a couple of reasons. The first is practical, in that the process of negotiating the transaction and performing necessary due diligence is resource-intensive, and, so, before committing those resources, the buyer should have a high level of confidence that the transaction will close. It is impossible to have such a level of confidence in an auction format. The second reason is that an auction format requires standardized bids, which removes the potential to craft the optimal transaction for both buyer and seller, making a satisfactory outcome less likely.

As a buyer, it is impossible to avoid auctions in some settings; exploration acreage in established or highly prospective basins is usually auctioned, and, given the high uncertainty and campaign nature of exploration activity, an auction process is suitable. Some jurisdictions require an auction. Petrobras, for example, is required by law to run an auction process for the sale of its assets. There is some scope for an exception here—Petrobras is allowed to negotiate sales if the terms of the transaction are non-biddable. One example of this was Statoil's (now Equinor) farm-in to the Roncador field in 2017 on the basis that it would employ its Improved Oil Recovery technology to increase the recovery factor from the field by at least 5%[135].

From a seller's perspective, the best approach is situation dependent. An auction format will provide information on the value of your asset and negates any potential internal criticism that the asset has been sold too cheaply. An auction format is a quick route to the highest cash value if the objective is to raise cash. There are some downsides to the auction. Many buyers will simply not participate in an auction process. Managing an auction process is labor intensive if run in-house and expensive if an investment bank is retained for that purpose. As your buyer pool and your competitor pool are the same, it is inevitable that you will educate your competitors.

On the other hand, a negotiated sale may provide a more tax-efficient solution, and, if the purpose of the sale is portfolio rationalization, then a negotiated sale may provide access to an interest in a coveted asset, which may be of greater value than the cash received from a straight sale. Another consideration is that complex assets, where value is hard to articulate, will not fare as well at auction as simple assets. Assets sold through an auction process at times of reduced commodity prices are also unlikely to receive their full intrinsic value; in this case, a swap or a negotiated share of future earnings will likely yield more value over the long run.

A third method of access is through bankruptcy, where assets are sold through either a court-monitored sale process or the acquisition of discounted debt in a target company. Distressed sales are a topic for a dedicated text[136].

5.9 ASSET MIX—INDIE OIL

What does Indie Oil's asset mix look like? Indie Oil is 100% oil focused, so adding some gas assets to its portfolio would provide some diversification and help smooth out earnings volatility. Indie produces around 80,000 barrels/day, so a transaction of 5,000 to 10,000 barrels or so/day would be material, and more than 20,000 barrels/day would be very significant.

Indie has a lot of firm scope and a lot of exploration activity, but it lacks development options, something that is in the Appraisal or Concept Selection phase. This is why it has a production gap opening in the late 2020s and struggles to deploy cash at high prices.

Indie's exploration program consists of high working-interest positions in two frontier or emerging basins. Indie would be better placed if it could farm-down these positions and pick up some additional acreage to spread risk—and the timing of its financial commitments. As identified in section 3.6., Indie is unable to fund both its exploration portfolio at $40/barrel at current working-interest levels, providing another reason to consider divestment.

All of Indie's existing production and exploration prospects are shelf or deepwater. Only Roosterfish and Tarpon, which have yet to be executed, are onshore. If Tarpon goes forward, it will be Indie's first attempt at onshore development and production, and the first oil and gas development in Uganda. Tarpon is key to delivering Indie's production promise for the next decade.

Indie is focused geographically on sub-Saharan Africa and South America, with most of its existing production in Ghana—more concentration than is comfortable. It has a couple of non-operated assets, but neither are material for Indie, merely contributing some legacy production.

5.10 ASSET MIX—APACHE

Trying to look back at the asset mix Apache would have been seeking is complicated as an exercise by knowledge of what choice they did make and how it actually turned out. However, we can attempt to put ourselves in their shoes and think about what asset characteristics would have been desirable, given where they found themselves in 2003.

Apache had a strategy of high-impact exploration, acquisition, and exploitation, and, so, it was likely to look for opportunities that were either early-phase exploration or existing, producing assets. Apache had an active exploration program, making 16 discoveries in 2002, and had also ramped up their development-drilling program over the prior three-year period. Apache did note that drilling costs were relatively high—high enough for them to consider curtailing development programs.[137] This may have resulted in greater emphasis on their wish to add production in a new region, but they seem to have been progressing smoothly with their twin exploration and exploitation strategy, with nothing to indicate a need to address one over the other, except, perhaps, that the opportunity presented itself.

Forties was part of a larger, negotiated transaction with BP that included some legacy BP assets in the United States Gulf of Mexico. While we don't know how widely shared the sale of BP's assets was, the author has found no evidence that it was part of a public-auction process. Apache are explicit in their annual reports that they will not engage in auctions, and, so, this approach was consistent with their philosophy[138].

Apache's reserves in 2002 were 51% gas[139], the kind of ratio that many companies were moving toward in recent years, but very gassy for the time. Therefore, it is reasonable to think that adding oil was a priority over gas. This predated the United States shale era, and Apache did not have any legacy of heavy oil production, so a conventional oil field was likely the target, if available.

Apache were producing around 440,000 barrels/day of liquids in 2002 and had a reserves base of 1.3 billion barrels. The total BP transaction involved adding 144 MMboe of reserves, an 11% increase, and 41,000 barrels/day of production, a 9% increase.[140] From either perspective, the transaction was material. The larger BP transaction, of which Forties was a part, was valued at $1.3 billion, the largest single transaction that Apache had undertaken. Apache's acquisition of the Forties field was, by any measure, material. It was certainly material enough to support a new geography for the company.

In 2003, Apache was concentrated geographically in North America, with exploration and production operations in Australia, Egypt, China, Poland, and Argentina. At the time, the North Sea was a mature province, with West Africa and Brazil both opening as deep-water provinces. Apache would certainly benefit from a geographic extension to their footprint and, in the UK sector of the North Sea, found a mature province with exploitation potential. The selection of the UK also represented a relatively low-risk venture for a United States company, with a common language, similar business culture, and the long-standing presence of other United States companies in the region.

Apache had experience operating both offshore and onshore, so the Forties field did not represent a technical step-out for them. In addition, under UK legislation, staff transfer with the asset, and, so, Apache inherited a very competent and functional organization.

Apache would require control in order to successfully execute their exploitation strategy. Apache was able to acquire a 97% interest in Forties, which would have given complete operational control and mitigated any risk of misalignment with a non-operating partner or partner-funding issues.

The prevailing fiscal regime would have given Apache considerable oil-price upside, and, as they highlighted in their subsequent annual reports, the acquisition did benefit from a backdrop of rising oil prices, although, as noted in section 2.4.1, the UK's fiscal regime has not always been a paragon of stability.

Apache raised debt and equity to finance the transaction, and, so, certainty that the transaction would go forward would be an important consideration in selecting both target and counterparty. The UK is open to foreign investment, and, as an established United States operator, there would be little concern about obtaining government approval. The fact that Apache was acquiring such a large working interest—97%—would have reduced the risk of the deal being pre-empted by the other partners.

The Forties acquisition allowed Apache to apply their exploitation strategy in a new region. That did not introduce many new risks for them, as the new region was, in many ways, similar to the areas where they already operated. It provided them with control of a proven material asset, with very little transaction risk. While we can't know their thought process at the time, when looked at using the framework described in this book, Apache's choice of Forties looks like a solid fit.

5.11 ASSET MIX—BHP

The challenge here again is that, while we are not privy to the internal deliberations behind the Petrohawk acquisition, we know how it turned out. Still, using the framework in this chapter, we can try to walk through what BHP might have been thinking at the time.

BHP's production and reserves in the 2008 to 2010 period were similar to Apache's in the 2000 to 2002 time frame. There were a couple of key differences, though. One is that BHP's petroleum business was one part of a larger conglomerate, and, so, any transaction would necessarily have to be larger to be classified as "material" at the BHP group level. The other is that, while Apache had to raise both equity and debt to support its transaction, BHP had a lot of surplus cash on its balance sheet. From this, it is fair to conclude that "material" for BHP would have been bigger than Apache's Forties transaction and larger than the overall Apache-BP. The amount of money available and the need for a large acquisition would steer toward large producing assets.

BHP's production split at the time was 60/40 oil to gas, which is oilier than is considered desirable today, but in line with other, similar companies at the time. BHP had LNG experience, although not as a field operator. It did not have unconventional or heavy oil production. At the time, both of these were seen as OECD resource plays, and so it would make sense for BHP to add exposure to either or both of these.

BHP had been struggling with its exploration funnel for some time. It had experience as a field developer and successfully executed deepwater developments in the United States Gulf of Mexico and Trinidad and Tobago. A successful developer needs a pipeline of projects, something which BHP lacked. This would make non-operated exploration interests in a number of new plays an obvious place to start. Discovered, undeveloped resources could also be attractive to a company with a strong development track record, and BHP's deepwater operated fields would have allowed it to qualify as an operator in all jurisdictions. One area where BHP differed from Apache is that it did not have a track record of exploiting older fields, which meant that the acquisition of legacy fields from one of the majors, as Apache did with Forties, was probably not on the menu.

BHP had a long track record of working as a non-operated partner, and, as it did not have specific methodology that it wanted to apply to whatever it acquired, as Apache did, then non-operated positions were perfectly viable. In addition, BHP did not have to fund the acquisition through new equity or debt issuance and so could afford to be patient, again opening the door to non-operated roles. As mentioned above, the struggle with exploration would recommend a series of non-operated exploration positions, and BHP's focus on Australia/United States also suggests the non-operated route could be a safer approach to achieve a broader international exposure.

The heavy exposure to Australia and the United States means that the portfolio would have had relatively high production costs but would have allowed BHP to capture price upside. Some more PSC exposure may be beneficial. Exposure to PSCs with less price upside but lower production costs could help BHP to smooth their earnings through the commodity cycle. The risk profile of BHP as a petroleum company at the time seems to be very much skewed toward technical.

As noted above, BHP could finance acquisitions through cash flow and, so, could afford to be patient and take greater closing risks. This would serve to expand BHP's choice of counterparties and regions where it could potentially operate.

Even with the benefit of hindsight, it is hard to see why BHP chose to bet so heavily on a series of shale acquisitions. There was clearly a place for shale, but as a smaller part of a larger portfolio, and as a means of learning about an emergent play type, rather than a transformational acquisition in its own right.

In the first instance, exploration should have been addressed through a series of non-operated exploration positions. This could have involved an explorer/developer relationship with a company like Cobalt, where BHP would develop any finds. The portfolio should also have included some discovered, undeveloped fields in a new geography—Brazil and West Africa both had deepwater opportunities at the time, and BHP could have entered in either an operated or non-operated role. The addition of a material, long-life resource through farming-in to Kashagan or participating in some of the Iraqi fields would have helped mitigate oil-price risk. While we can see how Kashagan turned out with hindsight, it would have made sense at the time. Finally, a foray into either shale or heavy oil, framed internally as a pilot to learn and establish viability, could have rounded out the portfolio.

As we know, this was not the path that BHP elected to take. The reasoning behind the Petrohawk acquisition was not clearly explained at the time; in fact, the Petroleum-division strategy was not clearly explained at the time. BHP were not the only company to act in this way: Exxon bought XTO for $41 billion the same year, and knowledge of that may have influenced BHP's decision-making. Mike Yeager, the President of BHP's petroleum division at the time, was an Exxon veteran and may have been acting on some of the same insights to bet the farm on shale.

5.12 CONCLUSION

If the discussion on portfolio health in Chapter 3 is all about identifying possibilities, and Chapter 4 is all about understanding what you are good at and where you could learn something new, this chapter is a little disheartening, in that it ends up becoming a list of all the things that you need to worry about. This may not be uplifting, but it is useful. If you were to go through the exercise outlined in Chapter 3, defining your desired portfolio, a few minutes spent with one of the industry's asset databases would provide hundreds, if not thousands, of target assets to evaluate. It is the process of defining competency and thinking about asset mix that imposes a necessary dose of realism that culls that list down to a few focus basins that you want to work in.

This process also helps the buyer or seller to articulate, both internally and for their counterparties, why they are taking the action that they are taking. A buyer will always want to understand why assets are available before investing time in evaluating them; a seller will want to understand how serious the buyer is before investing time in working with them.

In Chapter 6, we will look at how to put together the portfolio, competencies, and asset mix to construct notional portfolios and how to evaluate those to create a business-development strategy.

Chapter 6

DEVELOPING A STRATEGY

This chapter looks at how three concepts introduced in this book—portfolio health, organizational capability, and asset mix—can be combined to create a business-development strategy. The chapter starts by considering some established strategic archetypes from business literature and provides some examples of how joint ventures can be employed judiciously to enhance strategy through access beyond your current capabilities. The process of developing a strategy is best illustrated by example, and here we will pick up where we left off with Indie Oil to work through what their strategy would look like. This chapter closes with a final look at the Apache and BHP acquisitions and what can be learned from them.

6.1 BUSINESS-LEVEL STRATEGY

Following the guidelines in this book, the best strategy to adopt appears to be one where you target low-cost, low-risk, high-quality assets, in politically stable countries with very attractive fiscal regimes. Unfortunately, this insight is not unique, and the industry has been established for long enough that most of these assets were developed many years ago. But, as with every other apparently definitive statement in this book, there is ambiguity, as every now and then, one turns up. A couple of examples are Buzzard in the UK sector of the North Sea and, more recently, Johan Sverdrup, on the Norwegian Continental Shelf. Both are large, productive shelf fields in OECD countries, discovered in established plays in basins that were thought to have been picked over decades ago. Absent this kind of astonishing stroke of luck, you will be forced to make tradeoffs in the development of your strategy. You will have to pick your poison. That is, after all, the essence of a strategy: deciding what *not* to do.

Business strategy in general recognizes five strategic types, as illustrated in Figure 36, below[141]. This framework is as well suited to the oil and gas industry as it is to any other but can be difficult for those working in the upstream business to use, as it is traditionally applied in the context of customers. As we discussed earlier, upstream oil and gas is a commodity business; there is no way to differentiate your product, and, so, you must compete on price. The key differentiator between the upstream business and others is in resource access. Upstream companies do not really compete in the sale of their product, but in access to fields that allow them to produce that product competitively. If we think of the host-country government, rather than the buyer, as our customer, then we can apply the traditional strategic archetypes for how we compete for that access.

The traditional framework has five distinct strategies, based on whether they aim to serve the broad market or a narrow subset, and whether they aim to compete through low cost or some form of differentiation. The fifth strategy, called Integrated Cost Leadership/Differentiation, involves using the firm's inherent strengths to provide a differentiated product or service at a competitive cost. If we consider these strategies in the context of the upstream industry, we can see that some distinct trends have developed over time.

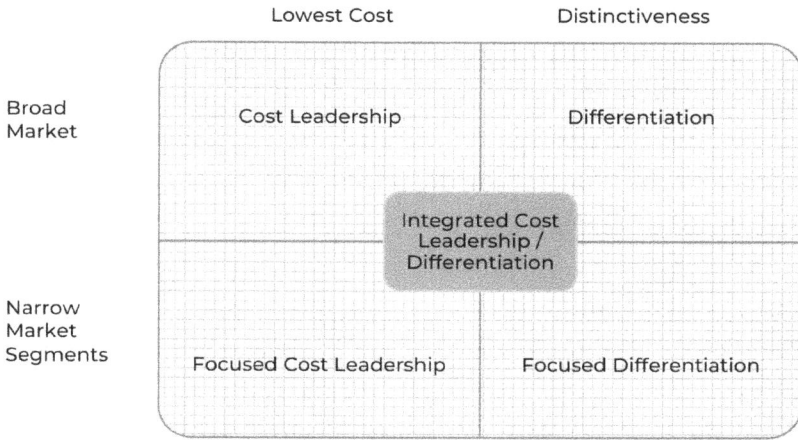

FIGURE 36: Types of Business-Level Strategy

6.1.1 Cost Leadership

Universal cost leadership is not a strategy that has emerged in the upstream oil and gas industry, as there is no one who tries to operate everywhere on the basis of lowest cost. The closest contender would probably be Exxon, but they are differentiated through their technology, and, so, this would not be an appropriate classification.

There have been examples of companies that tried to achieve cost leadership by adopting a strategy of holding only Non-Operated Working Interests. One recent example is Venari. The idea is that a non-operated model results in very low operating costs, which is a sound proposition. A small, centralized team can run operations through small, local representative offices. The problem with this approach is that non-operated partners have no control over their capital programs, which was fatal for Venari. Venari was unable to push any of its investments through development into production.

The companies that have the lowest global lifting costs—Qatar Petroleum, Saudi Aramco, Rosneft—tend to have a tight focus either by geography or hydrocarbon type, coupled with close ownership links with their host-country government. These companies realize their low costs through the quality of their fields, rather than the efficiency of their business operations. This combination of favorable geology and close government relations is unique to each of their geographies, preventing them from adopting an international cost-leadership strategy.

6.1.2 Focused Cost Leadership

While broad cost leadership has not been successfully adopted, focused cost leadership is another matter and is well established within the industry. Here an operator with a structurally lower cost-structure base acquires assets and extends their life by virtue of a reduced operating cost. Reduced operating cost can be achieved by eliminating functions such as exploration and development, focusing geographically or by theme, outsourcing key functions—or simply by virtue of having a leaner organization than integrated oil and gas companies. The focused-cost-leadership model has been adopted by a number of private-equity-backed companies in recent years, such as Chryasor and Siccar Point Energy, who have focused on late-life North Sea Assets. Apache is an example of a focused-cost-leadership company, with their commitment to acquiring and exploiting existing assets. Saudi Aramco would also fit in this category; with their focus on production in Saudi Arabia, they enjoy the lowest lifting costs in the world. Perenco is another example of a low-cost operator that has focused on production in former French colonies in Africa. Perenco alumni now lead many of the private-equity-backed firms that have adopted the cost-leadership strategy.

6.1.3 Differentiation

The premium operators, the majors, and supermajors have selected a broad differentiation strategy. They compete in all major markets

and field types and, given their reach and the size of their organizations, choose to compete on their technical and commercial
capability and on the strength of their balance sheets, rather than
trying to compete on cost.

This strategy leads these companies to focus on very large,
frontier projects, where they use their differentiated capabilities to
access opportunities that others can't. The scale of these investments
counterbalances their relatively high operating costs. The downside
for these companies is that they can struggle to compete in mature
basins once the large, frontier opportunities are exhausted—many
incremental-development opportunities are better left to others.
This leads many majors to exit established assets once they have
concluded that they can't add any incremental value. This is a
trend that has played out across the world over the years. Shell
and Exxon sold off their United States Gulf of Mexico shelf assets
and focused investment on more material assets in deepwater.
Shell and BP—and, lately, Exxon—have systematically exited
their mature positions in the UK and Norway, while continuing
to invest in high-margin frontier assets in the same basins. These
assets are sold on to companies like Apache, who have a lower
cost structure and can continue to invest in them, as we saw in
our Forties example.

6.1.4 Focused Differentiation

The specialist has a narrow focus and attempts to differentiate itself
by exploiting some technical or commercial niche. Occidental, while
in the news for their recent Anadarko acquisition, are one of the
world leaders in enhanced oil recovery; they exploit this niche in
their conventional and unconventional field developments both in
the United States and internationally. Occidental were able to use
their technical capabilities to access fields like Mukhaizna in Oman,
where they have been since the 1990s.

The other group who fit within this description are the companies like Tullow, Kosmos, and Cobalt, which differentiated themselves through their exploration capability. Their business model is based on entering frontier basins and finding hydrocarbons, before farming-down to have the field developed by a larger partner. Cobalt was originally built around this "find and flip" model but attempted to take the step of becoming a full-cycle oil company, a strategy that it was unable to execute successfully. In recent United States Gulf of Mexico license rounds, BP have partnered with Kosmos, who act as their exploration arm. This is an interesting new model for the industry.

6.1.5 Integrated Cost Leadership Differentiation

The only real example of a company attempting to follow an integrated cost leadership/differentiation model is Exxon. Exxon is widely regarded as having the most sophisticated subsurface characterization and drilling technology in the industry, while, at the same time, seeking to be the lowest-cost operator wherever they choose to operate. Exxon has been the largest traditional international oil company for the last two decades—in terms of both production *and* profitability—and has historically traded at an earnings multiple premium to its competitors.

There are a couple of things that Exxon does to differentiate itself from its competitors. The first is discipline and standardization. Exxon's system of governance is applied consistently everywhere that it operates. The second is a sophisticated and selective use of Non-Operated Working Interests. If Exxon can't be the lowest-cost operator in a region, it will come in as the non-operated partner of a company that can. This helps keep its production costs low. Exxon has a non-operated career path that helps its non-operated staff develop the skills required to be effective as a non-operating partner. Its non-operating joint ventures are run with every bit as much discipline as its operated ventures.

6.1.7 The Value of Joint Ventures

As illustrated by Exxon, the application of alternative commercial structures is the only path to an integrated cost leadership/differentiation model. One of the best examples is Aera, which is an incorporated joint venture between Shell and Exxon. Aera develops old heavy oil fields in California. The fields' operations are relatively straightforward, but margins are thin, and, so, they could not compete for operations in either Shell or Exxon's portfolio. The solution was to spin them off in their own incorporated joint venture and, thus, their own governance, processes, and cost structure. This approach allows companies with a broad, differentiated strategy to compete in a setting that requires a cost-leadership structure.

6.1.7 Conclusion

As this section illustrates, there are several different business-level strategies that a company can adopt successfully. Large companies with sophisticated technology and human capital tend to employ a differentiated strategy because this suits their strengths and their portfolio requirements. Firms that are differentiated more narrowly tend to adopt either a focused differentiation or a focused-cost-leadership approach, depending on where their capabilities lie. The creative use of joint ventures is the best route to an integrated approach and moving beyond your current capabilities.

6.2 DEVELOPING A STRATEGY

The previous section provided an overview of classic strategic archetypes, and it can be instructive to think through business-development strategies along one or two of these lines to see which is the best fit. The next step is more specific: business-development strategy involves determining which tradeoffs you are willing to make. The framework presented in this book introduced three concepts to use in making that determination—portfolio health, organizational capabilities, and asset mix. To define a business-development strategy, we need to define the notional portfolio or portfolios that lie at the intersection of these three concepts, as illustrated in Figure 37.

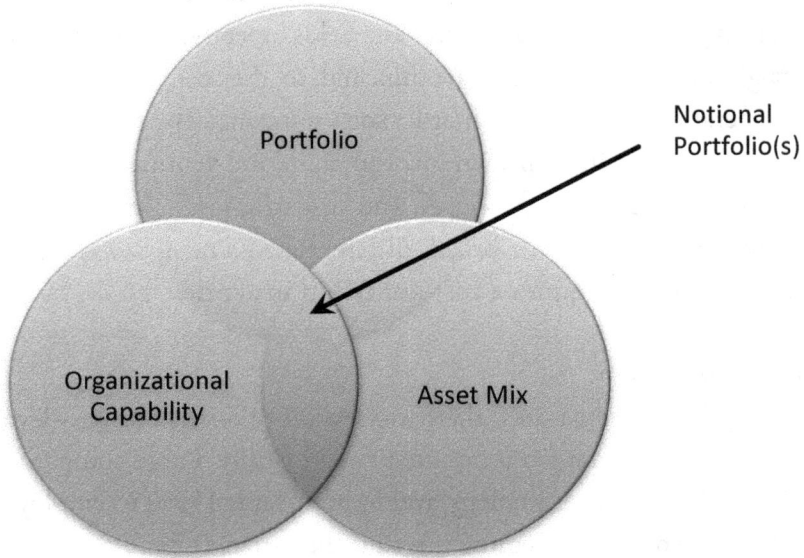

FIGURE 37: Business-Development-Strategy Framework

Determining where this intersection occurs is both a qualitative and a quantitative exercise, and we will return to Indie Oil to work through an example of this approach. We will start by examining the insights we derived from the analysis of Indie Oil in Chapters 3, 4, and 5 and develop actions to address those insights. We will then discuss the approach to building and evaluating a notional portfolio and work through an example with Indie Oil. Next, we will look at alternate notional portfolios and how to compare them. Finally, we will distill all of this into a business-development strategy, again using Indie Oil as an example. We will then look at our real-life examples—Apache and BHP.

6.3 INSIGHTS

The first step in constructing a notional portfolio is to examine the insights generated when considering portfolio health, organizational capability, and asset mix. There are some common results from scenario analysis, with recommendations on the best place to start constructing notional portfolios, as shown in Table 24.

INSIGHT	PORTFOLIO ACTIONS
Geographic concentration	Diversify through acquisition of geographically diverse assets, and divest most-exposed existing assets.
Surplus cash flow under optimistic scenario conditions	Acquire assets that can act as options.
Financial performance highly correlated with oil price	Divert assets with high oil-price exposure, like tax/royalty regimes, and acquire working interest in granting instruments which have some degree of price linkage.
Portfolio performance overly dependent on third-party decisions	Divest non-operated or low-control joint ventures, and acquire operated positions, with a controlling interest.

**TABLE 24: Common Scenario Analysis
Results and Corrective Action**

Next, we will look at the Indie Oil examples from Chapters 3, 4, and 5 to determine what portfolio actions may be required.

6.3.1 INDIE OIL EXAMPLE

Starting with Chapter 3, portfolio health, looking at the insights generated in sections 3.4.3, 3.5.2, 3.6.1, 3.7.2, 4.5, and 5.9, we can think about the adjustments that Indie Oil may need to make to their portfolio.

INSIGHT	PORTFOLIO ACTIONS
Indie Oil can meet its production target through Base Production plus Firm Investment over the next half decade.	Indie Oil has some time available to take the action required to address its portfolio.
Indie Oil has a production gap that opens in the second half of the decade, before options and exploration barrels can be brought onstream.	Indie Oil needs access to additional production in the second half of the decade.
Roosterfish and Wahoo don't screen.	Farm-out, exit.
Reliant on two exploration programs	Farm-down, and farm-in to additional exploration opportunities.
Heavy geographic concentration in Ghana.	Diversify geographically.
Indie can deliver the firm scope, plus the Tarpon option and some exploration at its $40/barrel price premise.	Indie Oil's portfolio is resilient at low oil prices; it does not need to make a shift out of higher break-even-price assets.
Indie is oil focused and would be exposed to a decline in global oil demand.	Diversify into gas.
In the high-price premise, Indie generates surplus cash flow, but in the mid-price case, Indie has little financial flexibility.	Indie needs additional investment options, but ones that have low upfront-investment cost.
Strong exploration track record in sub-Saharan Africa and Latin America.	Leverage capability by adding exploration acreage in those geographies.
Lack of gas-marketing and LNG expertise.	Consider non-operated positions in gas/LNG projects.
No prior onshore experience. Tarpon anchors production from the 2030s.	Farm-down, farm-out, cede operatorship, build capability.
Existing production and exploration portfolio is shelf or deepwater.	Leverage capability, or diversify position?
Limited non-operated exposure.	Has scope to expand the proportion of the portfolio that is non-operated.
Sensitive to financing costs.	Refinance to protect against a rise in interest rates.

TABLE 25: Indie Oil Portfolio-Health Insights

Roosterfish, as a discovered resource, has value which a sale should realize. In the case of Wahoo, there has been little improvement on the asset, with the exception of some desk work, and, so, an exit is the more likely outcome.

Indie Oil needs a producing or near-producing field to fill the production gap in the late 2020s. The lack of gas exposure and the exploration-risk concentration can be addressed simultaneously, by farming-down Bonefish and Giant Trevally, while maintaining operatorship and investing in other exploration opportunities, one of which should be gas. Indie has a lack of gas-marketing and LNG expertise, and has room to expand the portion of its portfolio that is non-operated; gas may be an area where it would be preferable to take a non-operated position.

The hardest point to address is the lack of upside options in the high-price premise case. The only asset types that really fit this bill are shale oil in the United States or OECD-discovered gas opportunities near existing infrastructure. In both cases, the leasing cost should be low if the external price is in line with the reference price. If the reference price persists, then Indie would undertake little to no development activity. If the price rises, then Indie can initiate development on very short cycle times, with production hedged. When prices fall back to the reference premise, Indie can curtail production. There is an option cost in acquiring access to the acreage and setting up local offices, but this is relatively small. The other option would be redevelopment of additional assets. Infill-drilling programs, even offshore, can be organized on relatively short notice, and, in most cases, the asset team will have some additional targets on the shelf because they don't screen. If this additional production can be brought onstream quickly and hedged, then this is another potentially profitable outlet for surplus cash.

Heavy geographic concentration could trigger some divestment, but, in this case, there is further investment in the pipeline, and the position is extremely good. Indie would be better served by finding opportunities elsewhere and try not to upset the apple cart.

Indie has a great track record in exploration in sub-Saharan Africa and Latin America, and deepwater capability. One approach would be to capitalize on this expertise and focus on remaining a predominantly shelf/deepwater operator, by targeting deepwater exploration acreage in West Africa and Latin America going forward. This decision needs to be made in conjunction with the decision on Tarpon, which is onshore, Indie Oil-operated, and responsible for the bulk of Indie's production in 2030. While Tarpon is an option, and Indie has no experience with executing this type of project, it anchors the portfolio in the next decade. Tarpon is also the lowest Unit Development Cost (UDC) opportunity on Indie's books and has one of the lowest break-even prices, so an exit would make the portfolio, as a whole, less resilient.

Indie could exit Tarpon and focus on leveraging its shelf and deepwater expertise, but this leaves a huge hole in Indie's portfolio, one that would be hard to fill. Alternatively, it could improve its chances of executing Tarpon successfully by building some onshore expertise on smaller projects. The third option, probably the best option, would be to cede operatorship to one of the partners, something that would be possible at this stage but would depend on who the partners were and their own appetite for that.

Finally, while not a business-development activity, sensitivity to financing costs can be addressed through locking in some longer-term debt at prevailing rates.

In section 6.4, we will show how to use insights to construct a notional portfolio and return to the Indie Oil example.

6.4 BUILDING A NOTIONAL PORTFOLIO

The notional portfolio, or portfolios, are based on the existing portfolio, but with adjustments designed to address the insights garnered from analysis of the current portfolio. At this stage, the focus should be on an asset type, rather than a specific asset, to understand what function the asset performs within the portfolio.

Depending on the situation, this can be a straightforward process or a very involved one. An otherwise-healthy portfolio that has some long-term production gaps will likely need additional exploration opportunities. Apache, at the time of the Forties acquisition, were comfortable with their exploration portfolio, but were on the lookout for material redevelopment opportunities at a good price. There is as much art as there is science to constructing these portfolios. It is best to avoid focusing on a particular asset, but, at the same time, the characteristics of the asset must be realistic.

Here you can use your own internal database, in conjunction with some industry data providers like Wood-Mackenzie, if required, to build an archetype based on a representative sample. The archetype doesn't represent a single asset but is broadly representative of the sort of thing that you are looking for, defined in enough detail as to assess its impact on the portfolio.

Once the portfolio has been assembled, screening can be undertaken, which follows the same process outlined in section 3.5. The screening of individual notional-asset archetypes within a portfolio should be undertaken using the company's normal evaluation metrics. Each notional portfolio should then be screened for conformance with the company's financial framework by testing cash flow, as outlined in section 3.6.

6.4.1 Indie Oil Example

In the Indie Oil example, the notional portfolio involves some divestment first, followed by some acquisition. An acquirer could afford to pay $125 million for Indies' 50% working interest in Roosterfish and still have a shovel-ready project that generated a rate of return of 15% at $60/barrel. Indie may be able to secure a better sale price, either up front or with some additional consideration based on future reservoir or price performance, but for the purposes of the analysis, we will assume that the sale generates $125 million. We will assume that Wahoo is relinquished with no compensation and that both Bonefish and Giant Trevally are farm-outs. We will assume that Indie is able to secure a 2:1 promote on both Bonefish and Giant Trevally, meaning that the farmee agrees to carry 100% of the exploration-program cost in exchange for a 50% working interest.

On the acquisition side, Indie will spend $50 million establishing a United States entity and leasing a 10,000-acre tract of land for 10 years at a 25% royalty in the early 2020s. Indie also enters two new Latin American exploration licenses and farms into a non-operated position on an East-African exploration license in a prospective gas block. Both of these prospects are less mature, with exploration drilling planned toward the end of the decade.

The United States property would satisfy Indie investment criteria at $60/barrel; they could deploy two rigs for five years to start, adding about $300 million/annum to their CapEx. At $40/barrel, the United States property would not reach Indie investment criteria, and, so, they would not invest further in the field. At $80/barrel, however, there would be surplus cash available for investment; Indie could raise activity to four rigs, and the program would profitably absorb $600 million/year in capital. Given steep declines, the wells would achieve their payout within a couple of years, over which period, production could be hedged at prevailing prices.

This acquisition addresses three of the issues with Indie Oil's portfolio. It fills Indie's near-term production gap, it provides flexibility to ramp activity up and down depending on oil price, and it provides onshore-development experience that can subsequently be applied to Tarpon.

The Latin-American exploration prospects are similar to, but less mature than, Bonefish and Giant Trevally. They serve to spread

COUNTRY	ASSET	MATURITY	OPERATOR	WORKING INTEREST	GROSS RESERVES/RESOURCES*
GHANA	Marlin	Operate	Indie Oil	25%	480 MMbbl
GHANA	Swordfish	Operate	Indie Oil	50%	160 MMbbl
GABON	Sailfish	Operate	Other	10%	600 MMbbl
EQUATORIAL GUINEA	Dorado	Operate	Other	20%	50 MMbbl
COTE D'IVOIRE	Tuna	Operate	Other	25%	40 MMbbl
UGANDA	Tarpon	Select	Indie Oil	25%	1200 MMbbl
GHANA	Marlin Expansion	Define	Indie Oil	25%	150 MMbbl
UNITED STATES	Shale	Define	Indie Oil	100%	100 MMbbl
GHANA	Swordfish Area	Explore	Indie Oil	50%	100 MMbbl
PERU	Bonefish	Explore	Indie Oil	50%	200 MMbbl
SURINAME	Giant Trevally	Explore	Indie Oil	40%	400 MMbbl
LATIN AMERICA	License 1	Explore	Other	50%	200 MMbbl
LATIN AMERICA	License 2	Explore	Other	50%	400 MMbbl
EAST AFRICA	Gas 1	Explore	Other	10%	4 Tcf

TABLE 26: Indie Oil Notional Portfolio

* Note: For the purposes of this table, reserves are used to define the expectation production from a post-FID asset, while resources are used to define the expectation production from the pre-FID asset.

Indie's exploration risk over more basins and support production later into the 2030s, without increasing either cost or production. In time, if prospective, Indie could farm-out and repeat the process, creating a production line of exploration opportunities. The East-African gas prospect is Indie's first step at diversifying away from oil. In this case, Indie paid the 2:1 promote and will fund the exploration program as a non-operator. As a result of the promote and the generally less-profitable nature of gas, this asset will not meet Indie's investment criteria, but Indie's board considers the move strategic and is willing to accept lower returns in order to diversify. Following these transactions, Indie's portfolio would be as shown in Table 26.

Figure 38, below, shows Indie's production at $60/barrel. As this forecast shows, the shale acquisition has filled the production gap that was emerging in the late 2020s. Production now remains more or less flat at 80,000 barrels/day through the late 2020s. The farm-out of Bonefish and Giant Trevally serves to flatten and extend potential peak production from exploration.

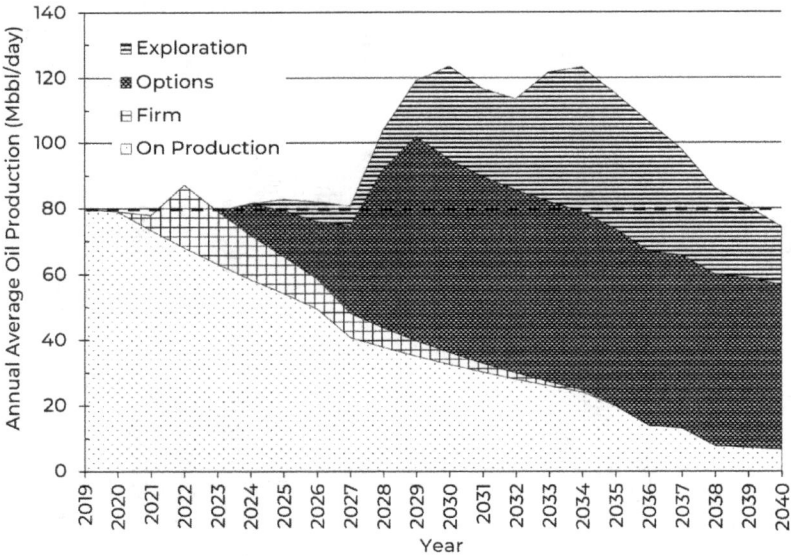

FIGURE 38: Indie Oil Production at $60/Barrel

This portfolio has a similar debt profile to Indie's conforming portfolio from section 3.6, with debt peaking at $2.9 billion in 2020 and declining from there, as shown in Figure 39, which is well within Indie's debt limit.

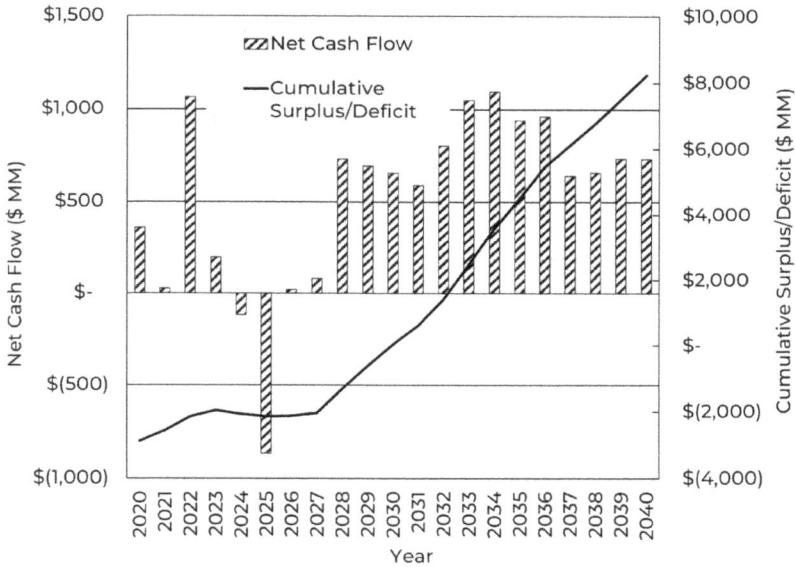

FIGURE 39: Indie Net Cash Flow and Debt at $60/Barrel

The notional portfolio smooths out Indie's production, spreads Indie's exploration risk over more acreage, starts a diversification into gas, and maintains a great deal of financial flexibility with respect to the debt limit. This notional portfolio also performs better than Indie's screened portfolio at Indie's cost of capital and $60/barrel, as shown in Table 27.

PORTFOLIO	NPV 14 @ $60 ($ MM)
Screened Portfolio	1, 610
Notional Portfolio	2, 338

TABLE 27: Economic Comparison of Screened vs Notional Portfolio

In a $40/barrel world, the United States shale acquisition would be just about break-even, so Indie would not move forward with it. Tarpon and the exploration opportunities would still satisfy Indie screening criteria, so these could move forward, provided Indie was able to fund them within its financial framework. Here we see some of the benefit from farming-down and re-phasing the portfolio, as Indie can now move forward with its exploration portfolio while maintaining its debt within $5 billion, as shown in the cash-flow plot in Figure 40.

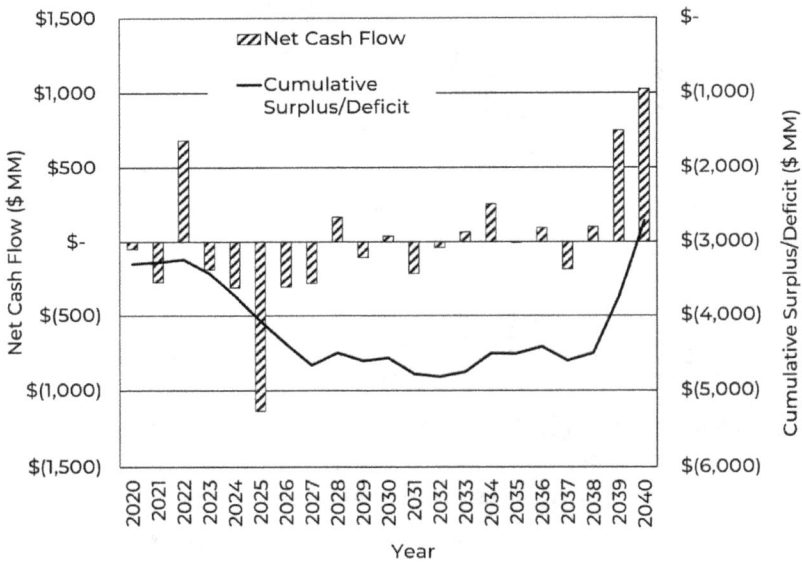

FIGURE 40: Indie Net Cash Flow and Debt at $40/Barrel

This provides a much healthier production outlook, as shown in Figure 41, positioning Indie to take advantage if commodity prices rebound.

At high prices, Indie is able to take advantage of the optionality in its United States shale asset to boost production beyond its 80,000 barrels/day target range toward the end of the decade, as shown in Figure 42.

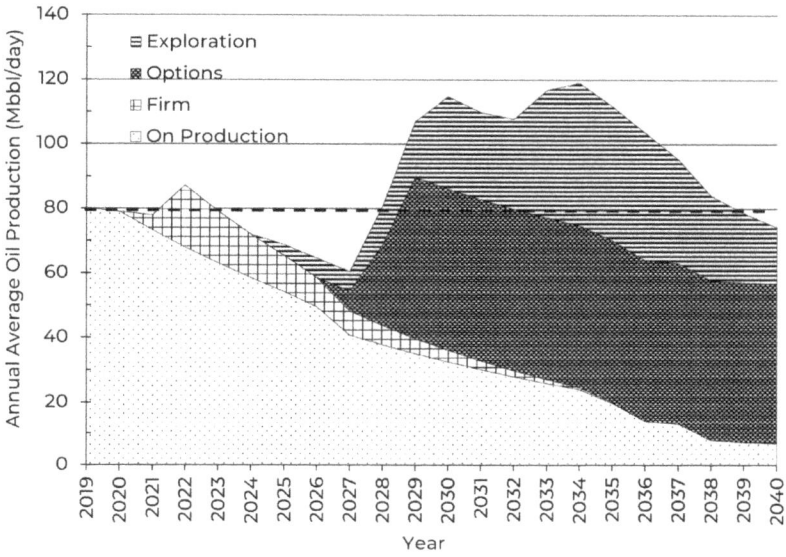

FIGURE 41: Indie Oil Production at $40/Barrel

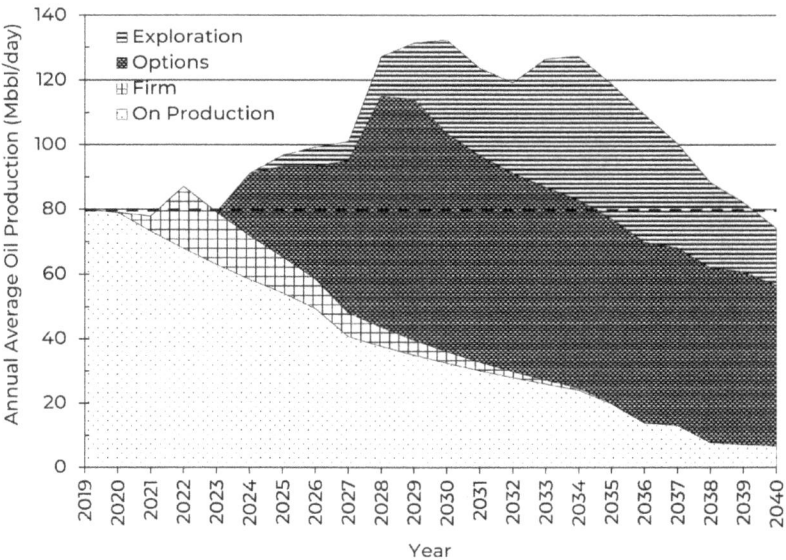

FIGURE 42: Indie Oil Production at $80/Barrel

As this section is designed to show, the adjustments made in the notional portfolio created for Indie Oil contained several benefits. Under the notional portfolio, at low prices, Indie could still progress with its exploration portfolio, better positioning the company for long-term survival and to take advantage of price upside. In the expectation-price environment, the addition of the United States shale asset allowed Indie to boost near-term production and gain some onshore experience in preparation for Tarpon. In the high-price case, Indie could boost its near-term production by raising activity on its United States shale asset, absorbing some of the excess cash that the portfolio threw off.

In the next section, we will look at how to develop other distinct notional portfolios and rank them, to select one or more notional portfolios that can be used to form the basis of a business-development strategy.

6.5 COMPARING NOTIONAL PORTFOLIOS

In practice, there are likely to be multiple different solutions, even at the archetype level, to address the insights that have been generated by the analysis of portfolio health, organizational capability, and asset mix. There will also be opportunities that pop up and new industry trends to investigate; what if, for example, Indie has an opportunity to pre-empt an acquisition where they already have some working interest? Some discipline is required here to keep this manageable, and the focus should be on creating notional portfolios that are genuinely distinct, not a large number of portfolios with archetypes that have slightly different properties. This workflow is summarized in Figure 43.

Here, it is useful to think in terms of some of the asset characteristics that were introduced in Chapter 4 and Chapter 5. Switching between two different frontier-exploration opportunities in the Latin-American deepwater does not change the notional portfolio, whereas substituting one for a deepwater Latin American redevelopment opportunity will make a big difference and should be considered as a distinct portfolio.

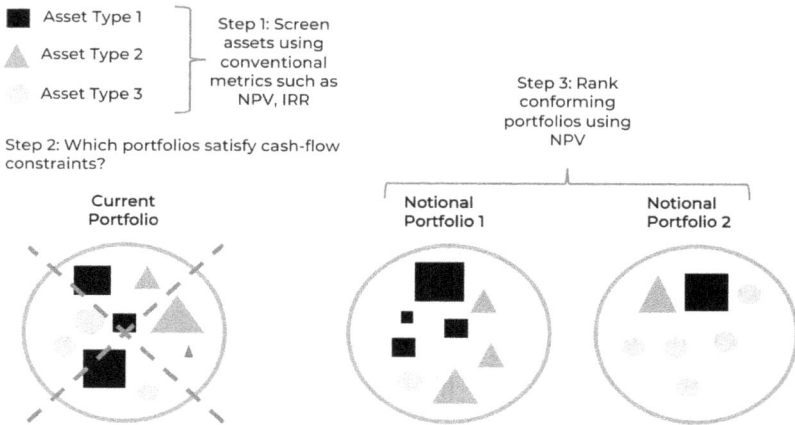

FIGURE 43: **Portfolio Screening and Ranking Summary Workflow**

Notional portfolios that have passed the screening stage can then be subject to ranking. This analysis should be undertaken using NPV or break-even prices, as the portfolio will consist of a series of investments and returns, which means other metrics such as payback and the profitability index are not meaningful. NPV can be calculated at whichever combination of price premise and discount rate the company uses.

Once again, the focus here should be on big differences; if there are two different portfolios that yield similar NPVs, then you have two plan A's. If you end up with three conforming portfolios with clearly different valuations, then you have a plan A, a plan B, and a plan C.

6.5.1 Indie Oil

If we return to the example of Indie Oil, there would have been multiple ways in which they could have addressed the insights identified in section 6.3. Let us say, for the sake of argument, that Indie Oil identified three distinct notional portfolios that addressed the insights they had identified and satisfied Indie's screening criteria. The screened portfolio is the current portfolio, with all assets that satisfy Indie's screening criteria, as described in section 3.6, and Portfolio A is the one that we assembled and analyzed in the previous section.

In Notional Portfolio B, Indie would divest the same asset as in A but would fill the late 2020s production gap with some late-life European gas assets, rather than United States shale. These would serve to plug the production gap and assist in diversification. Rather than pursue an East African gas-exploration asset, it would farm-in to the shale gas acreage in the United States, or Coal Bed Methane in Australia. This would avoid exploration risk but dilute returns. This would be the best-performing asset in a low-price environment but would be worse than the current portfolio at mid or high prices. Notional Portfolio C would plug the production gap by farming-in to existing Latin American deepwater production but eschew diversification into gas by retaining the higher working interest in Giant Trevally, rather than acquiring gas assets. Notional Portfolio C is stellar at high prices (and the implied assumption from our methodology that Giant Trevally comes in, at least to some degree) but performs very poorly at expectation or low prices. A comparison of these different portfolios is laid out in Table 28, below.

What does the table tell us? Both Notional Portfolio A and Portfolio B are more resilient to low oil prices than the current portfolio, with Portfolio B offering the most downside protection and Portfolio A offering better performance at all price points than the current portfolio. Portfolio C is the highest-risk, highest-reward outcome, but only in a high-oil-price environment; otherwise, it is worse than the current portfolio. This suggests that either Notional

Portfolio A or Notional Portfolio B—or perhaps some combination of those two approaches—would represent the best strategy. Portfolio A is better across the board, unless you are convinced that the world is in for a long period of low oil prices. In any case, it appears that divesting Roosterfish, Wahoo, Bonefish, and Giant Trevally is sound. In the next section, we will talk about how to convert this conclusion into an actual strategy.

PORTFOLIO	DIVEST	ACQUIRE	NPV 14 @$40	NPV 14 @$60	NPV 14 @$80
CURRENT CONFORMING	50% Roosterfish 50% Wahoo	-	($1.2) bln	$1.6 bln	$4.8 bln
NOTIONAL A	50% Roosterfish 50% Wahoo 50% Bonefish 40% Giant Trevally	100% United States Property 50% LATAM Exploration 1 50% LATAM Exploration 2 10% East Africa Gas	($0.7) bln	$2.3 bln	$5.1 bln
NOTIONAL B	50% Roosterfish 50% Wahoo 50% Bonefish 40% Giant Trevally	Europe Late Life Gas Shale Gas/ CBM	$ 0.2 bln	$ 1.3 bln	$ 1.7 bln
NOTIONAL C	50% Roosterfish 50% Wahoo 50% Bonefish	LATAM Deepwater Redevelopment	($1.9) bln	$2.7 bln	$6.4 bln

TABLE 28: Indie Oil Notional Portfolio Options

6.6 BUSINESS-DEVELOPMENT STRATEGY

This section will address how to take the insights from the analysis work that has been undertaken and convert it into an actual strategy. It is at this point that all of the careful analysis compiled and described over the previous chapters will make first contact with reality. The best business-development strategy is not the one that generates the highest NPV on the spreadsheet, but the one that is most likely to survive that first contact. The best business-development strategy is one that has flexibility and contains optionality.

The aspired portfolio will be defined specifically for divestment and far more broadly for acquisition. Divestment is more specific because you know which assets are being divested and on which aspired and reserve terms, together with a timeline. The acquisition process is going to be less specific, because it will involve looking for things with certain characteristics, rather than for something in particular. Timing and flexibility on timing are also key considerations here. There will be times when it is simply bad to be in the market—when prices are high or when nothing suitable is available. It is not realistic to expect a transformation like Indie's to be neatly completed by year end. It will take two to three years to move all of those pieces around, and, in the course of that two-to-three-year period, the divestment and acquisition targets may change; it is a continuous process.

The example is intended to highlight the importance of maintaining options with different characteristics in a portfolio. Business-development transactions in upstream oil and gas are multi-year affairs, and conventional projects, once sanctioned, take a minimum of two years to start producing revenue and many more years to pay out. The structure of the industry is such that, once a project is sanctioned, there is no turning back. Once transaction or sanction decisions are taken, capital is essentially locked in. External events move far more quickly than portfolio adjustments or project-execution timelines.

The average Brent Crude price between 2014 and 2016, as shown in Figure 44, illustrates the speed at which the external environment can change.

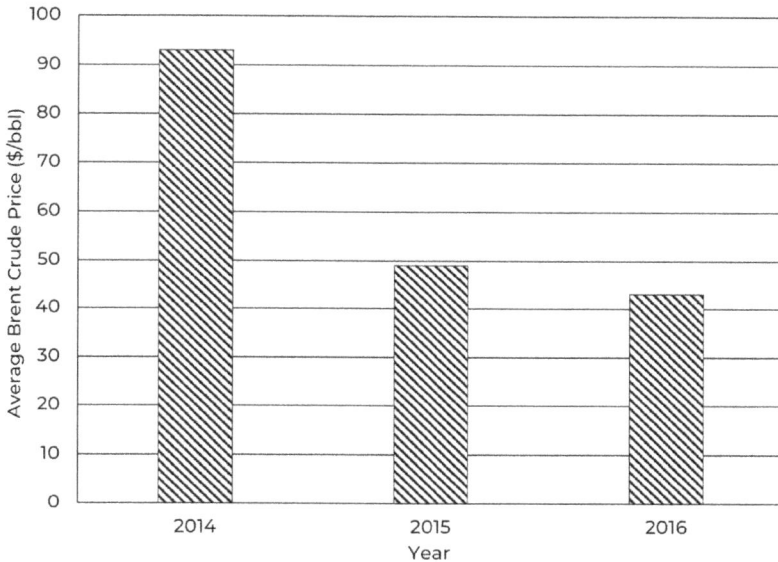

FIGURE 44: **Average Brent Crude Price (2014 to 2016)**

The alternative to developing a portfolio that is designed to withstand whatever the future holds is to react to events as they unfold, to be nimble—the *opportunistic* strategy. How does the opportunistic strategy work in practice? Let's start by asking how the opportunistic strategy works in the Indie Oil example. At $40/barrel, Indie was able to fund its firm work program and options, a great position to be in but seldom the case. If the assets can't be funded, then the alternative is to divest the asset that performed poorly at that price point. We can consider how those choices are likely to play out if undertaken in advance, as part of a portfolio action, or at the time that prices rise or fall.

If you are constructing a portfolio, then all of these decisions would be taken at a prevailing price of $60/barrel. If you decided to divest the asset, it would be profitable at prevailing prices, and you could reasonably expect to recover some of the value through a farm-down or farm-out. If you decided to acquire an asset that was profitable at low prices, you would have positive cash flow available to fund the acquisition; as the business is profitable, credit would also be available, and there would be little competition for assets that could not take full advantage of the prevailing commodity price.

Under the opportunistic strategy, you would attempt to undertake the portfolio adjustments once the fall in commodity price had occurred. At $40/barrel, the asset you are attempting to divest would not be profitable at prevailing commodity prices. Furthermore, every potential buyer would be experiencing the same shortage of cash as you, given the low-price environment, and credit may not be available. If you were unable or unwilling to complete the work program, then you would be forced to relinquish the asset, a situation any remaining potential buyers would also be aware of. It is unlikely that you would be able to recover any value from the asset. If you decided to try to secure an asset that was profitable at low prices, you would face a number of hurdles. Given the low commodity prices, you would not be able to fund the acquisition, credit markets would likely be closed, and, given the revised price outlook, there would be increased competition for assets that were profitable at low prices.

The situation is better in the high-oil-price scenario. You would benefit from the price upside, as the asset would have been in your portfolio, but you would still have missed out on the incremental cash flow available from acquiring the low-price break-even asset. The challenge in a high-oil-price environment then becomes acquiring additional assets to capitalize on the increased cash flow that high commodity prices bring. It is challenging because, in the same way a rising tide raises all ships, rising commodity prices raise all asset values. Every competitor is in the same position as you, flush with cash and looking to buy, and every host-country government is looking at their fiscal regime and starting to think it is too generous to the oil company. This is the very worst time to buy, but the pressure to put the excess cash to work will be intense.

Oil and gas companies cannot hope to adjust their portfolios this quickly. The only solution is to build enough flexibility into the strategy so that you accelerate or defer transactions to take advantage of or respond to the external environment, and that you focus on understanding and maintaining optionality within the assets in your portfolio. One of the reasons that Notional Portfolio A performs well across the range of oil prices considered here is that United States shale, by virtue of the way the asset is developed, allows activity levels to easily step up or down in response to price—it has the most optionality of upstream oil and gas assets.

6.6.1 Indie Oil

Returning to our Indie Oil example and bearing in mind the points made above on flexibility and optionality, how would we go about constructing a strategy that was flexible and provided optionality?

From the portfolio work, we know the "what." Pursuing a strategy built around the acquisition of different types of assets from two different notional portfolios in and of itself provides some flexibility there. The other dimension to consider is time. Here we will start by laying out the key decision-making timeline for the assets that Indie intends to relinquish. Here we are looking at when Indie needs to make the next financial commitment, what it is, and to what degree it can be deferred.

The Roosterfish concept-selection decision can legitimately be deferred 12 months without the need for external justification, as can the Giant Trevally exploration program. There is less flexibility with Wahoo and Bonefish, however, with both facing drill-or-drop decisions next year. This is not an issue for Wahoo, as the plan is to simply relinquish the acreage; on Bonefish, however, the plan is to farm-down and have a partner carry Indie on the well.

ASSET	MATURITY	NEXT DECISION	NEXT DECISION	MAXIMUM DEFERRAL
ROOSTERFISH	Select	FID	2022	2023
WAHOO	Explore	Well	2021	2021
BONEFISH	Explore	Well	2021	2021
GIANT TREVALLY	Explore	Well	2022	2023

TABLE 29: Indie Oil Divestment Targets Key Dates

The opposite approach is taken with the acquisition targets; here, the question is *When would they need to start contributing production?* Knowing this allows us to work back to build a target-acquisition window.

ASSET	FIRST OIL	ACQUISITION WINDOW	ENGAGEMENT WINDOW
UNITED STATES SHALE	2024	2021 to 2023	2020 to 2023
LATAM EXPLORATION	2036	2025 to 2027	2023 to 2027
EAST AFRICA GAS	2038	2022 to 2024	2020 to 2024
EUROPE LATE LIFE GAS	2024	2023 to 2025	2021 to 2025
SHALE GAS/CBM	2030	2027 to 2029	2025 to 2029

TABLE 30: Indie Oil Acquisition Targets Key Dates

The methodology applied in constructing the table above makes a number of assumptions. Both United States shale and shale gas/Coal

Bed Methane (CBM) can be brought onstream within a couple of years, whereas conventional oil is assumed to take 10 years and gas 15 years from the exploration well to first production. The acquisition window provides a three-year range, centered on the target-acquisition date, and engagement allows a start two years before the earliest acquisition date and running over the acquisition period.

We can put Table 29 and Table 30 together in the figure below.

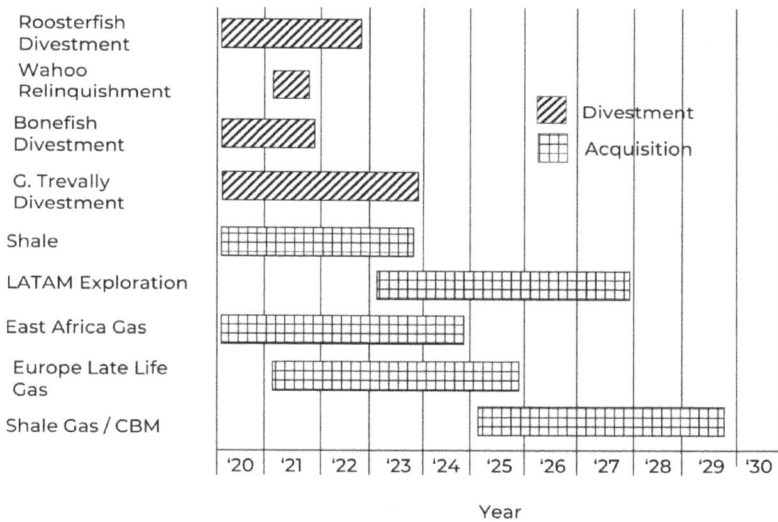

FIGURE 45: Indie Oil Business-Development Engagement Windows

Figure 45 allows us to look at the available timing flexibility in Indie Oil's business-development strategy. From the figure, we can also see that, for the first half of the decade, at least, Indie will need to update annually, depending on how the various transactions eventuate.

6.6.2 Indie Oil's Business-Development Strategy

Putting it all together, we can lay out Indie Oil's business-development strategy as follows:

Indie Oil is committed to increasing the resilience of its portfolio, while maintaining a production floor of 80,000 barrels/day, limiting debt to $5 billion and maintaining a $100 million annual dividend. To achieve this, Indie Oil will diversify (rebalance away from Ghana and invest in gas) and high grade its portfolio through select divestments (Roosterfish, Wahoo, Bonefish, and Giant Trevally) in the near term, and through acquisition of high-quality scalable assets (United States shale), a continued commitment to high-impact exploration (Latin American Exploration), and a focus on long-life gas assets in the OECD (Europe late-life gas/shale gas/CBM) over the rest of the decade.

At this point, we will go back to our real-life examples—Apache and BHP—to see how they articulate their business-development strategy.

6.7 APACHE

It is fairly easy to identify the strategy that Apache were following with their acquisition of the Forties field, as they explained it clearly and consistently in their annual reports at the time. A summary of their strategy, from their 2004 10-K filing[142], is provided below.

"**Over the years our strategy for achieving profitable growth has evolved. Over the most recent decade Apache has been an active acquirer of properties, following up with proactive exploitation operations, including workovers, re-completions, and drilling, to increase production, and efforts to reduce costs per unit produced and enhance profitability.**

Also over the past decade, we added an international component to our strategy, which exposed our shareholders to larger reserve targets and a greater ability to grow production and reserves through drilling. Our expenditures in 2003 were well balanced between acquisitions and drilling, with Apache having a robust year for both. During the year,

we invested over $1.6 billion in purchasing 267 MMboe. As for our active drilling program, Apache invested $1.5 billion drilling 1,449 gross wells to add 234.3 Mmboe. We plan on another substantial year of drilling activity in 2004, with a preliminary capital budget of approximately $1.8 billion. We do not budget for acquisitions because their timing is unpredictable; however, a significant part of Apache's growth strategy continues to be directed toward the purchase of properties to which we can add value and earn adequate rates of return. Because we maintained our financial flexibility (our year-end ratio of debt-to-capitalization was just over 26 percent), we are in a good position to take advantage of acquisition opportunities that may arise."

The strategy is clearly articulated and consistent from year to year. Apache has an exploitation strategy; it is looking for properties that it can acquire and enhance, through a combination of additional investment and cost reduction. The filing acknowledges that the strategy has evolved over the years as Apache has shifted its focus from the domestic United States to the international arena, in search of more material opportunities. The other point to note here is that both development and investment are opportunistic, but in a disciplined way. Acquisitions must have scope to add value and meet defined return targets, and Apache has organized its financial framework such that it can take advantage of these opportunities as they arise.

Their clearly articulated exploitation strategy was a form of differentiated cost leadership. They focused on material producing fields where there was additional development potential in which they could profitably invest. The same strategy was articulated consistently in Apache filings in prior and subsequent years.

6.8 BHP

It is harder to understand what BHP were doing with their unconventional acquisitions. For one thing, they do not articulate a strategy for their petroleum business, other than it should be present in high-quality assets. At the time of the Petrohawk acquisition, they did make the following statement:

> "The proposed acquisition of Petrohawk is consistent with our well defined, upstream, Tier 1 strategy and provides us with even greater exposure to the world's largest energy market, while also broadening our geographic and customer spread. Importantly, our offer and the associated substantial premium represent a unique opportunity for Petrohawk shareholders and recognize the growth opportunities embedded in its portfolio immediately."

The Tier 1 strategy is their reference to being present in high-quality assets, although it doesn't define what high-quality assets are. At the time of the Petrohawk acquisition, the assets could only be described as high quality based on projections; the underlying concept had yet to be demonstrated as economically viable. They make reference to broadening geographic spread, but the Petrohawk assets were located in the United States, where their petroleum-business head office was located, together with 29% of BHP's existing production. Even the statement is contradictory, as it talks about providing greater exposure to the world's largest energy market while broadening customer spread. There is a reference to growth potential, which there certainly was, which suggests that BHP were thinking along the same lines as Apache, just not as successfully.

The scale of the acquisition was transformational, but there were no obvious synergies, other than geographical, with their existing operations, and the play itself was not proven. BHP's petroleum business did not have the scale to compete across all categories, but at the same time did not distinguish itself as either low cost or differentiated. BHP did not appear to have a strategy for its petroleum business, and it remains unclear what the underlying motivation for its acquisition of the unconventional assets was.

Chapter 7

CONCLUSION

THIS BOOK HAS ATTEMPTED TO EXPLAIN, in the first instance, why having a business-development strategy is important in the upstream oil and gas industry, with BHP providing an example of what can happen when a large, well-capitalized firm with cash on its balance sheet acts without one. Apache is presented as a counterpoint, a firm that had less financial flexibility and didn't carry surplus cash but one that had developed and consistently applied a business-development strategy in a disciplined manner. Why do you need one? If you don't have a strategy, how do you decide which trade-offs to make, and how can you decide how to compete and where to compete? You can try to do everything, and do it better than everyone else, but you will fail. Even the world's largest companies, even at the dawn of the industry, didn't try to do that.

Having established the importance of a business-development strategy, we need to define what we mean. When we talk about business-development strategy in this book, we talk about how to compete and where to compete. In the context of the upstream oil and gas industry, this means how you compete and where you compete for *resource access.*

The cornerstone for defining your business-development strategy is understanding how your portfolio will perform, by testing it across multiple realizations, against your corporate financial framework. This yields insights into the changes that need to be made, what needs to be added, and what can be divested. Does your portfolio contain enough flexibility to cope with a sustained period of low prices? Does it have enough optionality to profitably absorb the fruits of a sustained period of high prices? This is the exercise that will tell you, in terms of production, CapEx, and Opex, where you need to acquire and divest.

The second step in defining the strategy is to understand how your organizational capabilities support the acquisition and divestiture of assets in a way that allows you to effectively build the portfolio that you need. This understanding of internal capability is the key to understanding where you can add more value to an asset than your counterparty, to arrive at the situation that Apache and BP did with Forties—a transaction that worked out for everyone. This step may include considerations on whether and how you need to expand your organizational capability, or to add skills that allow you to access new frontiers, such as deepwater or heavy oil. If you need to add those kinds of skills, how will you go about doing so?

This feeds directly into the third step: examining your asset mix in terms of the function that they perform within your portfolio and grouping them by type. This will tell you if you are overexposed to a certain commodity or country, if your portfolio already has too much of a non-operated component, or if you seem to be spread very thin.

Having determined what portfolio actions need to be taken and how you differentiate yourself, you can focus on defining the characteristics of the assets that you need to divest and acquire. Those three components, when combined, provide the basis for your business-development strategy. What type of assets do you need to shed, and what type do you need to acquire and on what kind of timeline?

Crafting a business-development strategy is as much an art as it is a science, and the performance of any commodity business is driven more than anything by fluctuations in the commodity price. However, if you follow the thought process outlined in this book, you should be positioning yourself to ride out the troughs and capitalize on the crests. At the very least, you should never find yourself in a position where, sitting across from your bankers, all you can think to say is, "I want to buy cash flow."

ENDNOTES

1. *The Prize*, Daniel Yergin, Simon & Schuster, 1991

2. "Oil Market Report" International Energy Agency, April 2020

3. "Permian Basin Decline Rates Have 'Increased Dramatically' Amid Ongoing Slowdown," *Journal of Petroleum Technology*, 12th December 2019.

4. "World Energy Outlook 2008 Executive Summary," International Energy Agency, November 12, 2008

5. "Global Energy Review 2019," International Energy Agency, 2019

6. "BP Statistical Review of World Energy," BP, 2019

7. "Global Merger and Acquisition Activity Decreased in 2019," Axios, Dan Primack

8. "Unit sales of Apple iPhone worldwide from 2007 to 2018," Statista

9. "Apple missed iPhone sales estimates, but it's making more money from iPhones than ever before," CNBC, Nov 1, 2018, Todd Haselton

10. "Xiaomi sold record 119 million smartphones despite market decline," Techinasia, Steven Millward, March 20, 2019.

11. "The Hidden Traps in Decision Making," *Harvard Business Review*, 2006, John S. Hammond, Ralph L. Keeney, and Howard Raiffa.

12. *The Intelligence Trap: Why Smart People Make Dumb Mistakes*, David Robson, W.W. Norton & Company, August 6 2019

13. "Driving value in upstream oil and gas," PWC, November 2013

14. "Technology industry worldwide: return on capital employed," Statista Research Department, January 20, 2021.

15. ROCE was calculated from data in "Financial Statements and Supplements, Independent Auditor's Report," Shell Annual Report and Form 20-F 2018

16. Apache Corporation, Form 10-K for the Fiscal Year ended December 31, 2003.

17. "Forties No. 2 for Apache" *Offshore Europe*, March 2003

18. "Forties at 40," Marc Thomas and Rhonda Duey, *Oil and Gas Investor*, Houston, Vol 36, Issue 1, January 2016

19. Apache Corporation, Form 10-K for the Fiscal Year ended December 31, 2003—Apache Corporation.

20. Chesapeake Energy 2012 Annual Report

21. "BHP Billiton and Petrohawk energy corporation announce merger agreement," News Release, July 15, 2011

22. BHP Annual Reports 2012 to 2018

23. "BHP sells United States oil and gas assets to BP for $10.5 billion," *Chemical Industry Digest*, 2018

24. *Earth Materials: Introduction to Mineralogy and Petrology*, Klein, C., and A.R. Philpotts, 2013, Cambridge University Press.

25. "Reservoir Engineering for Other Disciplines," MHA Petroleum Consultants LLC, Page 11-1.)

26. *Applied Reservoir Engineering*, Charles R. Smith, G.W. Tracy and R. Lance Farrar, OSCI Inc, February 2012, Chapter 3.

27. "Basic characteristics and evaluation of shale oil reservoirs," *Petroleum Research*, Volume 1, Issue 2, 2016, Zaixing Jiang, Wenzhao Zhang, Chao Liang, Yongshi Wang, Huimin Liu, Xiang Chen.

28. "Reservoir Engineering for Other Disciplines," MHA Petroleum Consultants LLC, Page 11-1.)

29. *Applied Reservoir Engineering*, Charles R. Smith, G.W. Tracy and R. Lance Farrar, OSCI Inc, February 2012, Chapter 3.

30. "Natural Gas Conversion Guide" International Gas Union, 2012

31. "Natural Gas in the Netherlands: From Cooperation to Competition" Aad Correlje, Coby van der Linde, Theo Westerwoudt, and the Oranje-Nassau Groep B.V., 2003

32. "Composition Variety Complicates Processing Plans for United States Shale," Bullin and Krouskop, Bryan Research and Engineering Inc.

33. "Reservoir Engineering for Other Disciplines," MHA Petroleum Consultants LLC, Page 11-37.

34. *Applied Reservoir Engineering*, Charles R. Smith, G.W. Tracy and R. Lance Farrar, OSCI Inc, February 2012, pp. 6-21.

35. "World Energy Outlook 2008" International Energy Agency, Chapter 12: "Natural Gas Resources and Production Prospects"

36. "North Field, Qatar: A Study of Condensate Blockage and Petroleum Streams Management," Arif Kuntadi, M.Sc. Thesis, Norwegian University of Science and Technology, Trondheim, 2004.

37. *Applied Reservoir Engineering*, Charles R. Smith, G.W. Tracy and R. Lance Farrar, OSCI Inc, February 2012

38. *Applied Reservoir Engineering*, Charles R. Smith, G.W. Tracy and R. Lance Farrar, OSCI Inc, February 2012, pp. 8-25.

39. "Reservoir Engineering for Other Disciplines" MHA Petroleum Consultants LLC, pp. 11-29.

40. *Applied Reservoir Engineering*, Charles R. Smith, G.W. Tracy and R. Lance Farrar, OSCI Inc, February 2012, pp. 8-27.

41. "Basic characteristics and evaluation of shale oil reservoirs," Petroleum Research, Volume 1, Issue 2, 2016, Zaixing Jiang, Wenzhao Zhang, Chao Liang, Yongshi Wang, Huimin Liu, Xiang Chen.

42. "High Recovery in a Volatile Oil Reservoir: Case History," B. Siti, L. Vignati and A. Usikalu, *SPE* 22361, 1992.

43. *Applied Reservoir Engineering*, Charles R. Smith, G.W. Tracy and R. Lance Farrar, OSCI Inc, February 2012, pp. 8-18.

44. *Applied Reservoir Engineering*, Charles R. Smith, G.W. Tracy and R. Lance Farrar, OSCI Inc, February 2012, pp. 8-22.

45. "Interpretation of an Unusual Bubblepoint Pressure Variation in an Offshore Field," Hadi Nasrabadi, Abbas Firoozabadi, Rogerio Oliveira, and Akexandre Jaime Mello Vieira, *SPE* 113574, 2008.

46. "Permian Basin Decline Rates Have 'Increased Dramatically' Amid Ongoing Slowdown," *Journal of Petroleum Technology*, 12th December 2019.

47. "Strategic Significance of America's Oil Shale Resource. Volume II *Oil Shale Resources*, Technology and Economics," Johnson, Harry R.; Crawford, Peter M.; Bunger, James W. (March 2004)

48. "Reservoir Engineering for Other Disciplines" MHA Petroleum Consultants LLC, pp. 11-29.

49. *Applied Reservoir Engineering*, Charles R. Smith, G.W. Tracy and R. Lance Farrar, OSCI Inc, February 2012, pp. 8-21/22.

50. *Applied Reservoir Engineering*, Charles R. Smith, G.W. Tracy and R. Lance Farrar, OSCI Inc, February 2012, pp. 8-24.

51. *Applied Reservoir Engineering*, Charles R. Smith, G.W. Tracy and R. Lance Farrar, OSCI Inc, February 2012, pp. 14-2.

52. *Applied Reservoir Engineering*, Charles R. Smith, G.W. Tracy and R. Lance Farrar, OSCI Inc, February 2012, pp. 8-27.

53. "Redevelopment of the compacting and subsiding Valhall and Hod fields," BP, Janne Saurdal Kvernstrom, Tron Kristiansen, Kent Andorsen, Olav Barkved and Jose Gil Cidoncha, May 2012

54. "Petroleum Concessions, Licenses and Leases: "Same-Same but Different?" *LSU Journal of Energy Law and Resources*, Volume 8, Issue 1, Fall 2019, Stanescu, Pereira, and Koenck.

55. "Global oil and gas tax guide 2019," EY, 2019

56. "The Taxation of UK Oil and Gas Production: Why the Windfalls Got Away," Dr. Hafez Abdo, Nottingham Business School, 2007

57. "Production Sharing Agreements: An Economic Analysis," Kirsten Bindemann, Oxford Institute for Energy Studies, 1999.

58. "Government Take in Upstream Oil and Gas: Framing a More Balanced Dialogue," Ivan Marten, Philip Whittaker, and Alvaro Martinez de Bourio, *BCG Perspectives*, December 2015

59. "Schlumberger to stop taking new field management projects: CEO," Reuters, 2019.

60. "Pemex ends plans to migrate more E&P contracts" Argus Media, June 2019

61. "Comparison of Selected Reserves and Resource Classifications and Associated Definitions," Mapping Subcommittee, Oil and Gas Reserves Committee, December 2005

62. "Exxon revises down oil and gas reserves by 3.3 billion barrels," Nia Williams, Reuters, February 22, 2017

63. "Randomness, serendipity, and luck in petroleum exploration," Alexei V. Milkov and William C. Navidi, *AAPG Bulletin*, v. 104, no. 1 (January 2020), pp. 145–176

64. "Government Take in Upstream Oil and Gas: Framing a More Balanced Dialogue," Ivan Marten, Philip Whittaker, and Alvaro Martinez de Bourio, *BCG Perspectives*, December 2015

65. "The Economic Folly of Chasing Schedules in Oil Developments and the Unintended Consequences of Such Strategies," Nandurdikar and Kirkham, *SPE* 162878, 2012.

66. *Corporate Finance | 11e*, Stephen A. Ross, Randolph W. Westerfield, Jeffrey Jaffe and Bradford D. Jordan, McGraw Hill Education, 2016.

67. "World Energy Outlook 2008 Executive Summary," International Energy Agency, November 12, 2008

68. "Permian has the lowest oil rate declines," Rystad Energy, August 30, 2019

69. "Permian Leads in Many Ways, Including Rapid Well Decline," *Journal of Petroleum Technology*, August 22, 2018

70. "Journey into Risk Country—The First 30 Years of Apache Corporation," Apache Corporation, 1985

71. "Against the Grain—Apache at 40," Apache Corporation, 1995

72. "Critical Mass: Apache at 50," Apache Corporation, 2004

73. "Form 10-K for the Year Ending December 31, 2002," Apache Corporation

74. "Form 10-K for the Year Ending December 31, 2001," Apache Corporation

75. "Form 10-K for the Year Ending December 31, 2003," Apache Corporation

76. "Form 10-K for the Year Ending December 31, 2002," Apache Corporation

77. "Form 10-K for the Year Ending December 31, 2003," Apache Corporation

78. "Form 10-K for the Year Ending December 31, 2004," Apache Corporation

79. "Form 10-K for the Year Ending December 31, 2000," Apache Corporation

80. "Form 10-K for the Year Ending December 31, 2000," Apache Corporation

81. "Form 10-K for the Year Ending December 31, 2002," Apache Corporation

82. "Form 10-K for the Year Ending December 31, 2002," Apache Corporation

83. BHP Website

84. "North West Shelf Venture," North West Shelf Gas Pty Ltd.

85. BHP Annual Reports 2008 to 2010

86. BHP Annual Report 2010

87. BHP Annual Report 2010

88. BHP Annual Reports 2008 to 2010

89. BHP Annual Report 2010

90. "Q3 2019 M&A Review & Outlook," *Enverus*, Q3 2019

91. Finbrook Database

92. "PV-X: WACCs for E&P Companies," Energy Valuation Insight Blog, Mercer Capital, August 2, 2016

93. "Oil and Gas Funding Is Evolving: An *Oil and Gas 360®* Special Report," Bevo Beaven and Richard Rostad, *Oil & Gas 360*, April 16, 2019.

94. "Borrowing Base Redeterminations Survey: Spring 2020," Haynes and Boone LLP, April 1, 2020.

95. "Proposed UK North Sea Acquisitions: Underwritten Financing and Extension of Credit Facilities," Premier Oil Press Release, January 7, 2020.

96. https://www.collegechoice.net/50-highest-paying-careers-college-graduates/

97. "Leading Creativity and Innovation," Jing Zhou, Ph.D, Jones Graduate School of Business, Rice University, 2018

98. *Offshore Oil History*, American Oil and Gas Historical Society

99. "Appomattox Deepwater Development, Gulf of Mexico," *Offshore Technology*

100. "Why Teams Don't Work," an interview with J. Richard Hackman, *Harvard Business Review*, May 2009

101. "Industry Profile: Oil and Gas," Center for Responsive Politics, 2019

102. Apache Corporation, Form 10-K for the Fiscal Year ended December 31, 2003

103. "Capital Structure and Determinants in Oil and Gas Companies: A study of factors critical to capital structures in the timeframe 1997-2014," Snorre Myhre, Copenhagen Business School, 2016.

104. "Annual Report and Accounts 2003" BP, February 9, 2004

105. "Form 10-K for the Year Ending December 31, 2003," Apache Corporation

106. "Apache Closed Forties Deal" *Oil Daily*, April 2, 2003

107. "BHP Billiton Annual Report 2012," June 30, 2012

108. "Capital Structure and Determinants in Oil and Gas Companies: A study of factors critical to capital structures in the timeframe 1997-2014," Snorre Myhre, Copenhagen Business School, 2016.

109. Koliander, W. (January 1, 2000): "The Metal Content of Crude Oils and Its Influence on Crude Oil Processing," World Petroleum Congress.

110. "Energy Outlook," 2020 Edition, September 2020, BP

111. "World Energy Outlook 2019," November 13, 2019, IEA, Paris

112. "International Energy Outlook 2019," September 24, 2019, Energy Information Administration.

113. "World Oil Outlook 2040," November 2019, OPEC

114. "2019 Summary Annual Report," ExxonMobil, January 1, 2020

115. "Shell Annual Report 2019," Royal Dutch Shell, 2020

116. "2019 Supplement to the Annual Report," Chevron, 2020

117. "BP p.l.c. Group results fourth quarter and full year 2019," BP, February 4, 2020

118. "Universal Registration Document, including the Annual Financial Report," TOTAL, March 20, 2020

119. "ENI Factbook 2019," ENI, 2020

120. "The Economic Folly of Chasing Schedules in Oil Developments and the Unintended Consequences of Such Strategies," Nandurdikar and Kirkham, *SPE* 162878, 2012.

121. "A Comparative History of Oil and Gas Markets and Prices," The Oxford Institute for Energy Studies, Jonathan Stern and Adi Imsirovic, April 2020.

122. "A Comparative History of Oil and Gas Markets and Prices," The Oxford Institute for Energy Studies, Jonathan Stern and Adi Imsirovic, April 2020.

123. "Natural Gas Conversion Guide," International Gas Union, 2012

124. "Natural Gas Conversion Guide," International Gas Union, 2012

125. "Global Gas Outlook to 2050," *Energy Insights by McKinsey*, February 2021.

126. "World Oil Outlook 2045," Organization of the Petroleum Exporting Countries, 2021.

127. "World Energy Outlook 2021," IEA, (2021) Paris

128. "Energy and Environmental Implications of a Carbon Tax in the United States," Columbia SIPA Center on Global Energy Policy, July 2018

129. "Global liquefaction capacity versus total LNG demand by scenario," 2010-2040, IEA, Paris https://www.iea.org/data-and-statistics/charts/global-liquefaction-capacity-versus-total-lng-demand-by-scenario-2010-2040

130. "Randomness, serendipity, and luck in petroleum exploration," Alexei V. Milkov and William C. Navidi, *AAPG Bulletin*, v. 104, no. 1 (January 2020), pp. 145–176

131. "AMLO reverses positive trends in Mexico's energy industry," Samantha Gross, Brookings Institute, 2019.

132. "Exxon quits some Russian joint ventures, citing sanctions" Reuters, Ernest Scheyder and Vladimir Soldatkin, February 28, 2018.

133. *Oil and Gas Fields in Norway, Industrial Heritage Plan*, Norwegian Petroleum Museum, 2011.

134. "Brazil's new local-content rules: 36 FPSOs and 21 billion barrels of oil unlocked for development," Wood-Mackenzie, May 2018.

135. "Statoil farms in to Roncador offshore Brazil," *Offshore Magazine*, December 19, 2017.

136. *The Art of Distressed M&A*, by H. Peter Nesvold, Jeffrey M. Anapolsky, and Alexandra Reed Lajoux, 2011

137. "Form 10-K for the Year Ending December 31, 2003," Apache Corporation

138. "Form 10-K for the Year Ending December 31, 2001," Apache Corporation

139. "Form 10-K for the Year Ending December 31, 2002," Apache Corporation

140. "Form 10-K for the Year Ending December 31, 2003," Apache Corporation

141. *Competing for Advantage*, Hoskisson, Hitt, Ireland, Harrison, Third Edition, 2013.

142. Apache Corporation, Form 10-K for the Fiscal Year ended December 31, 2003—Apache Corporation.

ACKNOWLEDGMENTS

Throughout this book, I have cited a number of expert sources, and these are acknowledged in the endnotes. However, there are several individuals who deserve special thanks for helping turn a collection of ideas into a book.

Dr. Feng Liang, a distinguished petroleum engineer, was kind enough to offer his time and expertise to review some early drafts of Chapter 2. His feedback was invaluable in producing a text that aims to highlight a few key points in a broad and complex subject. I am also indebted to Sophia for her willingness to review draft after draft of something I think we can all agree is not leisure reading, and for her encouragement and advice in turning it into something more approachable.

I'd like to thank the team at 1106 Design for all of their help and support in guiding me through the process of turning a manuscript into a book. When I finished the last draft, I thought I had reached the finish line. Little did I know that was just the end of the beginning.

The first few drafts of this book were written during the COVID-19 lockdowns of 2020—arguably the best and worst time for writing a book. After the initial outline, I found I would rather do almost anything other than write this book, literally any distraction was welcome. So, thank you Sophia, Alexander, and Jonathan for giving me the peace and quiet to work on it while (mostly) observing the "Do Not Disturb" sign hanging on the office door.

INDEX